MANCHESTER
UNIVERSITY PRESS

Jean-Jacques Beineix

PHIL POWRIE

Manchester University Press

MANCHESTER AND NEW YORK

distributed exclusively in the USA by Palgrave

Published by Manchester University Press
Oxford Road, Manchester M13 9NR, UK
and Room 400, 175 Fifth Avenue, New York, NY 10010, USA
www.manchesteruniversitypress.co.uk

Distributed exclusively in the USA by
Palgrave, 175 Fifth Avenue, New York,
NY 10010, USA

Distributed exclusively in Canada by
UBC Press, University of British Columbia, 2029 West Mall,
Vancouver, BC, Canada V6T 1Z2

British Library Cataloguing-in-Publication Data
A catalogue record for this book is available from the British Library

Library of Congress Cataloging-in-Publication Data applied for

ISBN 0 7190 5532 6 *hardback*
    0 7190 5533 4 *paperback*

First published 2001

10 09 08 07 06 05 04 03 02 01   10 9 8 7 6 5 4 3 2 1

Typeset in Scala with Meta display
by Koinonia, Manchester
Printed in Great Britain
by Biddles Ltd, Guildford and King's Lynn

Contents

List of plates

Series editors' foreword

To an anglophone audience, the combination of the words 'French' and 'cinema' evokes a particular kind of film: elegant and wordy, sexy but serious – an image as dependent on national stereotypes as is that of the crudely commercial Hollywood blockbuster, which is not to say that either image is without foundation. Over the past two decades, this generalised sense of a significant relationship between French identity and film has been explored in scholarly books and articles, and has entered the curriculum at university level and, in Britain, at A-level. The study of film as an art-form and (to a lesser extent) as industry, has become a popular and widespread element of French Studies, and French cinema has acquired an important place within Film Studies. Meanwhile, the growth in multi-screen and 'art-house' cinemas, together with the development of the video industry, has led to the greater availability of foreign-language films to an English-speaking audience. Responding to these developments, this series is designed for students and teachers seeking information and accessible but rigorous critical study of French cinema, and for the enthusiastic filmgoer who wants to know more.

The adoption of a director-based approach raises questions about *auteurism*. A series that categorises films not according to period or to genre (for example), but to the person who directed them, runs the risk of espousing a romantic view of film as the product of solitary inspiration. On this model, the critic's role might seem to be that of discovering continuities, revealing a necessarily coherent set of themes and motifs which correspond to the particular genius of the individual. This is not our aim: the *auteur* perspective on film, itself most clearly articulated in France in the early 1950s, will be interrogated in certain volumes of the series, and, throughout, the director will be treated as one highly significant element in a complex process of film production and reception which includes socio-economic and political determinants, the work of a large and highly skilled team of artists and technicians, the mechanisms of production and distribution, and the complex and multiply determined responses of spectators.

The work of some of the directors in the series is already known outside France, that of others is less so – the aim is both to provide informative and original English-language studies of established figures, and to extend the range of French directors known to anglophone students of cinema. We intend the series to contribute to the promotion of the informal and formal study of French films, and to the pleasure of those who watch them.

DIANA HOLMES
ROBERT INGRAM

Preface

I have never understood why the French critical establishment were so unhappy with Beineix's films. I happen to like them, just as I like Renoir's, Godard's, Truffaut's, or Tavernier's. I took pleasure in the excitement, both visual, but more than visual, which Beineix's films gave me and my students in the 1980s. This book is the result of my unease with French critical reactions to Beineix, and the compulsion to account for my pleasure in the positive terms which my students expected. That does not mean that I think that all of Beineix's films are 'good', even though I do happen to think that Beineix's first three films, *Diva* (1981), *La Lune dans le caniveau* (1983), and *37°2 le matin* (1986), although very different films, form a trilogy which help define a new sensibility in the 1980s. *La Lune dans le caniveau* in particular, much reviled in 1983, is, in my view, one of the great and essential films of the 1980s. The reader will therefore not find any further value judgements in this book, but an attempt to place Beineix's films within their various contexts, as well as a sustained attempt to treat those films as objects of critical enquiry, rather than as pawns in a politics of French cinema.

I would like to thank Jean-Jacques Beineix for allowing me to interview him and sustain correspondence with him, as well as allowing me a preview of his most recent film, *Mortel Transfert*, unreleased in the UK at the time of writing; David Laufer, Armel Gourvennec, and Carine Leblanc of Cargo Films, who gave me access to a large number of materials; the University of Newcastle upon Tyne for giving me research leave February–June 1999 to write this book; Caroline Jeanneau of the statistics department of the Centre National de la Cinématographie who provided the audience figures in the filmography; my students, who have taught me over the years to cock a snook at received ideas, and never to accept at face value the judgements that people like me like to establish. I have never much liked 'authority', and that is no doubt one of the many reasons why I like Beineix's films.

References include reviews from the BiFi (Bibliothèque du Film) database in Paris. These are newspaper clippings which are generally unpaginated.

P.W.
Newcastle upon Tyne

Foreword by Jean-Jacques Beineix

A l'heure où une polémique oppose un certain nombre de cinéastes français à leur propre Critique Nationale, je n'ai pas pu résister à l'envie de dire quelques mots sur le livre que Phil Powrie consacre à mes films.

Un Anglais qui sauve un Français du bûcher de la critique française, c'est un peu la revanche de Jeanne d' Arc ... Cela valait la peine d'être souligné.

J'ai en effet souvent pensé que les critiques français, contrairement au public, ne voyaient pas dans mes films ce que j'y mettais, qu'ils passaient, volontairement ou non, à côté du sens réel de mes histoires et de mes images – il est vrai que nul n'est prophète en son pays. J'ai souvent encore eu le sentiment que l'on me comprenait mieux à l'étranger que dans mon propre pays, et plus particulièrement en Angleterre ou aux Etats Unis.

Grâce à ce livre, je crois que certaines idées reçues sur mes films seront à reconsidérer, et que les motivations secrètes de mes images seront révélées. C'est très encourageant pour moi au moment où, après une longue période passée hors des plateaux de cinéma, je m'apprête à entamer un nouveau film.

Je pense que nous avons tous besoin d'être compris. La pire des choses c'est quand on nie le sens d'une œuvre – il m'a semblé que cela était souvent le cas. J'ai toujours volontairement caché des choses dans mes films. Phil Powrie a découvert certains secrets. Je ne me sens pas dévoilé, bien au contraire, je suis heureux de pouvoir les partager avec d'autres.

Le travail de Phil Powrie me rejouit, il m'encourage à faire des films, à continuer le dialogue avec les spectateurs. Phil Powrie se sert beaucoup de la psychanalyse dans son étude. Je trouve cette angle d'approche très à propos, c'est une des bases de mon travail et, cela tombe bien, c'est aussi le sujet de mon prochain film.

At a time when there is a polarised debate between some French film-makers and the French critical establishment, I was unable to resist the temptation to say a few words on this book which Phil Powrie has devoted to my films.

That it should be an Englishman who is rescuing a Frenchman from the stake of French critics smacks of Joan of Arc's revenge ... I think it is worth emphasising.

Indeed, I have often thought that French critics, unlike the French public, did not see in my films what I was putting in them, that they missed the real point, deliberately or not, of my stories and my images – it is true that no one is a prophet in his own land. I have often felt that I was better understood abroad than in my own country, especially so in the UK or the USA.

Thanks to this book, I think that certain received ideas on my films will need to be reconsidered, and that the hidden motivations of my images will be revealed. It is very encouraging for me at a time when I am preparing a new film after a long time away from feature film-making.

I think we all need to be understood. The worst thing is when the meaning of a work is denied – it seems to me that this has often been the case. I have always deliberately hidden things in my films. Phil Powrie has discovered some of those secrets. I don't feel I have been unveiled, quite the contrary, I am happy to share these secrets with others.

Phil Powrie's work delights me, it encourages me to make films, to carry on a dialogue with spectators. He has made considerable use of psychoanalysis in his study; I find this angle most appropriate, since it is one of the bases of my work, and, as it happens, it is also the subject of my new film.

A student once asked Joshu: 'If I haven't anything in my mind, what shall I do?'.
Joshu replied: 'Throw it out.'
'But if I haven't anything, how can I throw it out?', continued the questioner.
'Well', said Joshu, 'then carry it out'.

('Joshu's Zen' in *Zen Flesh, Zen Bones*)

Introduction

Most of Beineix's feature films to date were released in a single
decade, the 1980s, and he is generally seen as the best example of
what came to be known as the *cinéma du look*. This was one of the two
new types of film to emerge in the 1980s (the other being the heritage
film), to join the other popular French genres of the comedy and the
police thriller. For reasons which I shall explain, the *cinéma du look*
was placed by many, including Beineix himself, in a position of
confrontation with the cinema of the *nouvelle vague*. Just as Truffaut
had famously attacked the film-makers of the 1950s, the *tradition de
qualité*, so too thirty years later, Beineix attacked the *nouvelle vague*,
and the establishment critics who supported the modernist cinema it
represented, for being out of touch with contemporary, and especially
youth audiences.

Vincendeau defined the films made by Beineix and others as
'youth-oriented films with high production values ... . The "look" of the
cinéma du look refers to the films' high investment in non-naturalistic,
self-conscious aesthetics, notably intense colours and lighting effects.
Their spectacular (studio-based) and technically brilliant *mise-en-scène*
is usually put to the service of romantic plots' (Vincendeau 1996: 50).
The *cinéma du look* encompasses the films of two other directors, Luc
Besson and Léos Carax, the former, like Beineix, much maligned by
the critical establishment during the 1980s, while the latter was much
admired.

Unlike the other two directors, however, Beineix was from a
slightly older generation (Beineix was born in 1946, Besson in 1959,
and Carax in 1960), and had considerably more experience of film-

making, having served as assistant director on some fifteen films during the 1970s, before launching into his own career as a director with a short in 1977.

His first feature film, *Diva* (1981), enjoyed considerable success, becoming something of a cult film for the youth audience of the time, as well as launching the careers of Richard Bohringer and Dominique Pinon. It attracted the attention of one of the key theorists of post-modernism, Fredric Jameson, who called it the first French postmodern film. The French critical establishment, however, took a dislike to what were considered to be the more superficial aspects of a post-modern style, namely an attachment to objects and to surface effect at the expense of character psychology or moral message. Beineix was singled out as the representative of what became known, as a result of the supposed attachment to style and surface, as the *cinéma du look*, and the arguments that raged in the pages of the *Cahiers du cinéma* came to a head, as they did for Besson and *Le Grand Bleu* a few years later, at the 1983 Cannes Film Festival, where Beineix's second film, *La Lune dans le caniveau*, was booed when screened and more or less repudiated by its major star, Depardieu.

However, in 1986, Beineix's third feature, *37°2 le matin*, co-produced by his new company Cargo Films, became, as *Diva* had done five years earlier, an even more obviously cult film for youth audiences in France and abroad, thanks in part to the lead actress, Béatrice Dalle, who managed to capture the mixture of rebelliousness and innocence that characterised the 1980s youth *Zeitgeist*.[1] The enduring nature of the film can be seen in the fact that ten years later the three-hour-long director's cut was given an extended re-run of five performances at the National Film Theatre (NFT) in London in 1997, and it is frequently screened on the UK's major film-only satellite channel, Film Four. The brochure text for the NFT re-run signals why the film was a success, emphasising what many might think are stereotypes of Frenchness, the erotic – 'unabashed sexuality', 'energetic sex' – and the passionately romantic: the relationship descends into 'passionate outbursts', Dalle is 'a rollercoaster of pouting passion', Anglade, who plays Zorg, is 'the quintessential romantic Frenchman' (Adams 1997: 17).

1 Emma Wilson describes these two films as cult films in a recent book on contemporary French cinema (Wilson 1999: 148), and calls Dalle 'an icon of femininity in the 1980s' (Wilson 1999: 57).

Beineix's first three feature films had all been adaptations of novels. His next two feature films were based on original treatments in collaboration with Jacques Forgeas. *Roselyne et les lions* (1989), which some sought to place in the tradition of the *film animalier*, or animal-based film, is in fact a vehicle for the actress with whom Beineix was to share his life for a few years, Isabelle Pasco. Despite a story-line which on paper at least might seem to be calculated to please the *cinéma du look*'s youth audience – a young couple seek adventure in the world of the big top by training lions – the film did no more than averagely, as did Beineix's last feature film before an extended break, *IP5* (1992), again a narrative of initiation as two streetwise youths go on the road in search of romance, only to meet an old man, played by Yves Montand in his last role, apparently doing much the same thing.

Beineix did not make any other feature films during the remainder of the 1990s, turning instead to documentary film-making and political activity within the profession. In June 1994, he became the president of the *Association des auteurs, réalisateurs, producteurs* (ARP), a particularly vocal association for cinema professionals created by Claude Berri in 1987, and in July 1994 he was elected to the committee of Unifrance Film International, an association formed to promote French cinema internationally. He threw himself into the work, spending some 60 to 70 per cent of his time lobbying, according to him (Riche 1995). He very vocally sprang to the defence of French cinema, suggesting that French cinema was sufficiently important for the cultural life of the French that whenever the President or the Prime Minister travelled abroad, a representative from the industry should accompany them (Schwartzenberg 1994), and later in the year revealing how the European Union under pressure from the Americans had threatened the European audiovisual industry by suggesting modifications to the directive ensuring that television companies broadcast a majority of European films and television programmes (Mamou 1994: 9). In March 1995, the ARP took over the management of three screens in the new multiplex in Place Clichy, whose construction Beineix had chronicled in his 1994 documentary, *Place Clichy ... sans complexe*. The aim, according to Beineix, was to create a kind of cinema centre with a variety of activities, such as weekend events, a library, and so on (Anon. 1995: 25). This brief flurry of very public activity ended abruptly in May 1995 when Beineix resigned his presidency, although he returned to public lobbying over the issue of the cultural exception for French media products at the time of the Accord Multilatéral sur l'Investissement in early 1998.[2] He returned to feature film-making in 2001 with his own adaptation of a novel about a psychoanalyst, *Mortel Transfert*.

During the 1990s, Beineix has come to be seen, at least by English writers, if not the French, as a key director of the *cinéma du look*. It is characteristic, for example, that in Guy Austin's *Contemporary French Cinema* of 1996, which is otherwise a study of genres, Beineix, along with Besson and Carax, is studied as an auteur, rather than as an example of a particular genre, reflecting the importance that these directors have for a student audience in the UK; Austin's six pages on Beineix represent some 3.5 per cent of the book (see Austin 1996: 120–26). In France, however, the accepted view of Beineix is best exemplified by *Le Monde*'s critic, Jean-Michel Frodon. His comments on Beineix in his massive study for Flammarion's centenary of the cinema represent only about 1 per cent of the same period, 1968 to the present. Moreover, Frodon, in keeping with the position established by *Cahiers du cinéma* in the 1980s, uses Beineix as the best exemplar of what he calls 'le Visuel'. For Frodon, following the line established by critics writing for *Cahiers du cinéma* and *Libération*, 'le Visuel' is the abandonment of classic narrative for seduction by the image. The main complaint he has against this type of cinema is the intervention of technology (very mobile cameras such as the Steadycam and the Louma, as well as Dolby sound) which, in his view, distances the spectator from 'reality' (see Frodon 1995: 574–78).

This study of Beineix's work will consider the early 1980s debates concerning the film image which led to the view espoused by Frodon, after a brief account of Beineix's apprenticeship years. In doing so, considerable emphasis will be put on Beineix's first three feature films, in so far as they help explain the vicissitudes of that debate. These first three feature films, each very different, are key moments of French cinema in the 1980s, and the least successful of them, *La Lune dans le caniveau*, is a major film whose importance has been, in my view, much underestimated by scholars accounting for Beineix's work, or for French cinema in the 1980s.

2 See Labé 1998: 19.

My reading of Beineix's films, then, is fundamentally revisionist. It is also revisionist in the sense that I shall be taking issue with the standard, derogatory view of Beineix's work as all style and surface. Put simply, in my view, Beineix has been unjustifiably pilloried for reasons which have more to do with what critics felt was a crisis in French cinema, than as a result of a careful evaluation of his work. In the introductory chapter, I shall attempt to place Beineix's work within the context of the development of French cinema, and discourses on the French cinema, as they evolved during the 1980s. There follow six chapters, each devoted to one of the feature films. I have lingered more on the first three, which are likely to be of more interest to the reader. A final chapter will consider ways in which one can see Beineix's films as a kind of psychodrama.

References

Adams, Mark (1997), '*Betty Blue* (Director's Cut)', National Film Theatre Programme (September), 17.

Anon. (1995), 'L'ARP prend la gestion de trois salles au sein du futur supercomplexe Pathé', *Le Monde* (2 March), 25.

Austin, Guy (1996), *Contemporary French Cinema*, Manchester and New York, Manchester University Press.

Frodon, Jean-Michel (1995), *L'Age moderne du cinéma français: De la Nouvelle Vague à nos jours*, Paris, Flammarion.

Labé, Yves-Marie (1998), 'La création audiovisuelle française se mobilise contre l'AMI', *Le Monde* (13 February), 19.

Mamou, Yves (1994), 'La Commission européenne pourrait abolir la directive sur les quotas de diffusion', *Le Monde* (29 December), 9.

Riche, P. (1995), 'La diva de l'exception culturelle', *Libération*, 26 April.

Schwartzenberg, E. (1994), 'Beineix: "Le cinéma? L'enjeu des prochaines élections"', *Le Figaro*, 29 July.

Vincendeau, Ginette (1996), *The Companion to French Cinema*, London, Cassell and BFI.

Wilson, Emma (1999), *French Cinema since 1950: Personal Histories*, London, Duckworth.

2

Beineix in context

> Il appartient au clair de sortir de l'obscur, comme à travers un premier
> filtre auquel succéderont beaucoup de filtres
>
> (Deleuze 1988: 120).[1]

The apprenticeship years

Jean-Jacques Beineix's curriculum vitae begins laconically: 'Jean-Jacques Beineix est né à Paris le 8 octobre 1946. Après trois années d'études de médecine, il commence une carrière dans le cinéma'.[2] What these few words hide is an enduring love of the cinema, and a slow apprenticeship which Beineix has talked about in interviews.

That love of the cinema is one associated with Beineix's grand-parents, with whom he would go the cinema, and whom he associates with the notion of community and the popular:

> D'un côté je vivais chez mes parents, les beaux quartiers, voiture avec chauffeur, de l'autre, je découvrais Clignancourt, avec les caisses à savon! C'est pourquoi je ne me suis jamais senti bien ni chez les bourgeois, ni chez les pauvres. En allant chez mes grand-parents, je découvrais le monde des adultes, le métro, la ville, avec la loterie des anciens combattants, les vitriers, les marchands de peaux de lapins, les voitures à cheval et les terrains vagues, les décors de *L'Atalante* de

---

1 'Clarity has to emerge out of darkness, as if through a first filter that would be followed by many other filters' (Deleuze 1993: 91).
2 'Jean-Jacques Beineix was born in Paris the 8 October 1946. After three years' studying medicine, he began a career in the cinema.'

Jean Vigo et des *Portes de la nuit* de Marcel Carné. (Beineix 1989a: 151)[3]

As the passage makes clear, his parents were well off (his father was the director of an insurance company), and, interestingly, although his father gave Beineix a camera at the age of 10, and a film camera at the age of 15 (an 8 mm Paillard-Beaulieu), the purpose, as Beineix puts it, was scientific and technical rather than artistic. Thus, Beineix filmed on the one hand the monuments which his parents took him to visit on his father's many travels for business, and on the other, an Italian girl with whom he had fallen in love. These biographical elements are of considerable interest, since they hint at themes which I shall be developing in this book, the relationship with the father, and the apparent conflict between the technical and desire.

One of the key features of Beineix's relationship with the film image is the notion of seduction and the erotic, as we shall see. Much like André Breton's description of the erotic charge of a powerful image (which he describes as an 'aigrette de vent aux tempes susceptible d'entraîner un véritable frisson'; Breton 1992: 678),[4] so Beineix recalls the film image which haunted him in his youth, and which stayed with him. This image, of a young woman undressing in silhouette in *Marianne de ma jeunesse* (Duvivier, 1954), combined the impact of a revelation with eroticism, and he also describes how an erotic relationship for him is important when working with actors: 'La pire des choses qui puisse arriver à des amants, c'est de ne plus se désirer. Pour travailler avec des acteurs, qu'ils soient hommes ou femmes, il faut les désirer, c'est une relation de séduction' (Beineix 1989a: 155).[5]

3 On the one hand I lived with my parents, in the fashionable districts, chauffeured car, on the other, I discovered Clignancourt, with its old bangers. That's why I never felt at ease either with the bourgeois or with the poor. When I went to my grandparents, I discovered the adult world, the metro, the town, with the war veterans' lottery, glaziers, rabbit-skin vendors, horse-drawn carriages and wasteland, the decors of Jean Vigo's *L'Atalante* and Marcel Carné's *Les Portes de la nuit.*'

4 'A feathery wind brushing across my temples to produce a real shiver' (Breton 1987: 8).

5 'The worst thing that can happen to lovers is no longer to desire each other. To work with actors, whether male or female, you must desire them, it's a relationship of seduction.'

Love for the cinema changed into an intellectual curiosity when Beineix realised that, as he puts it, 'mes émotions étaient beaucoup plus fortes que ma capacité à les traduire' (Beineix 1989a: 155).[6] He attended films assiduously in a local cinemathèque where the audience discussed the films after watching them, seeing films from many national cinemas. He mentions, for example, Czech cinema, Brazilian cinema, Japanese cinema, Buñuel (Beineix 1989a: 155), as well as British cinema, such as the films of Richardson and Lester (Parent 1989: 175). He professes to adore Truffaut, and talks of *Les Quatre Cents Coups* as a revelation ('J'ai vu *Les Quatre Cents Coups* commentés par un instituteur. Ma passion pour Truffaut est née là';[7] Parent 1989: 175). Other high points of his childhood were the *amour fou* of *L'Atalante* and *Les Portes de la Nuit*. Such films, like his own, show us 'ordinary' people caught up in extraordinary situations.

Despite Beineix's love for cinema, curiously, he registered for medical studies in 1966. May 1968 put a stop to these studies. His reaction to the May events, in which he served as a stretcher-bearer (Beineix 1989b: 51) was as unconventional as his decision to take up medicine. Although he claims that he was one of the first to stand up and criticise the system, he also points out that he lost interest once he realised that professional agitators were manipulating the students (Beineix 1989a: 153). More surprisingly, he says that he was 'plutôt gaulliste', because 'De Gaulle, c'était quelqu'un qu'on pouvait admirer ... . De Gaulle était un héros. En même temps j'étais pour tout casser' (Beineix 1989b: 51).[8] He dropped out of university, began psychoanalytic treatment which lasted three years, and went through a succession of odd jobs in 1968–69 (for example, delivery-man for publishers, juice-seller at the 24 Hours of Le Mans; see Parent 1989: 176). He entered the competitive examinations for the Paris film school (IDHEC) in 1969, and was ranked twenty-first, although only the first seventeen were accepted.

Beineix's screen career began in 1969 as a trainee for a long-running television comedy series, *Les Saintes Chéries*, directed by Jean Becker. In the following ten years, he moved up to second assistant

---

6 'My emotions were stronger than my ability to translate them.'

7 'I saw *The Four Hundred Blows* commented on by a schoolteacher. My passion for Truffaut was born then.'

8 'More of a Gaullist ... De Gaulle was someone you could admire ... . De Gaulle was a hero. At the same time, I was all for smashing up everything.'

director, and then to first assistant director on some fourteen minor films, most of them comedies, working with a number of well-known directors, such as René Clément (*La Maison sous les herbes*, 1971; *La Course du lièvre à travers les champs*, 1972), Claude Berri (*Le Cinéma de papa*, 1970; *Le Mâle du siècle*, 1974), and more particularly Claude Zidi, which allowed Beineix to work with well-known comic actors (*La Course à l'échalotte*, 1975, with Pierre Richard; *L'Aile ou la cuisse*, 1976, with Louis de Funès; *L'Animal*, 1977, with Jean Rochefort).[9] Although Beineix has never made a feature-length comedy, the comic as a genre is often not far away in his films, and indeed, his very first film, in 1977, a short called *Le Chien de Monsieur Michel*, combines laconic, off-beat humour with the issue of the individual and his relationship to a community; Beineix describes it as 'a very bitter and mean' story, a parody of the song 'Le chat de la mère Michel' (Buckley 1984: 32).

Le Chien de Monsieur Michel tells the story of a loner who invents himself a dog so as to be able to ask the butcher for off-cuts, which he cooks for himself. The local community, however, believe his story and often enquire after the dog, whereupon Monsieur Michel feels obliged to give proof that it exists. This he does, first by barking occasionally, then staying up all night to do so, and, finally, by urinating on the stairs of the apartment block. After the outrage this causes, he reports that he has drowned the dog, half-believing it himself. The local community all contribute to buying him another. Monsieur Michel carries on asking for off-cuts, and the film ends with the dog, a fierce Alsatian, terrorising him because he will not feed it enough meat. The film's colours echo the wry, almost Kafkaesque narrative, with dimly-lit rooms and corridors, and a Monsieur Michel, played by Yves Afonso, who looks extraordinarily like Charles Aznavour as Charlie Kohler in Truffaut's *Tirez sur le pianiste* (1960). The link is perhaps not as tenuous as it might seem, since Beineix's first two feature films were both, like *Tirez sur le pianiste*, *films noirs*, and the second of them, *La Lune dans le caniveau*, like *Tirez sur le pianiste*, is based on a David Goodis novel.

These early years tell us a number of things about Beineix and his work. There is the emphasis on the comical, although it is a particular brand of comedy tinged with derision and irony. There is also the

---

9 Beineix has recounted his years as an assistant director in a long interview; see Beineix 1983b, and in interview to Denis Parent (see Parent 1989: 178–87).

attraction to community as a concept, but, yet again, whether in his personal life or the films, we shall discover that this attraction to community is counterbalanced by a strong sense of independence which manifests itself as marginality in his characters, and that marginality is tinged with a rebellious Œdipal streak. And, finally, there is the strong erotic charge of Beineix's work, one of the features most commented on, whether in relation to what his characters do, or the way in which his images are frequently calculated to seduce the spectator. All of these characteristics form part of the debate on postmodern cinema in the 1980s, and Beineix's work was seen by many establishment critics as typifying the worst excesses of this postmodern cinema.

The postmodern and 'postmodern cinema'

The fact that Jameson, one of the major theorists of the postmodern, called *Diva* the first French postmodern film, is no doubt partly responsible for the singling out of Beineix's work, and comments made by critics when *Diva* was released are heavily dependent on concepts familiar to theorists of the postmodern, as we shall see.

I shall therefore explore the concept of the postmodern, first in general terms, then in relation to film, before passing on to the specifically French focus on advertising, so that the reader may understand the context for the French cinema establishment's critique of Beineix's work. This I shall do in brief, since an extended analysis is well beyond the scope of this book. Of necessity, therefore, I shall not be questioning at length the term I am using, 'postmodern cinema', despite the fact that it is problematic.

Do I mean 'postmodern' here in the sense of an art form or, as Eagleton perceptively puts it, 'a style of thought' (Eagleton 1996: vii) which comes after what tends to be called 'modernism', so equivalent to the noun postmodernity? Or am I using it to describe features of a 'style of culture' (Eagleton 1996: vii), so equivalent to the noun 'postmodernism'? If the first, then logically all contemporary cinema is postmodern, depending on when you might think 'postmodernity' 'began'; but then since the postmodern is not dependent on the issue of origin, this is problematic. If anything, then, I am leaning towards a definition of a particular film style, and this mainly because it was an issue of some importance for the French cinema establishment during the 1980s, even if to some Anglo-Saxon critics it might, then and even more so now, seem to be a storm in a teacup. The reason it was of such importance to the French is that French national cinema is arguably the major cultural export of France, as the GATT negotiations of the early 1990s demonstrated very clearly, and as such a key component in the maintenance of French national identity. As we shall see, French critics disliked the postmodern style as exemplified by the work of Beineix because it could be seen, in their view, as a vehicle for consumer objects rather than high-cultural objects, and because the notion of a postmodern style transcended issues of national specificity, in a transnational and ahistorical cultural no man's land.

There is thus considerable irony in the fact that Beineix was to play a key part in defending French national cinema in the mid-1990s against the hegemony of Hollywood, and can be seen, as his inclusion in this series illustrates, as an auteur, with all the mannerisms that characterise a particular individual director's 'style', in the *Cahiers du cinéma*'s sense of the word.

The main features of the postmodern are the collapse of 'master narratives'; the collapse of the distinction between high art and popular culture; what one might call the imperialism of the technological image; and, as a corollary of all these, an attachment to the notion of surface. To each of these major themes of postmodern discourses, we can attach film-specific features.

At the ethical and philosophical level, what Lyotard, one of the two most influential French theorists of the postmodern, means by the collapse of master narratives is that there is considerable scepticism that all-encompassing philosophical or political systems, such as the Enlightenment project of emancipation, or Marxism, can explain the sheer messiness of life as we experience it, still less act as guides for living in a post-Holocaust, post-cold-war planet. In film terms, this might well translate into the violent amorality of Tarantino or Besson's characters, or the melancholic and often bitter rejection of society by Beineix's characters.

The postmodern is more often seen as a style, whether architectural, musical or cinematographic, and is usually contrasted with modernism. The aestheticism of modernism, where the consumer of the art object appreciates that object for its coherence at all levels,

whether moral, formal, structural (allowing that the refusal of traditional structure is still an adherence to the notion of structure, this
being particularly relevant to avant-garde art objects), gives way in the
postmodern to a greater heterogeneity, particularly in its mixing of
high and low culture. *Diva*'s opening sequence which mixes shots of
the Three Muses on the roof of the Paris Opéra with Jules's space-like
crash helmet is archetypal in this respect, as might be *IP5*'s long shot
of Tony covering a billboard with city-like graffiti in the middle of a
windswept rural landscape.

Partly because of its collocation with other types of object, and
partly because of its electronic reproducibility, the postmodern object
is an object in crisis. Indeed, it is the electronic reproducibility of the
object that makes this crisis of the object so different from the crisis of
the object in modernism during the 1930s. Baudrillard suggests that
when all objects can be reproduced and endlessly circulated (as
photocopies, or digitalised on computer screens or on television), the
user or spectator of the object loses sight of its origin, so that in the
postmodern, it can be said that there is no original and everything is a
copy, what Baudrillard calls the *simulacrum*, a term we shall come
across again in what critics had to say about Beineix's work.

The consequences of the image being divorced from a deep history
and divorced from a coherent aesthetic context are that images are
bound together by play on the surface of meaning, much like light
playing on water, and giving the same kind of instantaneous pleasure,
founded in the senses rather than the intellect. As Jameson puts it,
'depth is replaced by surface, or multiple surfaces (what is often called
intertextuality is in that sense no longer a matter of depth)' (Jameson
1993: 70). What might be meant by this is the insertion into a film of
quotations from other films, or indeed other media, which do not
appear to have a clear function other than to perform as quotations.
An example from *Diva* is the apparently motiveless quotation from
Wilder's *The Seven-Year Itch* (1955) where a Marilyn Monroe lookalike's
white dress billows up on the updraft from the Métro grill below her.[10]
If we follow the argument established by one of the few writers in

---

10 Beineix claims that this is not a reference to Monroe, but 'le dessous des choses.
   Une certaine idée de la sexualité. Moi je suis un voyeur. J'adore voir les robes de
   femmes se soulever' (Beineix 1983a), 'The underneath of things. A certain idea
   of sexuality. I am a voyeur. I love seeing women's dresses lift up'.

French to explore the postmodern in film, these kinds of allusion are not tied coherently to their contexts. The woman in *Diva* has not been seen before, and will not be seen again; the image itself signifies no more than what you see, it has no 'deep' meaning. Such images are emptied of content, to the extent that they could be replaced by any other filmic allusion. Their function is only to serve as allusions, as 'parodies d'un idéal perdu' (Jullier 1997: 28–29).[11]

The notion of parody and pastiche, raised here, is also of some importance in discussions on the postmodern. Jameson, in the article previously mentioned, tries to differentiate between the two in a well-known distinction:

> Pastiche eclipses parody ... . Pastiche is, like parody, the imitation of a peculiar mask, speech in a dead language: but it is a neutral practice of such mimicry, without any of parody's ulterior motives, amputated of the satiric impulse, devoid of laughter and of any conviction that along-side the abnormal tongue you have momentarily borrowed, some healthy linguistic normality still exists. (Jameson 1993: 73–74)

In practice, the two modes are usually elided in discussion; the key issue is not whether one mode is more critical than the other, so much as the fact that both modes depend on a gesture towards a vanished or vanishing original.[12]

A second point raised by intertextual allusions or quotations is that of fragmentation, since, logically, the more functionless intertextual allusions there are in a film, the more difficult it will be to perceive a coherent narrative. The film will appear to go off in an excess of unmotivated tangents, in a kind of parody of the European art film described by Bordwell. This is more apparent in the films of Carax than those of Beineix, however; Carax's second film, *Mauvais Sang* (1986) was criticised for threatening to collapse under the weight of its own intertextual references (see Powrie 1997: 131). Beineix's films, on the other hand, have a much stronger narrative coherence, usually based on quest narratives: the search for the cassette in *Diva*, the

---

11 'Parodies of a lost ideal.'

12 However, it is worth poining out that Susan Hayward retains Jameson's distinction, and applies it rigorously to Beineix among others. *37°2 le matin* is, for Hayward, an example of what she calls symptomatic or unoppositional cinema, because, in her view, it is 'completely constructed out of prefabricated images ... with images coming from directors as far apart as Huston, Cassavetes, Bergman and Malle' (Hayward 1993: 233).

search for a publisher in *37°2 le matin*, the search for the killer of the sister in *La Lune dans le caniveau*, the search for the ultimate performance in *Roselyne et les lions*, the search for love in *IP5*, the search for a resting place for a dead body in *Mortel Transfert*. These quests may well be, as we shall see, double, or split quests; but they are not fragmented into the centrifugal heterogeneity that has been seen as a major characteristic of the postmodern.

A more film-specific characteristic of a discourse whose aim would appear to be surface pleasure, founded in the senses, is a set of recognisable stylistic devices. Jullier isolates one in particular, which he sees as fundamental: the forward-tracking camera, whose purpose is to engage the spectator in the illusion of what he calls immersion. Contrasting the track forward with the 1960s and 1970s predilection for a zoom camera, which maintained a certain distance between spectator and object, Jullier points out how the track forward, particularly when associated with Dolby surround-sound, can affect the whole body, creating a dizzying feeling of exhilaration; his examples tend to be action sequences, as in the space battles of *Star Wars* (Lucas, 1977). Jullier is quite clear that not all track forwards have this effect. Certain conditions must obtain, and obtain as a group: the camera must not be associated with any object on the same forward movement as itself, nor must the movement be motivated by any obvious narrative goal; the camera must have a short focal length, and this must normally be combined with a set whose perspective emphasises the forward movement; an example might be Zorg pursuing Betty through the streets. Jullier suggests, following Daney, that such a style does not ask the spectator to construct a fictional world, but projects the spectator into the fictional world through the medium of sensation rather than reflection, and that this type of cinema is less centered on the character, than on the spectator (see Jullier 1997, chapter 3, for an extended analysis of the trope of immersion).

To this trope, we need to add excessive camera angles (extreme high or low angle camera, canted camera), frequently associated with close-ups, whose point is, again, to immerse the spectator in the screen space by creating an exhilarating disorientation. Effects of this type are not confined to the cinema of the 1980s, of course. Critics disliked the trope because Beineix used it as much for objects as he did for characters on screen, leading to the view that his cinema, by its predilection for the object, was symptomatic of alienation, and beholden to a style more familiar in advertising and music video clips.[13]

What all these points have in common is the immersion of the spectator, not in some kind of 'depth' but, paradoxically, in an infinite 'surface'. That surface is seen as the screen surface: the spectator does not go beyond the surface of the narrative, which functions more like a peg on which to hang the coat of style. The spectator does not go beyond the surface of the character, because it is not the psychological complexity of the character which gives pleasure, but the way in which the character behaves. In other words, what matters is what can be seen, what is presented, rather than what can be worked out, or constructed. Given the mistrust of the visual, which is prevalent in much of twentieth-century French intellectual work, as Martin Jay has shown (see Jay 1993), it is hardly surprising that French film critics took a dislike to this new style. There would have been deep-rooted political reasons for this dislike as well. The work of the situationist philosopher Guy Debord, whose *La Société du spectacle*, published in 1967, pre-dates much of Baudrillard and Lyotard's work, was an inspiration for many of the student revolutionaries during the May 1968 events. This work analysed the way in which spectacle, what the discourses of the 1980s called the image, had become all-powerful, driving out humanity, as the opening paragraph famously puts it: 'Tout ce qui était directement vécu s'est éloigné dans une représent-ation' (Debord 1971: 9).[14] Debord's vision is nothing if not apocalyptic; the final paragraph of the chapter devoted to consumer products endows these products with a life of their own: 'la marchandise se contemple elle-même dans un monde qu'elle a créé' (Debord 1971:

---

13 Here is an example among many, taken from a piece by Bonitzer from a *Cahiers* special issue on auteur cinema. Bonitzer implies that 1980s cinema is less complex than, say, 1950s Hollywood cinema: 'Lorsqu'on a compris que cinéma et disco, film et vidéo-clip, constituaient non des domaines foncièrement hétérogènes, mais les éléments d'un cocktail explosif (en termes d'adhésion populaire, de marketing et de box-office), le cinéma a pris un virage historique. En France, Beineix représente ce tournant' (Bonitzer 1983: 9). 'When people understood that cinema and disco, film and video clip, were no longer separate domains, but the elements of an explosive cocktail (in terms of public approval, marketing and box-office), cinema took a historical turn. In France, Beineix represents that turn.'

14 'All that was once directly lived has become mere representation' (1995: 12).

31).[15] This indicates to some extent, as did Baudrillard's early interest in the consumer society, the particularly French inflection in discussions on the postmodern, with their emphasis on the object, objectification or reification, and the most obvious context for this reification, advertising.

It is no surprise then that the issue of the postmodern image for writers associated with *Cahiers du cinéma* is, unlike those writing in the UK equivalent *Screen*, linked to the issue of advertising. The advertising image can be seen, in their view, as the perfect postmodern image,[16] and as a result Beineix represents everything which *Cahiers du cinéma* saw as most reprehensible in this new style of film-making.

Advertising

This was not helped by the fact that Beineix, like many directors during the 1980s,[17] made a number of television advertisements (some twenty or so are listed on his CV). These cover a wide range of consumer products. There is, for example, Suntory Cognac (1990) with Emmanuelle Béart, who had acted as a 6-year-old in one of the films Beineix worked on as second assistant director, Clément's *La Course du lièvre à travers les champs*. Other products covered are Bébé

---

15 'The commodity contemplates itself in a world of its own making' (1995: 34). Bonitzer, however, suggests that the situationist critique is not commensurable with the 1980s notion of the image: 'C'est par l'affirmation d'une différence, d'une coupure avec le monde réel que commence le spectacle. Le continuum audiovisuel en est par principe une négation' (Bonitzer 1988: 20). 'A spectacle begins by the affirmation of a difference, a cutting off from the real world. The audio-visual continuum is, on principle, a negation of the spectacle' (Bonitzer 1991: 233).

16 It is characteristic, for example, that Jullier, in his discussion of the functionless allusion, contrasts an image from *Le Mépris* (Godard, 1963), a Greyhound bus, with the same image in an advertisement for Levi's jeans (Jullier 1997: 28–29). A more meaningful contrast to pin down the postmodern image in films would have been the same image used in two feature films. It should be noted that Jullier is not a *Cahiers* critic, but an academic lecturing in film studies at the University of Metz, which only shows all the more how prevalent this connection between film and advertising is in film-specific discourses.

17 Other well-known directors working in advertising include Gainsbourg (Lux, Brandt, Woolite, Gini, Lee Cooper, Maggi); Rappeneau (Vie active); Chabrol (Winston cigarettes, Renault 5). See Schifres 1983: 42.

Cadum soap (with a well-known image of a father carrying his son in such a way that he looks like a pregnant woman), Apple computers, Renault cars. There are also a number of advertisements which use either out-takes from Beineix's feature films – Stéfanel clothes, 1987 and Douwe Egbert coffee, for example, both use elements from $37°2 le matin$ – or are heavily based on them: the advertisement for Valentine paints, for example, uses a black panther and Thierry Le Portier as the trainer, on whose biography *Roselyne et les lions* is based; Fujicolor in 1991 similarly has a circus-based theme. But there are also public utility advertisements, such as Médecins du Monde (where we see a plane inside the Roissy terminal building), and, more famously, an AIDS advertisement in 1987, with Gérard Sandoz, who was to play Thierry in *Roselyne et les lions*, holding a broken *Star Wars*-inspired red laser beam, with the motto 'Le SIDA, il ne passera pas par moi'.[18] Beineix returned to AIDS campaigning in 1990 with a series of short television advertisements, called 'Histoires d'amour'. In one of them, a young man looks in the mirror, saying, with deliberate ambiguity, 'Attention les filles, j'en ai plein les poches'.[19] Unlike the earlier moralising ad with Sandoz, this is, as Alastair Duncan points out, an example of how Beineix 'starts where he thinks young people are' (Duncan 1997).

The importance of advertising, both quantitatively and qualitatively, cannot be overemphasised. The 1980s were the consumer decade in France, as much if not more so than in other developed economies. General economic prosperity made advertising prosper. Over the period 1965–88, household expenditure (using a zero baseline) increased by 114 per cent, and this is paralleled by expenditure in advertising, which rose from 7 bn francs in 1970 to 58 bn in 1988, a 90 per cent increase, with some 50 per cent of that increase occurring during the 1980s (see Billard 1989). Advertising became a culture, as is suggested not only by the development of a specialised press (magazines such as *Médias, Stratégies, Communications Business*), but even more so by the television programme 'Culture pub', a one-hour Sunday show which started in 1988, devoted entirely to advertising, and Jean-Marie Boursicot's cult annual 'Nuit des Publivores', an all-night cinema showing of television and film advertisements.[20] By

18 'AIDS will not be passed on through me.'
19 'Look out girls, I've got a pocketful.'
20 And even crossing the Channel to London; see Rogers 1990.

1983, the French advertising guru Jacques Séguéla (who had written a book in 1979 ironically entitled *Ne dites pas à ma mère que je suis dans la publicité ... Elle me croit pianiste dans un bordel*, suggesting that to be in advertising was lower than the low), was able to say 'quant au publicitaire, hier farceur ou voleur, le voilà sacré sociologue ou artiste' (Séguéla 1983: 30).[21]

As Billard points out, the fact that advertising became fashionable in the 1980s is not only due to economic circumstances. Prominent intellectuals such as Barthes and Eco had, under the influence of 1970s structuralist linguistics, turned their attention to advertising, and the slow collapse of leftist ideologies in the decade, encapsulated publicly by the collapse of Communism in the Eastern bloc at the end of the decade, had also contributed to the discrediting of key concepts associated with Marxist ideology, such as the benefits of socialist community and the inevitability of alienation in a capitalist system. These factors led in France as elsewhere to the development of brash individualism. As Séguéla put it in 1983, the spirit of the 1980s is 'l'épanouissement personnel ... . La société de communication sera la société du "Moi Je"' (Séguéla 1983: 183).[22]

More particular to France during the 1980s was a penchant for advertisements where the product was at least in appearance considerably less important than the way in which it was advertised. The medium became more crucial than the message; or, rather, the medium became the message, with sophisticated visual and verbal displays showing a level of provocative creativity intended to dazzle. As Billard says, 'vedette de la société du look et des apparences, la publicité s'appuie sur l'arsenal surréaliste, l'érotisation de l'image et le non-sens pour nous offrir évasion, spectacle, humour' (Billard 1989).[23] It is a type of advertising much trumpeted in a famous catch phrase by Jacques Séguéla, the 'three r's', as he called them, 'rire, rêve, risque' (laughter, dream, risk). Indeed, in 1982 Séguéla had suggested that advertising should in this respect take over from cinema, which was no longer capable of creating myths (Séguéla 1982). Advertising, for

21 'As for the advertising executive, yesterday he was a joker or a thief, today he is hailed as a sociologist or an artist.'
22 'Personal fulfilment ... . The communication society will be the "me" society'.
23 'Star of the society of the look and of appearances, advertising relies on the surrealist arsenal, the eroticisation of the image and nonsense to offer escape, visual spectacle and humour.'

Séguéla, becomes a combination of seduction and derision (Séguéla 1983: 36). He frequently mentions Beineix among other directors, since for him Beineix typifies several of the elements mentioned: a style concerned with appearance, which combines the irreverent and the erotic so as to afford an immediate pleasure to the spectator. But whereas for Séguéla such characteristics are positive, for most establishment film critics, they were negative, as we shall see in the following chapters. The terminology used by critics is directly linked to key concepts in postmodern discourses, and to the language of advertising, as discussed in this chapter: the circulation of images without origin, images which give a sense of *déjà-vu*, images which collocate high and low culture, images which immerse the spectator, provoking pleasure and emotion rather than thought, images which are excessively stylised, images which fragment narrative, images used ironically.

   Cahiers du cinéma tried to counter what it saw as a 'dumbing-down' of the film image by a discourse on film and painting,[24] encouraged by a number of films which explored the connection between the two: *Passion* (Godard, 1982), in which a film director tries to recreate paintings by Rembrandt, Tintoretto, Goya, and others; *Un dimanche à la campagne* (Tavernier, 1984), which is about an ageing academic painter, and which, it should be said, *Cahiers* critics disliked;[25] *Thérèse* (Cavalier, 1986) in which *mise en scène* is calqued on paintings by Philippe de Champaigne. Focusing on painting arguably gives a 'thickness' to the image, a patina, which counters the glossy surface of the postmodern image. Clearly, however, this approach to the film image is 'high-modernist', and relies to a great extent on an aesthetic awareness which might typically be thought to appeal to a cultivated and intellectually aware public.

Youth

The trouble for *Cahiers* was that the majority of the cinema-going public in the early 1980s was aged between 15 and 24; as Séguéla

24 'Le cinéma depuis un moment semble vouloir chercher ses valeurs menacées du côté de l'expression plastique, de la peinture' (Bonitzer 1988: 20). 'Cinema seems to have been trying for sometimes [*sic*] to find its threatened values in the field of plastic art and painting' (Bonitzer 1991: 233).
25 See Powrie 1997: 21 and Lardeau 1984.

pointed out in 1983, the year of *La Lune dans le caniveau*, 'la société de communication, c'est ... savoir communiquer au nouvel âge. Un Français sur deux a moins de trente ans' (Séguéla 1983: 172).[26] Of the cinema-going public, 90 per cent of 18 to 20 year olds went to see films, and the 15 to 24 age group yielded more than 55 per cent of the total admissions figures. This age group, then as now, was reared on a different cultural diet, which includes attraction to the advertising image and the pop video, but also to romantic plots, as Vincendeau reminds us in the quotation which began this introduction. By incorporating such elements in their films, Beineix (and Besson) ensured a following among the youth class. As Beineix later wrote, in a provocative defence of advertising, and the advertising aesthetic:

> La publicité n'a jamais rien inventé sinon ce que les artistes ont inventé. En revanche, elle a su capter, détourner, parodier, copier. Elle s'est approprié le Beau que le cinéma de la nouvelle vague avait rejeté, ce qui fait dire à certains critiques ignares que beau c'est pub. Elle a kidnappé la couleur que le cinéma n'arrivait plus à transgresser, tout occupé qu'il était à faire vrai, ce qui fait dire à certains critiques crétins que la couleur c'est pub. Elle a expulsé l'histoire, dont le cinéma, crispé sur le récit, ne pouvait se défaire, ce qui fait dire à certains critiques débiles que le cinéma sans histoires c'est pub. Enfin ... elle a plus généralement capté la jeunesse, dont le cinéma qui vieillissait ne traduisait plus les aspirations, ce qui fait dire à certains critiques qui sont vieux et qui ne s'intéressent qu'à ce qui est mort, ou à ceux qui sont morts que le cinéma de la jeunesse, c'est pub. (Parent 1989: 222, 224)[27]

26 'The communication society is about knowing how to communicate with the new age. One French person out of two is less than 30 years old.'
27 'Advertising has never invented anything except what artists have invented. On the other hand, it has been able to capture, inflect, parody, imitate. It appropriated the Beautiful which the cinema of the New Wave had rejected, which makes certain ignorant critics say that beautiful equals advertising. It kidnapped colour, which the cinema no longer violated, so preoccupied was it with being true to life, which makes certain cretinous critics say that colour equals advertising. It dispensed with stories, which the narrative cinema was unable to do without, so some stupid critics are saying that a film without a story equals advertising. Finally ... it generally captivated young people, whose aspirations the ageing cinema no longer translated, so that some old critics who are only interested in what's dead and gone, or those who are dead and gone are saying that youth cinema equals advertising.'

Beineix and Besson's films also managed to reflect the contemporary mood of cynicism and alienation prevalent in the youth class, which felt disenfranchised (see Hayward 1998: 23–27), as films like *La Haine* (Kassovitz, 1995) in the 1990s have continued to underline. Beineix's combination of passion and derision, therefore, corresponded with the prevailing mood of youth audiences: 'Roman et cynisme, c'est un mélange des deux. C'est un romantisme auquel on ne croit pas vraiment' (Beineix 1987: 43).[28] Prédal's assessment underlines the social effect of Beineix's irony: 'Il aime ... distancier son récit par l'ironie et la dérision. Ses personnages parviennent en effet à la fois à se prendre très au sérieux et à se regarder de l'extérieur, relativisant ainsi leur intégration au milieu où ils vivent' (Prédal 1991: 468).[29]

The 'neo-baroque'

By the end of the decade, the passion raised by the postmodern youth cinema had run its course. As Daney put it in 1988, 'après *La Lune dans le caniveau* ... on se lassa de l'opposition manichéenne entre l'art du cinéma et l'esthétique publicitaire. Non qu'ils se soient réconciliés mais parce que la pub a fini par gagner' (Daney 1992: 47).[30] Faced with the inevitability of the postmodern, some commentators began to reassess its potential. Hutcheon, for example, among others, pointed out that postmodern parody is double-coded since it 'both legitimizes and subverts that which it parodies' (Hutcheon 1989: 117). As Dominic La Capra puts it:

Irony and parody are themselves not unequivocal signs of disengagement on the part of an apolitical, transcendental ego that floats above historical reality or flounders in the abysmal pull of aporia.

28 'Romantic and cynical, it's a mixture of both. It's a romanticism you don't really believe in.'
29 ' He likes to distance his narrative by the use of irony and derision. Indeed, his characters manage at one and the same time to take themselves very seriously and to see themselves from the outside, relativising their integration into their milieu.'
30 'After *La Lune dans le caniveau* ... people got tired of the Manichaean opposition between the art of cinema and the advertising aesthetic. Not that they had become reconciled but because advertising had ended up as the winner.'

Rather a certain use of irony and parody may play a role both in the critique of ideology and in the anticipation of polity wherein commitment does not exclude but accompanies an ability to achieve critical distance on one's deepest commitments and desires. (La Capra 1987: 128)

Even the *Cahiers du cinéma* adopted a more conciliatory position, as can be seen by the editor's comment on 1980s French cinema in 1991:

La fin de l'artisanat, la peur du téléfilm – ou de ce que l'on perçoit comme relevant vaguement d'une esthétique télévisuelle – la relative facilité pour monter des films chers, la crise des sujets, et bien sûr l'air du temps, l'air de la pub, du clip, de la forme courte, du zapping, sont autant d'éléments qui poussent le cinéma vers un 'tout à l'image' ... . (Ceci) a l'avantage d'offrir une troisième voie, entre le retour à 'la qualité française' opérée par un certain nombre de cinéastes des années 70, et le cinéma d'auteur marginalisé. (Toubiana 1991: 47)[31]

There was also a revaluation of the *cinéma du look*, which was placed in a different theoretical context, paradoxically, given in particular *Cahiers du cinéma*'s emphasis on painting during the 1980s, a fine art context, that of the baroque. Some of the points raised by that discussion will help us define Beineix's cinema in more detail.

Several reviewers had used the word baroque in relation to *Diva* in 1981. It was not until 1989 that the issue was explored in some depth by Bassan, writing for the *Revue du cinéma*. He makes a number of polemical points. The first is one which Beineix himself had made during the 1980s on several occasions (see, for example, Beineix 1981), that artists use whatever material is to hand in the world around them, and that therefore it would be illogical to criticise Beineix's use of 'low'-cultural material. He also points out that Beineix's fetishisation of objects is not confined to objects, but includes locations (such as the loft in *Diva*) as well, and therefore constructs a new urban myth, rather than slavishly pastiching advertisements. His major point, however, is to outline the way in which the style of the films of

31 'The end of artisanal filmmaking, the fear of the telefilm – or what was seen as being vaguely related to a televisual aesthetic – the relative ease with which expensive films could be made, the crisis in good subjects, and of course what was in the air, advertising, pop videos, short films, zapping, were all elements which pushed cinema towards "the image and nothing but the image" ... (This) has the advantage of being a third way between the return to the French quality cinema of some directors from the 1970s, and the marginalised auteur cinema.'

the *cinéma du look* can be called neo-baroque. He quotes the Larousse dictionary definition:

> En art le baroque veut étonner, toucher les sens, éblouir, et y parvient par des effets de mouvement et de contraste lumineux, de formes tendues et contrariées jusqu'à suggérer l'éclatement de perspectives jouant du trompe-l'œil; architecture, sculpture, peinture tendent à se fondre dans l'unité d'une sorte de spectacle dont le dynamisme scintillant traduit l'exaltation. (Bassan 1998: 49)[32]

Bassan's analysis, which Prédal has since hardened into a critical orthodoxy (see Prédal 1991: 468–69), came in the wake of a resurgence of interest in the baroque sensibility. A number of books appeared in French (see Buci-Glucksmann 1984; Buci-Glucksmann 1986; Deleuze 1988; Scarpetta 1988). The interest was not confined to France, however. Calabrese's book on the neo-baroque was published in Italy in 1987, and several of the points he makes are useful in thinking about Beineix's cinema.

Calabrese's book is less about the baroque than about the postmodern as an echo of the baroque. He explores contemporary culture to isolate what are now considered typical postmodern effects, such as excess, fragmentation, vortical turbulence and metamorphosis, which he links to show how the postmodern seeks to avoid the centre by excessive fragmentation. This creates monstrous forms, in the baroque sense of a combination of the marvellous and the enigmatic (Calabrese 1992: 92–93). The other point to retain from Calabrese is his insistence on structures of complexity such as the knot and the labyrinth, whose interest lies in what he calls 'constructed undecidability' (Calabrese 1992: 139): the pleasure to be gained from such structures 'is primarily the obvious pleasure of getting lost, of wandering, of renouncing that final principle of connection that is the key to the solution of the enigma' (Calabrese 1992: 140). Fragments 'become more relevant than the whole to which they belong and constitute excessive, baroque, hyperbolic forms of estrangement, (which) strive to reach a missing center, and multiply endlessly by means of infinite

---

32 'In art the baroque seeks to astonish, touch the senses, dazzle. It does so by using effects which rely on movement and contrast of light, forms which are stretched and strained to the point where perspective is disrupted and mutates into trompe-l'œil. Architecture, sculpture and painting tend to blend together into a unitary spectacle whose dazzling energy conveys euphoria.'

replication and differentiated repetitions' (Degli-Esposti 1998: 8). In this sense, *Diva*, with its double narrative strands, which intertwine in a complex puzzle, really is a perfect postmodern film, as suggested by Jameson, but it is equally applicable to the darkly operatic *La Lune dans le caniveau* and the glisteningly repetitive and allegorical *Roselyne et les lions*.

Deleuze's book is more about Leibniz than about the baroque; nevertheless, the point to hold on to is the key figure of the fold which gives the book its title. Rather like Calabrese's notion of the labyrinth or knot, Deleuze, who, like Calabrese, also uses the image of the labyrinth (Deleuze 1988: 5/1993: 3) and turbulence (Deleuze 1988: 7/ 1993: 4), sees the fold as archetypally baroque, leading matter to 'détours et ... replis' (Deleuze 1988: 52).[33] As he pithily puts it, 'par rapport aux plis dont elle est capable, la matière devient matière d'expression' (Deleuze 1988: 52),[34] dependent on light, illusory depth and fabric or texture. Moreover, this turbulence of matter gives rise, almost literally, to the spiritual: 'L'âme dans le Baroque a avec le corps un rapport complexe: toujours inséparable du corps, elle trouve en celui-ci une animalité qui l'étourdit, qui l'empêtre dans les replis de la matière, mais aussi une humanité organique et cérébrale ... qui lui permet de s'élever, et le fera monter sur de tout autres plis' (Deleuze 1988: 17).[35] Deleuze is most insistent on the spiritual side of the decorative: 'Les plis du vêtement prennent autonomie, ampleur, et *ce n'est pas par simple souci de décoration*, c'est pour exprimer l'intensité d'une force spirituelle qui s'exerce sur le corps, soit pour le renverser, soit pour le redresser ou l'élever, mais toujours le retourner et en mouler l'intérieur' (Deleuze 1988: 166–67; his emphasis).[36] Of particular

33 'Meanders and detours' (Deleuze 1993: 37).

34 'In relation to the many folds that it is capable of becoming, matter becomes a matter of expression' (Deleuze 1993: 37).

35 'In the Baroque the soul entertains a complex relation with the body. Forever indissociable from the body, it discovers a vertiginous animality that gets it tangled in the pleats of matter, but also an organic or cerebral humanity ... that allows it to rise up, and that will make it ascend over all the other folds' (Deleuze 1993: 11).

36 'Folds of clothing acquire an autonomy and a fullness *that are not simply decorative effects*. They convey the intensity of a spiritual force exerted on the body, either to turn it upside down or to stand or raise it up over and again, but in every event to turn it inside out and to mould its inner surface' (Deleuze 1993: 122).

interest here is Deleuze's view of the baroque house, which he sees as 'l'apport baroque par excellence', 'le monde a deux étages seulement, séparés par le pli qui se répercute des deux côtés suivant un régime différent' (Deleuze 1988: 41),[37] the lower floor, with its five windows representing the five senses, and therefore being open onto the world, representing matter, and the upper floor, a *camera obscura*, enclosed and heavy with the folds of drapery, representing the soul; the upper floor resonates, 'comme un salon musical qui traduirait en sons les mouvements visibles d'en bas' (Deleuze 1988: 6).[38] Beineix's films are vehicles which express not just disillusion with the world as it is, but also aspirations to a better world, a striving for an utopian perfection, so strong that it is analogous to what Deleuze means by the 'spiritual'.

Essentially, this book is grounded in the belief that there is much more to Beineix's films than the following fairly characteristic appraisal:

> Passion, dérision, sur-excitation, ombres chaudes à l'intérieur et dureté des extérieurs, contre-rythmes tour à tour languissants et frénétiques, couleurs à la fois violemment opposées et subtilement complémentaires, imposent non seulement l'esthétique mais une véritable éthique publicitaire, celle d'une fureur de vivre très mode où cynisme et romantisme font bon ménage, où on s'éclate dans l'alcool et le sexe, mais avec la sincérité d'une jeunesse avide d'écraser les gros porcs exploiteurs comme les clients bêtes et méchants d'une pizzeria. (Prédal 1991: 467)[39]

What the discussion of baroque and neo-baroque suggests is that, in addition to the heady mixture of passion and derision, and the idealism of youth, there is also light, excess, monstrosity, fragmentation,

---

37 'The Baroque contribution *par excellence*', 'a world with only two floors, separated by a fold that echoes itself, arching from the two sides according to a different order' (Deleuze 1993: 29).

38 'As if it were a musical salon translating the visible movements below into sounds up above' (Deleuze 1993: 4).

39 'Passion, derision, over-excitement, warm shadows inside and hardness outside, counter-rhythms which are listless and frantic by turns, colours which are violently contrasted and subtly complementary, impose not only an advertising aesthetic but the ethics of advertising: fashionable fast living where cynicism and romanticism are bedfellows, where people have a good time drinking and having sex, but with the sincerity of youngsters eager to squash the capitalist bastards as well as the stupid and nasty customers in a pizzeria.'

pleasure, the lost centre of a complex labyrinth, the body transformed. These are all elements to which I shall return when discussing Beineix's films in detail.

References

Bassan, Raphaël (1989), 'Trois néobaroques français', *Revue du cinéma* 449: 44–50.
Beineix, Jean-Jacques (1981), 'La métaphore de l'alpiniste', *Le Monde*, 9 March. Interview with Claire Devarrieux.
Beineix, Jean-Jacques (1983a), 'Je défie le jury de la critique', *Libération*, 13 May. Interview with Louis Skorecki.
Beineix, Jean-Jacques (1983b), 'Les confessions d'un enfant du siècle et du cinéma', *Première* 75: 119–21, 130–35.
Beineix, Jean-Jacques (1987), 'Interview', *Séquences*, 129: 40–47.
Beineix, Jean-Jacques (1989a), 'Jean-Jacques Beineix', in *L'Aventure du premier film*, edited by Samra Bonvoisin and Mary-Anne Brault-Wiart, Paris, Barrault, 148–59.
Beineix, Jean-Jacques (1989b), 'Entretien', *Revue du cinéma* 448: 50–54.
Billard, Pierre (1989), 'Les pouvoirs de la pub', *Le Point*, 895: 54–58.
Bonitzer, Pascal (1983), 'Standards d'émotion', *Cahiers du cinéma* 353: 9–12.
Bonitzer, Pascal (1988), 'Les images, le cinéma, l'audiovisuel', *Cahiers du cinéma* 404: 17–21.
Bonitzer, Pascal (1991), 'Images, cinema and the audio-visual scene', in *Cinema and Television: Fifty Years of Reflection in France*, edited by Jacques Kermabon and Kumar Shahani, London, Sangam, 228–36.
Breton, André (1987), *Mad Love*, translated by Mary Ann Caws, Lincoln and London, University of Nebraska Press.
Breton, André (1992), *Œuvres Complètes*, vol. 2, Paris, Gallimard. 1987.
Buci-Glucksmann, Christine (1984), *La Raison baroque*, Paris, Galilée.
Buci-Glucksmann, Christine (1986), *La Folie du voir: De l'esthétique baroque*, Paris, Galilée.
Buckley, Michael (1984), 'Jean-Jacques Beineix: An Interview with Michael Buckley', *Film In Review* 35/1: 29–33.
Calabrese, Omar (1992), *The Neo-Baroque: A Sign of the Times*, Princeton, New Jersey, Princeton University Press. Originally published in Italy as *L'età neobarocca*, Rome, Laterza, 1987.
Daney, Serge (1992), 'Beineix Opus 1', in *Devant le recrudescence des vols de sacs à main: Cinéma, télévision, information (1988–1991)*, Lyon, Aléas, 47–48.
Debord, Guy (1971), *La Société du spectacle*, Paris. Editions Champ Libre. Originally published Paris, Buchet-Chastel, 1967.
Debord, Guy (1995), *The Society of the Spectacle*, translated by Donald Nicholson-Smith, New York, Zone Books.
Degli-Esposti, Cristina (1998), 'Postmodernism(s)', in *Postmodernism in the*

Cinema, edited by Cristina Degli-Esposti, New York and Oxford, Berghahn, 3–18.

Deleuze, Gilles (1988), *Le Pli: Leibniz et le Baroque*, Paris, Editions de Minuit.

Deleuze, Gilles (1993) *The Fold: Leibniz and the Baroque*, translated by Tom Conley, London, Athlone.

Duncan, Alastair (1997), 'Representations of AIDS in health campaigns in France', unpublished paper, Conference on French visual identity, University of Stirling, Scotland, July 1997.

Eagleton, Terry (1996), *The Illusions of Postmodernism*, Oxford and Cambridge, Massachusetts.

Hayward, Susan (1993), *French National Cinema*, London and New York, Routledge.

Hayword, Susan (1998), *Luc Besson*, Manchester, Manchester University Press.

Hutcheon, Linda (1989), *The Politics of Postmodernism*, London, Routledge.

Jameson, Fredric (1993), 'Postmodernism, or the cultural logic of late capitalism', in Docherty, Thomas (ed.), *Postmodernism: A Reader*, New York and London, Harvester Wheatsheaf, 1993, 62–92.

Jay, Martin (1993), *Downcast eyes: The Denigration of Vision in Twentieth-century French Thought*, Berkeley and London, University of California Press.

Jullier, Laurent (1997), *L'Ecran post-moderne: Un cinéma de l'allusion et du feu d'artifice*, Paris, L'Harmattan.

La Capra, Dominic (1987), *History, Politics, and the Novel*, Ithaca, New York, Cornell University Press.

Lardeau, Yann (1984), 'Le dimanche d'un tâcheron', *Cahiers du cinéma* 359: 36–37.

Parent, Denis (1989), *Jean-Jacques Beineix: Version originale*, Paris, Barrault Studio.

Powrie, Phil (1997), *French Cinema in the 1980s: Nostalgia and the Crisis of Masculinity*, Oxford, Clarendon Press.

Prédal, René (1991), *Le Cinéma des Français depuis 1945*, Paris, Nathan.

Rogers, B. (1990), 'Breaks with tradition', *The Independent* 30 November, 16.

Scarpetta, Guy (1988), *L'Artifice*, Paris, Grasset.

Schifres, Alain (1983), 'Les dessous de la "pub" à la télévision', *Le Nouvel Observateur* 975: 42.

Séguéla, Jacques (1979), *Ne dites pas à ma mère que je suis dans la publicité ... Elle me croit pianiste dans un bordel*, Paris, Flammarion.

Séguéla, Jacques (1982), *Hollywood lave plus blanc*, Paris, Flammarion.

Séguéla, Jacques (1983), *Fils de pub*, Paris, Flammarion.

Toubiana, Serge (1991), 'Le cinéma présent: Trajectoire en 20 points', *Cahiers du cinéma* 443–44: 42–48.

3

Diva (1981)

Synopsis

Jules the postman makes a pirate recording of the famous black diva
Cynthia Hawkins at the Opéra, observed, unknown to him, by two
Taiwanese. He obtains her autograph in her dressing room where he
steals her white dress, and returns to his loft (an old garage) to listen
to the previously unrecorded diva on his hi-fi system. He is unaware
that two Taiwanese saw him record the diva, just as he is unaware
that Nadia, a prostitute, has, before being killed by two thugs, Spic and Le
Curé, dropped a tape which would reveal the identity of the boss of a
drug and prostitution racket into his mobylette.

Jules makes friends with Alba who borrows the tape of the diva so
that her boyfriend Gorodish can listen to it; Jules's flat is ransacked by
the Taiwanese who want the diva's tape. Saporta, the police chief, who
is also the head of the racket, instructs the thugs to get Nadia's tape
before his detectives do. The Taiwanese try to blackmail the diva into
signing a record contract by revealing the existence of Jules's tape
while Jules is with her. Jules remorsefully leaves to collect the tape, is
pursued first by the detectives, then, having listened to what he
thought was the tape of the diva, but was in fact Nadia's tape, by the
thugs. He is saved at the last minute by Gorodish who takes him to a
lighthouse to recover.

Gorodish listens to Nadia's tape, and forces Saporta to pay him for
it at a meeting in an empty warehouse. The Taiwanese take the
cassette, but Saporta blows up their car. Jules is caught by the thugs,
who take him to his loft where one of the two detectives, Paula, is still
on a stake-out. Paula kills Le Curé and wounds Spic. He is finished off

by Saporta, who is himself killed by Gorodish. Jules remorsefully returns the diva's tape to her in the empty Opéra.

Background

After making *Le Chien de Monsieur Michel* in 1977, and winning the first prize for it at the Festival de Trouville, Beineix decided to stop work as an assistant director and prepare a script with Olivier Mergault whom he had met on set. This was the story of a honeymoon gone wrong, with the newly-weds grounded in Paris by a strike (see Beineix 1983: 133). They sent the script to a variety of producers, among whom was Irène Silberman, who, with her husband Serge were the producers for Clément's film *La Course du lièvre à travers les champs* on which Beineix was second assistant director. She, like all the other producers, rejected the script, which Beineix and Mergault sold to the television channel TF1.[1] Beineix kept in touch with the Silbermans, and began working on adapting a *série noire* police thriller which had been proposed to him, only to find a few months later that the author had sold the rights to another producer. Beineix worked on his last film as assistant director, *French Postcards* (Huyck, 1979), to make ends meet. In August 1979 Irène Silberman phoned Beineix to ask him whether he had read Delacorta's *Diva*. Beineix liked the novel, and a contract was drawn up.

Beineix was given a co-writer (against his will), the Belgian Jean van Hamme; the two of them spent a couple of months working on the script together in Bruxelles, although Beineix subsequently finished the treatment by himself. Silberman decided that more money should be invested in production values than in actors, and accordingly there were no major stars (Rouchy 1981). Beineix and Bohringer had worked together on Zidi's *L'Animal* in 1977, where Bohringer had a small part.[2] Subsequently, Bohringer had acted in, among others, *Le Dernier Métro* (Truffaut 1980; where he plays the Gestapo officer), *Inspecteur La Bavure* (Zidi 1980), and *Le Grand Pardon* (Arcady 1981). Jacques Fabbri (Saporta) was a minor actor with some twenty-four films to his credit since 1949. Frédéric Andréi (Jules) had acted in a

---

1 It was later made for television by Fabrice Cazeneuve.
2 Although they had met a few years previously in the street, and a friendship had developed; see Parent 1989: 190.

couple of TV series, and Gérard Darmon (Spic) in one film. Dominique Pinon (Le Curé), An Lu Thuuy (Alba), and Wilhelmenia Higgins-Fernandez (Cynthia Hawkins, the diva) all made their débuts in this film. Beineix had seen Higgins-Fernandez in the role of Musetta in a Paris Opéra production of *La Bohème*; he modelled her performance on those of Jessye Norman (Beineix 1989: 156). Shooting lasted some ten weeks on a budget of seven million francs, and went well, although Beineix frequently felt frustrated by Serge Silberman's production decisions.

Adaptation

Beineix and Van Hamme stayed close to the voice of Delacorta's novel, with its mixture of ironic asides and fetishistic attachment to consumer objects. This, for instance, is the description of Jules's illicit recording equipment, which in the novel he hides in a violin case: 'N'allez pas croire que Jules passait son temps à insuffler du nerf à son *staccato*. Il aimait trop la musique pour chatouiller un Stradivarius de bazar. Dans sa boîte, il n'y avait ni violon ni archet, mais tout simplement un Nagra avec ce qu'on trouvait de mieux comme micros: des *Shoeps*' (Delacorta 1981: 15).[3] The novel has a postmodern mix of shopping sprees by Alba and Gorodish on the one hand and constant references to classical music on the other (a passion shared by Jules and Gorodish). This is echoed by the film's attention to objects and music. There are many iconic objects, such as the wave machine and the antique bath in Gorodish's loft;[4] the limousine murals on the walls of Jules's garage; the white Citroën, Parisian statues. Objects are more often than not presented with musical accompaniment, such as the tape-deck and other objects in Jules's loft when he replays the Catalani aria of the opening sequence. Satie-like piano music is

---

3 The translation omits the two first sentences, which I have attempted to translate within square brackets: '[Don't go thinking that Jules spent his time breathing spirit into his staccato. He liked music far too much to scratch and scrape on an imitation Stradivarius.] There was no violin in his case. It contained a Nagra tape recorder with the best microphones he could find: Shoeps' (Delacorta 1997: 6).

4 Inspired, Beineix later pointed out, by the theatre director, later turned film director, Patrice Chéreau's use of space (Beineix 2001: 56).

associated with Jules and the diva's night-time ramble through the streets of Paris, whose emphasis is on tourist sites (the Arc de Triomphe, the Luxembourg, the Place de la Concorde) and statues.

There are changes to the novel, however. Some are relatively minor, although significant, such as the fact that Alba is in the novel a 13-year-old blonde, rather than of Vietnamese extraction; Jules is a courier for a record company rather than a postman; and we are given considerable information about Gorodish's past and about his plans for the future. He has been an apprentice baker, a classical pianist, a nightclub pianist, chauffeur to Saporta, and artist-photographer, and is now planning 'un grand coup' (Delacorta 1981: 12/1997: 4). These changes are significant because in Alba's case they introduce a further complication in race issues to add to the novel's black diva (with a characteristic Beineixian irony in that Alba's name means 'white'). Where Jules is concerned, the change emphasises two key issues: the film is about mixed messages, and Jules is the messenger who ties two very different worlds together. As Forbes points out, the change from courier (who delivers objects from one client to another) to postman (who delivers messages to a whole network) makes the film postmodern, because 'it demonstrates that it is the circulation of information rather than its production which motivates both the narrative and social organisation' (Forbes 1992: 65).

In Gorodish's case, the film develops his enigmatic side by leaving out any sense of a personal history or motivation. These are replaced by a mythical history as the White Knight, according to Beineix: 'J'ai bien le droit de voir en Gorodish ... le Chevalier blanc. La traction avant, c'était un cheval blanc!' (Parent 1989: 232).[5] This mythical reference is doubled by a cinematic reference to Feuillade, both to the white horse ridden by by the eponymous hero in *Judex* (1916), as Tom Milne points out (Milne 1982: 191), but even more to the enigmatic criminal Fantômas in the crime series of the same name (1913–14), as suggested by Auty (Auty 1982: 302). Fantômas's chief characteristic is his elusiveness, bordering on the magical, which Beineix recreates by eliminating explanatory dialogue, and, more particularly, by the sequence where Gorodish appears as if from nowhere to knock Le Curé out with chemical gas as the thug is about to kill Jules (whereas

5 'I have the right to see Gorodish as the White Knight. The Citroën front-wheel drive was a white horse !'

in the novel, Jules rather more prosaically manages to escape from police and thugs before phoning Gorodish). Similarly, it is Gorodish who in the film tricks Saporta into his metaphoric and real fall, whereas in the novel it is Paula, the policewoman, who shoots him as he walks through the door of Jules's flat, gun at the ready.

Saporta is two characters in the novel, Saporta the mobster and Boulanger the police chief, whereas the film, intent on exploiting moral paradox among other types of duality, reunites the two in one character.

Locations, rather than characters, are where Beineix has changed the novel most. The exterior locations are much the same (the Opéra, followed by the Bouffes du Nord for the opera sequence, the Champs-Elysées, the métro which is the place in both novel and film where Jules is chased by the police). But one of the film's most striking features is its use of space, something Beineix has emphasised: 'Tout a été filmé en décor naturel. Mais nous avons considéré ces derniers non pas en relation avec leur finalité de lieu, mais en les traitant comme des volumes mis à notre disposition' (Beineix 1981: 26).[6] Jules's flat which in the novel once belonged to a painter, and which has paint splashes all over the floor, becomes a disused garage in the film, filled with all the clutter you might expect of a garage (it was a working garage in reality), with the addition of 1950s-style limousines painted on the walls. Gorodish's eight-room flat in the novel, which he slowly fills with furniture, much against Alba's wishes, because he likes to feel comfortable, becomes a vast loft space with only a few iconic items of furniture, such as the bath with feet, or the wave-machine. Saporta and Gorodish exchange money and tape on top of a water-tower in the novel, whereas the film's meeting occurs in a large disused hangar,[7] emphasising once again the use of vast interior space. The water-tower is one of the novel's more startling locations, and it is no surprise to see it resurface as the film's lighthouse, whereas Gorodish's hide-out is a large country house in the novel. The lighthouse was chosen for its light, because it was North-facing, which meant that the sun would both rise and set over the sea (Parent

6 'Everything was filmed on location. But we considered locations not in relation to their purpose, but as volumes for us to do as we liked with.'

7 As it happens, the old Citroën factory, quai de Javel in Paris, the very factory, Beineix has pointed out to me, which manufactured the Citroën 'traction avant' featured in the film.

1989: 231–32), but also because Beineix had visited it by chance with his girlfriend a few years before (see Beineix 1983: 134).

Finally, although I have mentioned some narrative changes when discussing changes to characters and to locations, it is worth pointing out one major change which concentrates the action: Nadia's tape is dropped into Jules's mobylette much later in the novel than in the film (in chapter three of eleven chapters), as the novel introduces the characters slowly. The effect is to establish the intertwining of the two worlds (Jules and classical music, Saporta and criminality) within the film's first fifteen minutes.

Reception

The film was released in March 1981. Many reviewers pointed out the newness of *Diva*'s style, which was felt to reflect a contemporary aesthetic. Billard, for example, in one of the few reviews with unqualified praise, lamented the fact that what he considered to be one of the most original films of the year, in a 'modern baroque' style, seemed to have passed unnoticed, with only average audiences (Billard 1981: 23). There were other supporters: the Communist *L'Humanité* which, unlike many, signalled the film's coherence (Vaugeois 1981), and the weekly what's on *Pariscope*, whose reviewers called the film 'un grand moment de cinéma' (Halimi 1981),[8] underlining the prodigious talent shown by Beineix (Bescos 1981).

Most reviewers were either cautious or overtly hostile. The photography and décor were generally praised, but it was pointed out that the film was quite obviously mannered, uneven and excessive in its iconography: 'Maniéré, recherché, emphatique ..., gratuité splendide de l'image, ... fascination pour les cadrages distingués, ... goût forcené de l'insolite' (Bosséno 1981: 30).[9] This was at the expense of a message: '(La) prééminence de l'image ... s'établit ... aux dépens de la signification, du "message" que l'on attend, peu ou prou, aujourd'hui de tout film' (Ramasse 1981: 68).[10] Terms connected to the notion of

8 'A great moment of the cinema.'
9 'Mannered, recherché, emphatic ... resplendent gratuitousness of the image ... fascination for good-looking compositions ... exaggerated taste for the unusual.'
10 '(The) pre-eminence of the image ... is at the expense of meaning, of the "message" which is expected from more or less every film nowadays.'

excess occur time and time again: 'surenchère', 'surcharge' (Chazal 1981), 'trop-plein de sophistication' (Coppermann 1981), 'démésurée dans l'hyperréalisme des décors' (Siclier 1981).[11]

Critical reactions were in fact sharply polarised. There is no better example of this than the reaction of one of the standard film journals, *Cinématographe*, which, unusually, ran two reviews, one very hostile, complaining about the overly mobile camera-work of the opening sequences, the stereotyped characters, and the overwhelming photography ('on ne remarque qu'elle'),[12] leading to the implied anti-postmodernist criticism, with its emphasis on the image as commodity: 'on croit qu'on regarde un film, on fait du lèche-vitrine' (Cuel 1981: 76).[13] On the same page, a more positive review complimented Beineix for the same features, pointing out that the film's principal tonality was irony:

> Clinquant, outré et dérisoire, moderne dans chaque excès de la modernité, *Diva* réunit tous les stigmates d'un film de son temps ... . (Beineix) ne se contente pas d'inventorier, avec une candeur enthousiaste, le catalogue des mythologies les plus immédiates et les plus précaires: il montre qu'il n'en est pas dupe. (Carcassone 1981: 76)[14]

Broadly speaking, most reviewers adopted one or the other of these two positions, so that where for one reviewer the film is like a cartoon, and this is bad because the characters have no depth (Schidlow 1981: 31), for another this is a positive quality (Vaugeois 1981). There was a similar reaction to the film's nightmarish quality (see Cuel 1981 for a negative reading, and Rochereau 1981 for a positive reading), and to its mixture of genres and intertextual allusions (Coppermann 1981 is positive; Leirens 1982 is negative, describing the film as a series of anthology pieces).

The *Cahiers du Cinéma* reviewer astutely pointed to a paradox: one of the film's strengths might be its quality of strangeness, but in this it was disappointing because it was less troubling (the hallmark of

11 'Extravagant', 'overloaded', 'overly sophisticated', 'excessively hyper-realist decor'.
12 'That's all you notice.'
13 'You think you are watching a film; you are just window-shopping.'
14 'Flashy, extravagant and derisory, over-emphatically modern, *Diva* combines all the faults of a film of its time. Beineix does not just catalogue, with enthusiastic ingenuousness, modish and transient mythologies, he shows that he is not fooled by them.'

strangeness in the Freudian sense of the *unheimlich* or uncanny) than familiar (Sainderichain 1981: 66). It is this familiarity, the feeling that the images of *Diva* were 'already-seen', a hotch-potch of recirculated bric-a-brac in line with Baudrillard's simulacra, that was at the core of the discussion in the pages of *Cahiers du Cinéma* during the remainder of the 1980s, and which, with hindsight, implicitly gestures towards the issue of originality and its interface with what the *Cahiers* saw as the importance of the auteur. The problem for *Cahiers* was how could someone who apparently used ready-made images from other media, especially those connected with advertising, and thus showed a lack of 'originality', possibly be considered an auteur, given that the premise of an auteur cinema was that it should distinguish itself from commercial cinema discourses?

The matter might have rested there, if the film had remained an average first film, with average takings and average success. This certainly looked as though it would happen. The film was released two weeks before its due date, and as a result publicity was not extensive. The film managed to attract a small score of 17,400 spectators in Paris and the Paris region; audience figures then sank over a period of ten weeks, levelling out at about one thousand spectators a week in two cinemas (thanks partly to one exhibitor, Pierre Braunberger, of the Panthéon cinema, who was a fervent supporter of the film). The film stayed at one thousand spectators a week until its 47th week. Nominated for the Césars in that week, the film began attracting large numbers of spectators, rising rapidly from one thousand a week in its 47th week to 11,500 in its 51st week. The film received four Césars (France's equivalent of the Academy Awards) at the end of that week (Best First Film, Best Decor, Best Lighting, Best Sound), and the next three weeks saw the numbers of spectators rise massively again from 23,400 to 26,400, to almost 32,000 in its 54th week, eventually giving a total of some 775,000 spectators in the Paris region, and some 1,500,000 in France as a whole. Against Silberman's advice, Beineix took the film to the Toronto Festival, where it did extremely well, subsequently doing well in the United States too, grossing $6 m, making it the third best-performing French film in the USA since 1975 (Saint Bris 1983).

Critical work

Diva is the only film by Beineix to have solicited considerable scholarly attention. I shall in this section give brief summaries of the major scholarly statements made, before moving on to my analysis.

Postmodern analyses (Jameson 1982; Forbes 1992; Hayward 1993; Austin 1996, Greene 1999)

Partly no doubt because of the film's success in the USA, it drew the attention of one of the foremost theorists of the postmodern, Fredric Jameson. His article is less a sustained analysis of the film than a meditation on the cultural specificity of the postmodern. He points out that the film marks a turn which corresponds to the accession to power of the left for the first time in thirty-five years. The film is for Jameson, on one level at least, a political allegory. He contrasts Gorodish with Jules. Gorodish is the 'hip new counter-cultural businessman' (Jameson 1992: 56), who although he meditates like a throwback to the 1960s, also, and more importantly, very actively masters the technological for profit. Jules, on the other hand, is the opposite of Gorodish. He is more passive, and represents the more traditional figure of the *enfant du peuple*, or innocent, tied to a local community by his job as a postman, and tied to the post-war period by his economic and sensible mode of transport, the mobylette. Broadly speaking, then, Jules represents the old, and Gorodish the new, 'post-Sixties multinational modernity versus a traditional French left populism' (Jameson 1992: 58), and Jameson links this to the opposition between the right-wing *nouveaux philosophes*, who embrace modernity, and the cultural agenda of the left under Mitterrand, which tried to appeal to the electorate by a return to past values. He points out, however, that although Gorodish and Jules may be in some sense opposed, the two sides they represent are brought together by an aesthetic synthesis. The two sides combine in *Diva* to work together in 'a curious new kind of solidarity, mediated by the theme of techno-logical reproduction ... and by a range of Third World women figures' (Jameson 1992: 59).

Jameson thus shifts his argument away from political allegory, to a consideration of what makes *Diva*'s postmodernism different from other types of postmodernism. Here, he draws a distinction between

Diva's images and those of what he considers to be a more obviously postmodern film such as Brian de Palma's *Blow Out* (1981). *Diva*'s images in their 'extraordinary luminosity' (Jameson 1992: 60) mark a return to an 'older Bazinian aesthetic' (Ibid.), where the objects in shot signal 'the restitution of a world transformed into images rather than infected and fragmented by them' (Ibid.). As he neatly puts it, when contrasting the images in *Diva* and *Blow Out*, 'the latter gleam while the former glow' (Jameson 1992: 62). In *Diva*, Jameson argues, the images help the spectator see the world differently, rather than simply gesturing to themselves auto-referentially so that all the spectator can do is to marvel at the display. Staying with the issue of auto-referentiality, he points out that the enthusiasm felt for the new age of mechanical reproduction cannot be represented in the same way that machines were represented in the 1920s (a computer casing does not embody energy in the way that the wing of an aeroplane might have done, for example). A film like *Blow Out*, then, Jameson suggests, focuses its narrative entirely on issues of reproduction; it 'sends us back to the reproductive machinery which is its own pre-condition' (Jameson 1992: 62).[15] In *Diva*, on the other hand, technology is not the paranoid centre of the film's narrative, but simply a theme among others:

> The new-technological content of postmodernism has been recontained, and driven back into the narrative raw material of the work, where it becomes a simple abstract *theme*: the Diva's horror of technological reproduction, along with the incriminating posthumous testimony on the other tape – these have become 'meanings' inside the work, where analogous material in *Blow Out* is scarcely meaningful or thematic anymore at all, generating on the contrary a whole celebration and 'acting out' of the reproductive process as form and as the production of sounds and images. (Jameson 1992: 62)

Jameson's point, then, is that *Diva* is not straightforwardly postmodern; rather, it is 'a curious mixture of old and new' (Jameson 1992: 62), positioned on the cusp of a political change as well as a cinema-specific change in the image. But whereas for *Cahiers du*

15 Jack (John Travolta) is a sound technician who works on B-movies. He records evidence of a crime, and gradually unravels a conspiracy which puts him in danger. The film does for sound what Antonioni's *Blow Up* (1966) did for photography, and also reprises, in a good example of postmodern intertextuality, Coppola's *The Conversation* (1974).

cinéma, *Diva*'s images were an end in themselves, for Jameson, more generous, and more attuned to the way the images are part of a culturally specific socio-political context, the images are a return to something which *Cahiers* believed in, the Bazinian aesthetic, but of which they refused to accept Beineix as an example.

If Susan Hayward, as noted above, adopts the same view as *Cahiers*, other British writers on French cinema, such as Austin have tended to agree with Jameson (see Austin 1996: 120). Forbes implicitly suggests that the technological content of the film makes it quintessentially postmodern in the same way that *Blow Out* is, and, returning to Jameson's distinction between pastiche and parody, suggests that the film is more pastiche than parody, for example in its stereotyped police-thriller side. Nevertheless, she also points out how *Diva* is complex. The film has a moral dimension in Jules, with whom we sympathise because we recognise that it is poverty which drives him to steal in his aspirations for something higher; and, something hinted at by Jameson, but passed over, the film has a most untypical *femme fatale* in the form of a black opera singer (Forbes 1992: 63–66).

A recent commentator, Naomi Greene, has picked up on the *Cahiers* view and on Jameson's analysis. She makes the important point that the political context was not as clear as Jameson makes out, since 'the difficult choices awaiting the Socialists – choices that Jameson places at the core of Beineix's 1981 film – were by no means apparent when they first assumed power' (Greene 1999: 171). She also shows how the film alludes less to the only political film mentioned by Jameson, Renoir's *Le Crime de Monsieur Lange* (1935) than to René Clair's 1930 comedies, such as *Le Million* (1931), and that this suggests a nostalgic return to the Golden Age of French cinema. However, in agreement with the *Cahiers* view of Beineix's films as surface spectacle, she sees Jules as no more than an '"emblem" of a populist character ... . An improbable creature of the present, he bears only the "look" – and the memory – of a vanished past' (Greene 1999: 173).

Feminist analyses (Zavarzadeh 1983; Kelly 1984; White 1988; Dagle 1991; Rowe 1991; Yervasi 1993)

Jameson's refusal to acknowledge issues of race and indeed gender is much criticised by Rowe, who considers that 'the most troubling aspect of the film ... is that it blatantly romanticizes the woman of colour as the last refuge for the white male' (Rowe 1991: 10), a point made by Zavarzadeh in 1983. He considers that the film exemplifies a crisis in male–female relationships. Since Western women have achieved considerable autonomy, they can less easily serve male fantasies of the 'nurturing mother and seductive mistress' (Zavarzadeh 1983: 56). Men's response, as exemplified in *Diva*, is twofold. White women are punished, either literally by death in Nadia's case, or by being presented as un-sensuous in the case of Paula, the policewoman, who rejects her companion's advances on the stake-out. Moreover, Paula, as Zavarzadeh points out, is on screen more than any other white woman, but, like the other white women, plays a relatively passive role. Dark women, on the other hand, are presented as caring and sensuous. Paula searches Jules's flat for the tape in the hope of cornering him, whereas Cynthia, who has more to lose from what she calls a rape, almost inexplicably forgives him, and protects him from the outside world in the cocoon of her music. Similarly, Alba cares for Gorodish, literally encircling him as she skates around him in the loft, and is sexually and socially uninhibited, as the sequence with the nude photographs of her suggests. Gorodish, the coolly analytical, and Jules, the intuitive romantic, both of them at ease with the modern world and its technology, represent, for Zavarzadeh, 'the two complementary sides of the European mind' (Zavarzadeh 1983: 59), and their 'colonization' of women of colour is legitimised by being associated, along with those women, with the forces of good, whereas other men and more particularly white women, are associated with the forces of evil. But, Zavarzadeh reminds us, Gorodish and Jules are just as greedy as the others: Jules steals the diva's voice and her gown, and Gorodish 'steals Alba from Indochina' (Zavarzadeh 1983: 59).

There are problems with this analysis, in that its logic collapses at key points. Paula's rejection of her companion's macho advances is hardly negative for a feminist analysis. Moreover, not all women of colour are associated with the good (Karina the prostitute, for example, who betrays Jules, admittedly under compulsion), and not all Western men are associated with good either: the thugs may be stereotypes, and Spic an unpleasant racial stereotype of the Spaniard, he is still a Western man, as is Saporta. Nevertheless, Zavarzadeh's analysis points usefully to issues of race which, as Kelly reminds us, underpin what might otherwise not have seemed to be anything more than a surface image. As Kelly points out, the diva may be black, but nothing is made of this, apart from the short 'Queen of the Night' sequence in the café (interestingly, not in the novel). Zavarzadeh shows how the image is charged with ideological power, demonstrating 'the emotional and sexual colonization of the dark woman' (Zavarzadeh 1983: 55).

Kelly's analysis revolves less around issues of race than around issues of female solidarity. Alba and the diva are, as Kelly puts it, 'social isolates' (Kelly 1984: 39); they do not have contact with other women in their group, nor do they have contact with each other, and both depend for affection on one (white) man. The exceptions to this rule are the prostitutes, with whom spectators are less likely to identify, if only partly because they betray Jules. Not only are the main female characters isolated, they are not portrayed as close to the men with whom they have relationships. These relationships are presented to us ambiguously: although the novel makes it very clear that Gorodish eventually makes love with Alba, and that the diva initiates lovemaking in the opera auditorium (a point Kelly does not make), the film tantalises the spectator with the spectre of sexual relationships, but these are never shown and remain unclear.

Kelly seems to be suggesting that women are presented as deficient; her subsequent analysis of the men correlatively suggests that the men gain what the women lose. She points out how Gorodish and Jules show feminine traits or are demasculinised. Gorodish is a home-maker, he knocks Le Curé out with chemical gas; Jules is puny, rides a downsized version of the more macho motorbike, and loves opera, which, says Kelly, is 'not a traditionally working class musical favourite' (Kelley 1984: 40). Although Kelly accepts that the eco-politics of the film are positive, in that the individual is in the end shown to be superior to technology, her view is that the film's gender politics are negative. The film isolates women and gives agency as well as femininity to the men, and shows, stereotypically, that men on the whole take, whereas women tend to give.

Yervasi takes this point one step further by focusing on what she calls the 'capturing process' (Yervasi 1993: 39), whereby the film constantly objectifies women, rather than men, by establishing representations of them, or associating them with representations of objects. Yervasi distinguishes between two types of representation, the first being what she calls permanent representations which not only objectify, but mythify the women, placing them within an 'eternal feminine': 'There are permanent images (photos, statues, paintings) and voices (recordings) that allow the "real" to leap out of its temporality and make itself eternal or mythical' (Yervasi 1993: 43). The second type is the mirror-image (the diva in the glasses of the Taiwanese, Alba in Gorodish's loft, Jules and the diva in the diva's hotel room), which, although they do not 'fix' the representations due to their ephemeral nature, nevertheless, according to Yervasi, 'attempt to efface the "real" and to offer the viewer the facility to accept the representation in the place of the "real"' (Yervasi 1993: 44–45). The 'capturing process' is paralleled in the narrative's insistence on the traffic in women, whether in women's bodies (the prostitutes) or their voices (the diva), or as Rowe puts it, 'female flesh and female cultural production' (Rowe 1991: 10). For Yervasi, it is logical that the film should end where it began, in the Opéra, since this 'conveniently frames the closed circuit of the patriarchal system' (Yervasi 1993: 46).

White bases her analysis on Doane's work on the female voice (see Doane 1980). She contrasts the diva's attempt to control her voice, and the patriarchal forces of (male) fantasy, technology and commerce ranged against her. These attempt to divorce the voice from the body and to turn the body into spectacle. The film thus becomes an 'allegory of women's submission to the ruling patriarchal order' (White 1988: 38), but with an utopian possibility: 'the holding of voice to body is figured as an idealized plenitude of non-divided female presence that resists male control' (White 1988: 38). Does this make the film 'progressively self-conscious' or 'regressively self-mystified', however (White 1988: 39)? In other words, is the film somehow analysing women's oppression critically, or is it colluding in that oppression by turning it into fantasized spectacle? White does not answer this question directly, but suggests the latter when she points out that the disjunction between Nadia and the diva's voice and body is presented to us from the very start of the film, so that 'this division of voice and body is the constitutive condition of (the film's) fictional narrative' (White 1988: 38). Dagle, similarly, reprising White's question, implies that the film's ambiguity is at the expense of women: 'Taping the song is an act of separation, of fragmentation (and this is how the diva understands it), but it is simultaneously an act meant to *re*constitute unity and coherence – for Jules' (Dagle 1991: 29; Dagle's emphasis).

Dagle's article focuses principally on a split other than the division between voice and body, however: that between race and gender. Dagle notes that feminist/psychoanalytic critiques of the film do not address issues of race (she is referring to White 1988 and to two critiques which I shall be considering in the following section, Lang 1984, Silverman 1988). Conversely, those which do explore issues of race (Zavarzadeh 1983; Kelly 1984) do not engage 'the theoretical dimensions of representation and gender' systematically (Dagle 1991: 32). Echoing White's query concerning progressive self-consciousness/regressive self-mystification, Dagle asks whether the apparent occlusion of race in the film itself is positive or negative: 'Either the film (projects) a liberal utopianism (constructing a potential world in which race does not matter) or the film (projects) a postmodern bourgeois cultural chic (taking advantage of an internationalised pop culture ethic wherein post-colonial signifiers indicate sophistication) – or some muddled combination' (Dagle 1991: 30–31). Like White, and like Dagle herself in the section of her article which deals with gender, she does not answer this question directly. What by default then is 'a muddled combination' of liberal utopianism and postmodern chic is read as a symptom. The conflict between positive–negative does not need to be resolved, because it is significant in itself; the racial other 'helps to unsettle the narrative's attempt at resolution' (Dagle 1991: 32). Dagle reaches this conclusion by a close analysis of a key sequence of the film, the Queen of the Night sequence, the only sequence where allusion is made to the diva's ethnic origins.

The sequence is constructed as a romantic interlude, and the spectator is deliberately misled during its course to assume that Jules and the diva will sleep together. This deception is maintained until the very end of the sequence when we see the diva asleep in her bed, followed by a shot of Jules also asleep under the same coloured blue sheets (shots 423–24 in Leclère 1991: 17). Dagle points out how the sequence 'can be read as revealing the contradictions inherent in Jules's desire derived from his constitution of her as both maternal and sexual Other' (Dagle 1991: 32); indeed, the sequence is followed by the diva's practice of Gounod's 'Ave Maria', which, when contrasted with Catalani's aria of doomed passion from *La Wally*, underlines the dichotomy between the maternal and the sexual. The sequence, however, insists on the diva's ethnic origin: she is wearing an African dress and beads, and is called 'Queen of Africa' by the street-seller N'Doula. Jules responds to this by calling her 'Queen of the Night'. Dagle points out how Jules's response is ambiguous. Although it could be read as an echo of 'Queen of the Night', emphasising the diva's blackness, it is just as likely that it represents Jules's attempt to reinstate the maternal–erotic dichotomy ('since either a mother or a lover might be metaphorically designated "queen of the night"'), or his attempt to reinstate what Dagle calls 'an operatic "lineage"', since 'Queen of the Night' is also 'the name of Mozart's evil queen/mother in *The Magic Flute*' (Dagle 1991: 33). Either way, in Dagle's view the effect of this sequence is that 'the racially-marked body interposes itself in the maternal/sexual dichotomy and ... is what prevents the contradictions from achieving narrative resolution' (Dagle 1991: 33). These contradictions are maintained in the final sequence on the stage of the Opéra, where Jules and the diva's embrace is ambiguously maternal as well as erotic. In an acute reading of what follows the last images we see on screen, however, Dagle suggests that the film does try to resolve these contradictions, although it does so by occluding race:

> The credits appear, the visual image fades to black, but the taped aria continues. The voice and its song constitute the final gesture effacing the contradictions of desire and race. Thus by suppressing the visual image and leaving only the voice, the film seeks to 'leave behind' the narrative and its lack of resolution and locate the fulfillment of desire, however self-divided, in a 'pure space' of 'pure presence'. (Dagle 1991: 33)

The voice is also crucial to psychoanalytical readings of the film.

Psychoanalytical analyses (Lang 1984; Silverman 1988)

Several of the feminist critiques allude to psychoanalytical frameworks. For example, Rowe points out that the ambiguity of the film's ending can be read through an Œdipal scenario. A conventional romantic thriller, she suggests, would have brought the two young protagonists, Jules and Alba, together at the end. Indeed, although she does not mention this, their meetings are suffused with sexual innuendo: the nude photographs which form the basis of Jules's opening gambit with Alba; Jules explaining the romantic song to Alba in his loft; Alba undressing in front of Jules in the water-tower.

Despite all of these cues, as Rowe points out, 'the film unites the two child-lovers with their older, more Œdipal partners' (Rowe 1991: 11). In this light, the diva serves as a mother for Jules, just as Gorodish serves as his 'good father' who has defeated the 'bad father', Saporta (Rowe 1991: 11).

In a similar vein, Silverman sees the emphasis on the diva's voice as 'an imaginary return to infantile plenitude, or, to be more precise (given the generational gap between Jules and the diva) the maternal voice' (Silverman 1988: 87). This is a view which Lang had elaborated a few years previously. Lang suggests that the primacy of music in particular can be interpreted as a return to the pre-Œdipal relationship with the mother, for both Jules and more importantly for the spectator: 'It is a return to the pre-mirror stage where there is no perceived difference between one's body and the rest of the world that Jules craves and which is part of what draws us to the cinema' (Lang 1984: 76).[16] Lang adduces the obvious cocooning effect of much of the music in the film, pointing especially to the 'amniotic bath' taken by Jules at the diva's hotel, and Gorodish's bath 'in the placental gloom of his loft' (Lang 1984: 77), both baths being associated with the mother-like diva singing. Gorodish's aural pleasure is doubled by the oral pleasure of his cigar.[17]

16 The relationship between music and the maternal has been discussed by Barthes and Kristeva, among others. See my account of this debate in Powrie 1997: 23–24.

17 As Lang implicitly suggests, although he misrecognises the prop: 'with a cigarette, he has every prop for the experience of perfect pleasure, if not of bliss' (Lang 1984: 77). There are a surprising number of mistakes in Lang's article, which it might be as well to point out here. He claims that the music which accompanies Jules as he arrives at the opera is internal diegetic (Lang 1984: 73), meaning that it represents what Jules hopes to hear, whereas it is diegetic: it emanates from the audiocassette machine on Jules's mobylette, as is made clear when he reaches forward to turn it off; just in case we did not catch this aural trick, it is repeated, more obviously, when Jules returns to his flat. The mistake would not matter were it not for the fact that Lang uses it to make a general point about music being frequently 'in the head' of the character, as established by this shot. Lang also claims that the diva is reflected in Jules's sunglasses, whereas she is reflected in the sunglasses of the Taiwanese; Jules does not wear any (Lang 1984: 73). Finally, Lang suggests that Gorodish and Saporta meet in a disused railway station, whereas it is a disused factory (Lang 1984: 75). It should be said that Lang is not the only writer to have made mistakes. Greene consistently calls Gorodish 'Godorish'; Jameson thinks that Jules listens to the tape of the diva on a water-sofa in his flat (Jameson 1992: 57). And both Lang

Pre-Œdipal bliss is a logical impossibility, of course, although as Lang says, music's emphasis on the voice, and therefore on the body, is a more likely vehicle to approximate it. Nevertheless, the film's narrative makes it clear that it is impossible: in the final opera sequence, the auditorium is empty, underlining that Cynthia's 'possibility of being completely "at one" with an audience as a pre-mirror phase child is "at one" with the world, has been forever lost' (Lang 1984: 76). Jules surrounds himself with the diva's voice (whether in his flat or on his mobylette), and smothers himself with her dress, but at the end of the film, they remain standing, holding hands, and, although occasionally moving to clasp each other, they very pointedly do not kiss, still less make love, as in the novel (see Delacorta 1981: 223/Delacorta 1997: 135–36).

In Lacan's mirror phase, the child sees an ideal image which s/he will spend the rest of her/his life trying to capture. As Lang says, 'the self can only be seen in reflection' (Lang 1984: 72). In *Diva*, the voice is used, Lang has suggested, to somehow get closer to what preceded the emerging identity glimpsed in the mirror, but, clearly, the film is also about reflections, as Hagen's piece explores.

Spatial analyses (Hagen 1988; Revie 1994)

Hagen points out how the film's centre is a performance space with a disappearing centre (except for the final establishing shot of the opera, interior spaces are fragmented and never presented as wholes;

---

and Kelly unwisely base general points on mistranslated sub-titles. Thus, Gorodish maintains his independence, as is suggested, says Kelly, by the epithet of 'The Lone Ranger', which is a mistranslation for 'un rasta', meaning, in the context, someone who is different from the others (Kelly 1984: 39). Lang suggests that Alba says 'out of sight' when she hears the diva's voice for the first time, but Alba has said 'le pied!'. This does not mean the literal foot, as one might have thought, but is a familiar expression based on the phrase 'prendre son pied', which in fact means to take one's share ('pied' in the sense of the measure, as in the English 'foot' of 12 in), and by extension, to make love. The expression, irrespective of its now obscure erotic origin, means to take pleasure. This somewhat diminishes Lang's point when he uses the sub-title's approximation of the vernacular, 'out of sight', to make the point that 'it is an experience which (unusual for the cinema) has little to do with sight' (Lang 1984: 75). This may be true, but the expression carries a sense of desire, which is not far removed from the pleasure afforded by sight.

indeed, the 'opera' is, in the opening sequence, two separate locations, the Paris Opéra and the Bouffes du Nord), and which is structured on a complex series of duplications and replications:

> Two tapes, two white Citroëns, two pairs of villains, two pairs of positive characters (Alba/Gorodish and Jules/Diva), the police team, the performance and the tape, the dead Nadia and her tape, Alba and her nude shots, the Diva and her prostitute substitute – linked by the Diva's gown – the prostitute and her nude bust, the head of a statue in the Tuileries and the close-up of the Diva, also looking to the left, the poster of the Diva, the various 'looks' of the Diva associated with her changing hair-do ... , the puddle that reflects the white Citroën, the back of the chrome headlight that reflects the same car, Jules's shiny helmet, the windows of the Ritz and the arcade, the reflective sunglasses of the Taiwanese. (Hagen 1988: 157)

Hagen suggests that Gorodish, as master of space, light and illusion, is an avatar of the director, and that through his performance (emblematised by the zen art of buttering bread sequence), he brings order, centrality and stability to a chaotic, decentred and unstable space.

Revie, similarly, places Gorodish, or rather his values – a paradoxical lack of concern with material possessions combined with a constant preoccupation with money – at the centre of the film's concerns, pointing out how classical music functions in the film to legitimise Gorodish's amorality. By comparing the novel and the film, he shows how Alba, who is relatively important in the novel, is accorded little importance in the film. Revie's major concern, however, as the title of his piece suggests, is to explore the way in which Paris is presented to the spectator. Reminding us how Paris in French films had, at least until the 1980s, tended to be mythologised as romantic, and community-oriented, Revie underlines the alienating qualities of *Diva*'s Paris, 'a succession of crowds devoid of human contact and value', 'a theatre of hostility' (Revie 1994: 31). Hostile exteriors are contrasted with interiors of fantasy (the dreamy loft spaces). The function of music in the film is not only to give Gorodish plus-value, but to 'transcend the hard spaces which separate the characters' (Revie 1994: 32). In that respect, Revie suggests, it works in the same way as fantasy and parody in the film, to reclaim a fragmented, alienated space.

What emerges from the variety of readings of *Diva* is, first, the fact that they exist at all. The film is quite clearly a problematic, indeed provocative object for commentators, who more often than not emphasise its contradictions and paradoxes. Second, the readings offer heterogeneous and often conflicting interpretations, suggesting that the film is not only an object of fascination, but that it is pivotal, the symptom of a turn. It is a turn in cinematographic terms, with the emphasis on the image and spectacle. It is a turn in cultural terms with the emphasis on postmodern effect (parody/pastiche, image at the expense of narrative). It is a turn, finally, in film studies terms; the 1980s was the decade of a key debate between the two principal interpretations of the film, the postmodern on the one hand, and the feminist/psychoanalytical on the other.

The analyses of which I have tried to give an account above may well be heterogeneous; they do, however, all have one thing in common, and it will be my point of departure in the next section.

Towards a new approach

All of the analyses outlined above have in common the notion of binary opposites and doublings, whether it is Jameson's old/new, Greene's old cinema/new cinema, Zavarzadeh's uncaring and therefore bad white women/caring but stereotyped and colonised dark women, Kelly's women alone/men together, Yervasi's real/representation, White's voice/body, Dagle's gender/race, Hagen's list of reflections, Revie's alienation/fantasy, or Lang's implied mother/son dichotomy, resolved inadequately by the oral, itself opposed to the visual (or, to use the psychoanalytical terms employed by Lang, the invocatory versus the scopic), the oral/visual dichotomy in turn inadequately resolved by the kiss we never see.[18] *Diva* is therefore built on a structuring absence, equivalent to the slash I have used to separate the binaries above, a gap or cut whose function is to underline difference and the impossibility of escaping splitting, the most primal of these splittings being that between the infant and the mother. The film proliferates excessively and melodramatically (very literally, since it is a film partly about music) in its narrative and iconographic systems the cut which is at the heart of film, the cut

18 This formula is Lang's, who points out that spectators crave closure in films, often provided by the terminal kiss of romantic comedy, which brings together the oral and the scopic; see Lang 1984: 77.

between different shots, drawing attention not only to the constructedness of film, but to the constructedness of identity, and to the way in
which the two interact.

Using the materials suggested by the scholars whose work I have
tried to summarise above, I shall show how this cut or split at the
heart of *Diva* can be used to theorise the film's operations. Much like
Lang, who sees the film as a return to the pre-Œdipal (and indeed
Silverman, who views the cut in film more generally as a symptom of
loss),[19] I see the film as an enactment of the attempted return to the
Kleinian oral mother, but with the difference that the drama of the
film is less the obvious point that this cannot be achieved, with all the
melancholy and nostalgia that this entails, so much as the very real
tussle between, to use a Kleinian term, different imagos (good/bad
father, good/bad mother) as the child struggles to cope with its
emerging selfness. Further, into this basic Kleinian structure, I would
like to return to issues connected with the baroque to show how the
film cannot be reduced to a psychological template, but is also an
aesthetic object with spiritual impulsions.

Essentially, then, I am proposing two ways of reading the film. The
first is based on psychoanalysis, and is therefore dependent on one of
the major types of interpretation in film studies, operative since the
early 1970s, and, although much contested and revised during the
1980s, still used by writers in film studies today. However, most
writers use Freud and Lacan as the basis for such psychoanalytical
work, whereas my interest here is to use Klein, who was championed
by a number of feminist writers during the 1980s,[20] and I shall

19 'Since suture has been advanced as a means of accounting for cinematic syntax,
  and since cinematic syntax obviously exceeds the shot-reverse shot formation,
  we might simply formulate it as the relationship between a shot and the missing
  element (syntagmatic or paradigmatic) by which it is perceived as a shot. To
  push the analogy between castration and the cinema a bit further, I would like to
  suggest that the missing element by which a shot is defined as a shot might well
  be the cut. Seen in these terms, cinematic activity comprises a constant
  fluctuation between the imaginary plenitude of the shot, and the loss of that
  plenitude through the agency of the cut' (Silverman 1980: 4). Silverman places
  the moment of the shot in the context of the Œdipus, as a form of castration,
  whereas I will be suggesting that the splitting procedure of which the cut is
  evidence is less the entry into the symbolic, as Silverman goes on to point out,
  than the pre-Œdipal moment of loss defined by Klein.
20 The paperback editions I am using were published in the mid-1980s; see the
  references, p. 69.

outline the principal interest of her work for a feminist analysis of film in the next section.

The second interpretative scheme I am using is also rooted in the 1980s, that of the neo-baroque. Whereas the psychoanalytical framework uses a film's narrative more than its iconographic systems, conversely, an approach based on the neo-baroque will tend to privilege the iconographic over the narrative. The two approaches should therefore complement each other, as well as provide interpretations using discourses which were operative during the 1980s.

Klein and 'memories in feeling'

The reason for using Klein's work, however, is not principally because it somehow corresponds neatly to the films of Beineix in terms of epoch. Rather, Klein's work emerged as an important strand of feminist thinking during the 1980s. It thus at least started to counter the hegemonic Freudianism and Lacanianism used by both literary and film theorists. It is, then, the fact that Klein throws a different light on old structures which interests me here, for I remain unconvinced that the psychoanalytic paradigm used in film studies since the mid-1970s has been exhausted.[21] In particular, I think that that the paradigm manages to explain the peculiar pleasures of film in ways which other paradigms do not. The theoretical problems encountered, principal among which are the assumed maleness of the gaze and the use of the Œdipus complex as a fundamental structure, both of which have as a consequence the disempowerment of the female spectator, can be avoided if one uses a structure which precedes the Œdipus. Studlar attempted to do this by invoking masochistic structures, using Freud and Deleuze's work on Sacher-Masoch (Studlar 1985). This was treated sceptically by some theorists;[22] their differences,

21 I have used Klein's work before; see 'Reading for Pleasure: Marie Cardinal's *Les Mots pour le dire* and the text as (re)play of Œdipal configurations' (Powrie 1990: 163–76) and '*Un dimanche à la campagne*: Nostalgia, Painting and Depressive Masochism' (Powrie 1997: 38–49).

22 Silverman, for example, who was also working on masochism in this period, considers that Studlar 'conflates Deleuze's oral mother with the pre-Œdipal mother of object relations psychoanalysis, and extrapolates from that conflation a highly dubious argument about the origin of masochism. According to Studlar, that perversion has its basis in the (male) child's relationship with the

which were outlined in footnotes, and which I have myself relegated to a footnote, are complex, and in a sense unimportant, because the model I am suggesting avoids the complexities which arise out of using the Œdipus as a model, and is in many ways much simpler to understand.

Basing her theories primarily on the empirical observation of young children playing, Klein outlined splitting procedures which occur in the first few months of life, prior to the Œdipus complex. During the first three months of life, the infant ego lacks cohesion and has sadistic phantasies directed against the mother and the primal object, the mother's breast (or the bottle). The infant copes with parts of the self which are felt to be bad and destructive by projecting these parts into the mother, phantasising aggressive attacks on her, and very quickly on the father, as well as other people or objects.[23] Parts of the self which are felt to be good are also projected in this way; indeed, the primal object, the breast, is not only seen as bad, but as good, and idealised, partly to compensate for what is felt to be its persecutory nature. Klein came to call this process projective identification, and it forms the basis of what she calls the paranoid–schizoid position. In

---

actual mother prior to the advent of the father, a relationship predicated upon his helpless subordination to her, and the insatiability of his desire for her. Masochistic suffering consequently derives from the pain of separation from the mother, and the impossible desire to fuse with her again, rather than from the categorical imperatives of the Œdipus complex and symbolic law. This is a determinedly apolitical reading of masochism, which comes close to grounding that peversion in biology' (Silverman 1992: 417 n. 50). Rodowick agrees with Silverman's critique, and points out that 'in opposing masochism to sadism as a model of filmic pleasure, Studlar fundamentally misconstrues (his) critique of Mulvey ... reinvoking an agonistic logic of binary terms that (he) insist(s) must be rejected' (Rodowick 1991: 143 n. 11).

23 'The phantasied onslaughts on the mother follow two main lines: one is the predominantly oral impulse to suck dry, bite up, scoop out and rob the mother's body of its good contents ... . The other line of attack derives from the anal and urethral impulses and implies expelling dangerous substances (excrements) out of the self and into the mother. Together with these harmful excrements, expelled in hatred, split-off parts of the ego are also projected on to the mother, or, as I would rather call it, *into* the mother. These excrements and bad parts of the self are meant not only to injure but also to control and to take possession of the object. In so far as the mother comes to contain the bad parts of the self, she is not felt to be a separate individual but is felt to be *the* bad self' (Klein 1986: 183; her emphases).

this position the infant feels persecutory anxiety as a result of its phantasied attacks on the mother, because it fears retaliation (as Klein points out, 'the infantile dread of magicians, witches, evil beasts' is a later modification of these early phantasies; Klein 1986: 117). Splitting, which leads to the fear of retaliation for the attacks on the mother, is also a way of defending itself against that fear, because bad parts are split off from the self. Essentially, the infant is feeling something like this: 'I hate the breast/mother because it is not satisfying me, there-fore the breast/mother is hateful. But because I am attacking it in phantasy, this means that it will attack me in return, so I had better carry on projecting its hatefulness back onto the mother, as well as seeing it as a bountiful breast and taking solace in that breast (which is also persecuting me because it hates me)'. Of course, my attempt to summarise the mechanisms involved is fundamentally flawed in that it presumes a coherent ego, whereas the infant at this point is frag-mented, disintegrated, 'falling into bits' as Klein puts it (Klein 1986: 179).

The paranoid–schizoid position is followed by what Klein calls the depressive position in the fourth to sixth months of life. At this point the ego splits less and works towards greater integration as the infant adapts to the reality of the outside world. Parts which were previously split and separated from each other (the loved mother/breast, the hated mother/breast) are more likely to be felt as a complete rather than part object. The infant is said to introject this complete object (to take it into itself in a process of identification), and as a result the infant feels guilt for its attacks on the mother and her breast (and all the other objects which follow it), which is now felt to be the loved object. This leads to an increased feeling of loss and mourning as the infant feels something like this: 'Why ever did I attack the object I love, even if I admittedly also hate it ? Now it will go away and I will have lost it forever'.

There are two key issues for my purposes in Klein's work: the first is that the mechanisms which she describes are not gender specific (despite the fact that, coming before second-wave feminism, she uses 'he' constantly to talk about the infant). This, together with the fact that these mechanisms are in operation before the Œdipus complex, means that the problems associated with the psychoanalytical struc-tures used hitherto in film studies, as exemplified by Mulvey's work and the various debates to which it gave rise during the 1980s and early 1990s (briefly: what does one do about the female spectator if the gaze is 'male'?), do not occur. The gaze becomes only one of the ways in which object relations are mediated. Whereas for psycho-analytic film theorists the fetish is of crucial importance, and is dependent on a very specifically male gaze, in the structure I am proposing, what is important is not the fetish object which is linked to castration as part of the Œdipus, but objects which are as much felt (smell, touch, taste, hearing), as they are gazed upon, and which form part of the infant's experience well before the Œdipus.

The second key issue is that Klein stresses that these are *positions*: they can occur simultaneously, and they recur throughout one's life. As Mitchell points out, unlike the Freudian emphasis on libidinal stages through which the infant must pass, Klein 'substitutes a structural for a developmental notion. This facilitates the making of a connection between adult psychosis and infant development – a "position" is an always available state, not something one passes through' (Klein 1986: 116); or, as Klein herself explains, 'processes of introjection and projection in later life repeat in some measure the pattern of the earliest introjections and projections: the external world is again and again taken in and put out' (Klein 1988: 155). This means that it is considerably easier to use Klein's theories as a synchronic structure to explain why a film is pleasurable (even if that pleasure is mixed with pain) for the spectator at a given point in time, as I hope to show in what follows.

Klein herself used her structures to talk about literary texts. In one of the three such pieces she wrote, 'On identification' (1955), which is an exploration of a novel by the French writer Julien Green, she analyses the adventures of the hero, Fabien, 'almost as if he were a patient' (Klein 1988: 152). I should stress, however, that it is not my intention to do the same thing with Jules; rather, I am using Klein to show how the film works as a structure which returns the spectator to the same kind of positions (the paranoid–schizoid, the depressive) as might have been experienced in infancy, and which carry on being experienced throughout life. The film works, and has endured, in other words, because it articulates a powerful structure, what Klein elsewhere calls 'memories in feelings' (Klein 1988: 180). Klein was obscurely aware that her work could be used in this way. In her penul-timate, unfinished piece of work, 'Some reflections on *The Oresteia*' (1963), she wrote that 'the creative artist makes full use of symbols;

and the more they serve to express the conflicts between love and hate, between destructiveness and reparation, between life and death instincts, the more they approach *universal form*' (Klein 1988: 299; my emphasis), a form she attempted to isolate in Aeschylus's trilogy. *Diva*, then, like the part-object (the mother's breast), powerfully evokes pre-verbal emotions and phantasies, what she also calls, 'fundamental situations', which, in analysis, allows the past, the 'memories in feelings', to be retrieved and articulated, or, as I have put it elsewhere,[24] 'the spectator is placed in a position of recall, recognition, and recovery' (Powrie 1997: 45):

> In taking the analysis back to the earliest infancy, we enable the patient to revive fundamental situations – a revival which I have often spoken of as 'memories in feeling'. In the course of this revival, it becomes possible for the patient to develop a different attitude to his early frustrations … . The weakening of projections, and therefore the achieving of greater tolerance, bound up with less resentment, make it possible for the patient to find some features and to revive pleasant memories of the past, even when the early situation was very unfavourable. (Klein 1988: 234)

Beineix himself has said that in making *Diva* he wanted to recover the 'grandes émotions d'enfant' (Tranchant 1982).[25] The pleasure gained from viewing *Diva* is, in my view, largely due to the fact that it revives, as 'memories in feelings', the pre-Œdipal paranoid–schizoid position, characterised by multiple splitting procedures, projection, aggression on part-objects, and works through (to use a Freudian term also employed by Klein)[26] to the depressive position characterised by guilt,

24 Although my argument there was to account for the power of the intertextual use of paintings, rather than the more general point I am making here.

25 'The great emotions of childhood.'

26 'I have attempted to show that by analysing over and over again the anxieties and defences bound up with envy and destructive impulses, progress in integration can be achieved. I have always been convinced of the importance of Freud's finding that "working-through" is one of the main tasks of the analytic procedure, and my experience in dealing with splitting processes and tracing them back to their origin has made this conviction even stronger' (Klein 1988: 231). Klein stresses elsewhere that 'working through' is not confined to patients with mental problems, but occurs 'to some extent in normal individual development … . Depressive and persecutory anxieties are never entirely overcome; they may temporarily recur under internal or external pressure, though a relatively normal person can cope with this recurrence and regain his balance' (Klein 1988: 255–56).

and the introjection of the complete object. And, much like the analyst helps the patient articulate those memories, some of which may well be painful, the present analysis will, I hope, articulate the way in which the film positions us. In this respect, working through the splitting mechanisms is analogous to Aristotelian catharsis.

I am all the more convinced that the film works in this way, because so many reviews of the film stressed its visual attractiveness while at the same time denigrating the importance of the narrative, which was felt to be confused. This view of the narrative is almost incomprehensible, since the narrative structure is relatively simple: two tapes, both of which are betrayals, are interchanged, bringing two worlds which would otherwise not have been connected, the upper (class) world of classical music and the lower (class) world of criminals, into close contact. Much French comic theatre relies heavily on this kind of upstairs/downstairs parallelism, which is not so much complex and confusing as a staple narrative structure. My conclusion, then, is that the view that the narrative is confusing is a defence mechanism, a way of protecting oneself from a powerful 'memory in feeling',[27] and the displacement onto the visual is a means of avoiding the power of the narrative and the soundtrack, as vehicles for 'feeling'.

Finally, before I embark on a Kleinian analysis, the reader might be forgiven for thinking that I am using a sledgehammer to crack a nut. One of the more respected Parisian reviewers, however (and he alone to my knowledge), points out the psychoanalytic overtones of

27 Here is a sample from some of the reviews. The narrative is 'totalement farfelue'/ (totally far-fetched') (Anon 1981a), 'un peu complexe' ('somewhat complex') (Anon 1981b), 'bien compliquée' ('very complicated') (Baignères 1981), 'un méli-mélo' ('a mish-mash') (Anon. 1981c), 'artificiellement tortueux' ('artificially convoluted') (Sarran 1981); 'tout s'embrouille' ('everything is confused'), says another (Rochereau 1981), and yet another ironically writes that the story is so confusing that 'il évite au critique le mieux intentionné de (le) résumer' ('even the critic who has the best of intentions will not be able to summarise it') (Rolin 1981). More surprising still is the suggestion by at least two reviewers that the adaptation from the novel is more complex than the original: 'une variation folle et débridée sur l'histoire simple, inspirée d'un roman de Delacorta' ('a wild and unbridled variation on a simple story, inspired by a Delacorta novel'), says one (Baudin 1981), while one of *Le Monde*'s critics complains of 'changements de l'intrigue (inutilement compliquée)' (changes in the story-line which make it pointlessly complicated') (Siclier 1981; this statement is repeated in Siclier 1991: 256), which makes one wonder whether they read the original novel.

the film. His allusions to a deep structure are couched in vituperatively ironic tones, with unpleasantly racist touches, as though, yet
again, a defence mechanism were being invoked:

> Il y a de la sorcellerie psychanalytique dans le scénario de *Diva* et je me
> garderai bien d'essayer d'en élucider les mystères. Qu'on sache
> simplement que le jeune homme a demandé à une autre prostituée de
> passer la robe de la diva avant de faire l'amour ... , que le réseau de
> traite des Blanches qui le poursuit (les prostituées que nous voyons
> sont noires, mais je crois qu'il faut dire traite des Blanches) est dirigé
> par une figure paternelle de style jupitérien appartenant à la police et
> que la diva frustrée de sa robe et de sa voix finit par se prendre pour lui
> d'une affection toute maternelle. (Pérez 1981)[28]

This is an extraordinary piece of writing. A psychoanalytic framework
is invoked and rejected at the same time (it is no more than 'witchcraft'), and it is the familiar Œdipal scenario where the young boy
phantasises making love with his mother, displaced onto a prostitute.
This kind of analysis will normally mention the desire to kill the
father, here alluded to as Saporta. But the God-like ('Jupiter') Saporta,
unnamed, and unharmed, apparently survives (when part of the
dénouement of the film is precisely that he should die), and it is
wrongly implied through ambiguity (although I am sure that Pérez
did not intend it, but there again ...) that the diva develops affection
for him, not Jules. Much is made of prostitutes in this text, and in his
desire to make the film's narrative cohere (although it is his own
narrative which is seeking for the coherence of plenitude, the complete
object), Pérez emphasises the trade in prostitutes at the expense of
drug-trafficking, which is at least as prominent in the film's dialogue.
He goes off at an inexplicable tangent (all the more inexplicable
because the text is desperately seeking for coherence) by cracking a
dubious joke about slave trading. He is calling the prostitution racket
a slave trade, which normally alludes to trading black slaves, but, having

---

28 'There is psychoanalytic witchcraft in *Diva*'s screenplay and I shall be careful
not to try and elucidate its mysteries. Know simply that the young man has
asked another prostitute to put on the diva's dress before making love ... , that
the network which deals in trade in white women and which is after him (the
prostitutes we see are black, but I think that one should say trade in white
women) is directed by a father-figure in Jupiterian style who belongs to the
police and that the diva who has lost both her dress and her voice ends up by
developing a very maternal affection for him.'

pointed out that all the prostitutes we see are black (erroneously, since Nadia is white), he insists that we should call this the white slave trade, which means the trade in white women sold into prostitution. The text works hard, then, to establish the parental couple while at the same time purporting that this is nothing but 'witchcraft'. Having done so, it emphasises the father figure (who is a god), and denigrates the mother figure (is she white? is she black? does it matter anyway? because it's all 'witchcraft'). Typically, the review later complains that the visual side of the film is excellent, and that it is a pity that it has been put to the service of 'une entreprise si débile' (Pérez 1981).[29] The narrative is only 'débile' because Pérez has made it so. He has realised that the film can be analysed as a deep psychoanalytic structure, but dismisses it, invoking a simplistic Freudianism which we are supposed to dismiss as preposterous. He tries to make the film's narrative, and his narrative cohere into a structure which eliminates digression and fragmentation, while at the same time paradoxically digressing himself.

If I have dwelt on this review, it is because I find its strategies to avoid coming to terms with its implications fascinating, and even more because the strategies employed prove *a contrario* what I am positing: that the film's attraction is precisely because it invokes mother and father figures, good and bad, and works to resolve the splittings, the 'bits' as Klein calls them, not in some simplistic incest fantasy, but in what Klein calls 'gratitude', which 'is rooted in the emotions and attitudes that arise in the earliest stage of infancy, when for the baby the mother is the one and only object' (Klein 1988: 187). That one and only object in *Diva* is the diva, with whom I shall begin to investigate the multiple splittings of the film. The splittings are summarised in tabular form below, see p. 60.

The diva is the focal point of attention at the beginning of the film, with an elaborate set of tracking and panning shots which have her at its centre, a set which is echoed as Jules listens to the recorded diva in his garage space, her dress draped over him, as if to emphasise the attempted fusion with the mother. The diva is presented to us very literally in a blue light, the light of the idealised mother, who represents the perfection of pre-Œdipal bliss. Quite apart from the fact that the metaphoric use of blue recalls very forcefully the symbolist poet Mallarmé's use of the word 'azur' to signify the ideal, Beineix has

29 'Such a moronic venture.'

stressed how he strove to make a blue film, and has emphasised all the technical difficulties to which this self-imposed ideal gave rise:

> Le concept de départ était la réalisation d'un film 'bleu' en tant que dominante mono-chromatique. Cette idée n'est pas novatrice en elle-même. L'originalité résidait plutôt dans notre persistance, car malheureusement, sur un tournage, on abandonne au moins 80% du concept de base. Pour lutter contre cette fâcheuse tendance, nous avons établi un cahier de charges, et nous nous en sommes tenus à ses prescriptions jusqu'à la fin du tournage. (Beineix 1981: 26)[30]

At the same time as the film suggests fusion with the idealised good mother, it is clear that the mother is split. First, she has been robbed of her voice and her dress, which we can explain by 'the phantasied onslaughts on the mother' described by Klein, one of which is 'the predominantly oral impulse to suck dry, bite up, scoop out and rob the mother's body of its good contents' (Klein 1986: 183).

Second, she is represented by or associated with specific spaces. Klein points out how 'in the analysis of every child ... things represent human beings, and are therefore things of anxiety' (Klein 1986: 89). Therefore, when I shall speak of splitting procedures, I shall be comparing and contrasting not just human figures in the film, but also objects, and in this case more particularly spaces, which can be taken to represent human beings. As is typical of splitting procedures, the mother is injured: not only is she captured visually in the glasses of the Taiwanese and her voice robbed by Jules, but the uterine spaces which are associated with her, the opera and Jules's garage space, are both 'damaged'. One of the more curious features of the opera space is that its painterly dome contrasts very markedly with the stage sets (they are two separate locations as I pointed out above), which, daubed roughly in paint, appear to be incomplete. That sense of 'damage' is even clearer in Jules's garage space, which, as he tells Alba, is 'le désastre de luxe' (Leclère 1991: 23).[31]

Third, the diva is multiply split. As good mother, she has a split in the form of Alba, the 'white' to her black (Alba's function in the film is

---

30 'The concept we started with was of a "blue" film as the dominant colour. This is not a novel idea in itself. What was original was our persistance, because sadly when you are shooting a film you drop 80 per cent of your starting concept. To counter this unfortunate tendency, we drew up contractual obligations and we stuck to them right to the end of shooting.'
31 'Deluxe disaster.'

considerably less important than in the original novel, confirming the diva's centrality). The two are linked by the opera: the diva sings in the opera, Alba wears the opera on her body. Alba too is split; her name means 'white' (as well as 'dawn'), but she is Vietnamese rather than Caucasian. The split established between the two women is paradox-ically 'repaired' by the fact that both she and the diva are 'Third World women figures' (Jameson 1992: 59). But the diva is further split, and doubly so, into the bad (because prostituted) mother in the form of (white) Nadia, whose voice is also recorded on a tape, and (black) Karina, Nadia's prostitute friend, who consents to wear the diva's dress for Jules. The prostitutes quite literally stand in front of and for the diva (*pro-stare*), actualising the virgin–whore dichotomy starkly.

The issue of prostitution, as Pérez obscurely felt, is at the heart of the film, inscribed not only in split female figures, but in the issue of commerce. One of the film's sub-plots is the marketing (trading) of the diva's voice. Not much is made of this issue in the dialogue – all that is said is the diva's statement at her press conference that 'c'est au commerce de s'adapter à l'art et non pas à l'art de s'adapter au commerce' (Leclère 1991: 33)[32] – so it is all the more surprising that Beineix confessed himself to be pleased with the film's dialogues, and particularly pleased with what is said about art and commerce: 'Je n'en suis pas mécontent de ces dialogues. Il y a notamment un discours sur l'art, sur le commerce et sur le commerce de l'art dont je suis rétrospectivement assez fier' (Parent 1989: 266).[33] And yet, Beineix's insistence on this aspect of the film's dialogue emphasises its func-tional importance.

The good mother represents an ideal of untainted but unattainable purity, split, logically, into her opposite, her body twice prostituted in the form of sexual contact (Nadia, Karina) and in the form of her voice, recorded and used for barter, which she herself calls a rape in the press conference (Leclère 1991: 34). Her unattainability is stressed by the fact that she never meets her split-off parts, Nadia and Karina, nor the good father (Gorodish) or the bad father (Saporta). Indeed, what is a drama within the world of the good mother, the stealing of

32 'It is up to commerce to adapt itself to art and not up to art to adapt itself to commerce.'
33 'I am quite pleased with these dialogues. There is in particular a discourse on art, on commerce, and on the commerce of art of which retrospectively I am quite proud.'

her dress, in other words the violence done to her body, seems out of place in the world of the fathers: the headline on the board of a newspaper kiosque, proclaiming that the diva's dress has been stolen, inevitably raises laughter in the film's audience. This is because, no doubt, it appears very literally 'out of place', a melodramatic moment from a woman's film at odds with the film's *polar* streak. It is all the more obviously out of place for occurring in the street, the place of the *polar*, rather than the opera, the place of the diva.

The blue world of the diva as good mother is echoed by the world of the good father, Gorodish, dominated by trade and money, but who also inhabits a large music-dominated and blue-dominated space, as well as a phallic lighthouse.[34] Unsurprisingly, Gorodish is presented to us at the beginning of the film as an echo of the diva: he is as if at the centre of a stage, watched by both the camera and by Alba, as was the diva by the camera and Jules. Unlike the diva, Gorodish is not split into other good parts (except, perhaps, for the contrast between the two major spaces he inhabits, the uterine musical space of his loft, and the phallic lighthouse), confirming, within this frame of reference, the point Revie makes about his centrality (Revie 1994: 29). He is split, however, into a bad father, Saporta, whose office is shot through a very heavy yellow filter, contrasting markedly with the film's overall blueness. However, as we have already seen, what is split is usually also conjoined in other ways. In the case of the bad father Saporta and the good mother, their spaces are brought together, as were the opera and the station, by similar figure compositions: the diva's dressing-room and Saporta's office are both relatively claustrophobic spaces, unlike the other spaces they control, the opera and the underworld. Like the diva, the bad father is betrayed (in Kleinian terms injured) by a tape, although the contents of the tapes are contrasted. In the case of Saporta, the bad father who must be attacked, Nadia's testimony will undo his power. The content of the diva's tape, on the other hand, in

34 In this respect, the so-called 'motiveless' reference to the *Seven Year Itch*, with the Marilyn Monroe lookalike's dress lifted by the updraft from the Métro, is in fact motivated. The reference introduces Gorodish's negotiation with the two thugs beneath the street. It therefore establishes a connection between two parallel spaces, the upper world of the Opéra, dominated by the diva as good mother (literally the goddess), and the rather more shadowy underworld dominated by Gorodish as the good father (whose name might well put us in mind of 'God'). The dress which lifts up to signal that underworld makes clear that we are dealing with two parallel mother-dominated spaces.

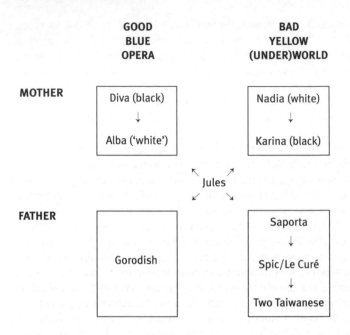

	GOOD BLUE OPERA		**BAD YELLOW (UNDER)WORLD**
MOTHER	Diva (black) ↓ Alba ('white')		Nadia (white) ↓ Karina (black)
		Jules	
FATHER	Gorodish		Saporta ↓ Spic/Le Curé ↓ Two Taiwanese

consonance with the good mother she represents, is presented to us, at least until Jules explains the Italian words of the song, as pre-verbal, redolent of the 'unsatisfied longing for an understanding without words – ultimately for the earliest relation with the mother' (Klein 1988: 301), and which is suffused with 'the depressive feeling of an irretrievable loss' (Klein 1988: 301), as the words will eventually make clear. Jules explains these to Alba: 'C'est une femme ... elle veut mourir ... elle a un chagrin d'amour et elle chante. Elle dit "Je vais m'en aller au loin, très loin, là-bas où les nuages sont dorés, là-bas où la neige est blanche ... Sans doute ne me reverras-tu plus, plus jamais ..." C'est tragique ... Et à la fin, à la fin elle se jette dans un couloir d'avalanche' (Leclère 1991: 25).[35]

---

35 'It's a woman ... she wants to die ... she has had an unhappy love affair and she is singing. She says "I will go far away, very far, where the clouds are golden, where the snow is white ... No doubt you will never see me again, never again ..." It's tragic ... And in the end, in the end she throws herself down an avalanche corridor.'

The kinds of splitting mechanisms I have been describing occur constantly. Indeed, they are already there embryonically from the very first shots of the film, and within the first establishing sequences. In the first shots of the film, we see first the Three Muses, a shot whose classicism is immediately contrasted with a lateral view of Jules's helmet, which, until we realise that it is a helmet he wears for a mobylette, looks like a space-helmet.[36] There is a similar contrast in the soundtrack with what appears to be non-diegetic music turning, when Jules obviously switches it off on his mobylette, into diegetic music. Similarly, at another level, that of the sequence, the whole of the opening sequence in the Opéra is contrasted both in terms of music, colour (an all-pervading blue) and a domed interior space, with the translucent exterior space of the station and the road outside, suffused in the yellow light of day, these to a techno-rock soundtrack. What remains the same, obeying the need to keep together what is at the same time split, are the figures: the diva–Nadia, the two Taiwanese–the two thugs, the anonymous crowds, and the fact that they do remain the same only serves to remind us of the differences, both between the figures, and more obviously between the sequences.

As Hagen points out, and as I recorded above, there is constant splitting at all levels in the film; the instances are far too numerous to list. My concern here is to account for them as part of the theoretical structure I am using. Klein, considering the constant proliferation of symbols in the splitting procedures, points out how these are founded in anxiety:

> Since the child desires to destroy the organs (penis, vagina, breast) which stand for the objects, he conceives a dread of the latter. This anxiety contributes to make him equate the organs in question with other things; owing to this equation these in their turn become objects of anxiety, and so he is impelled constantly to make other and new equations, which form the basis of his interest in the new objects and of symbolism.
>
> Thus, not only does symbolism come to be the foundation of all phantasy and sublimation but, more than that, upon it is built up the subject's relation to the outside world and to reality in general. (Klein 1986: 97–98)

---

36 As will be underlined later in the film when Alba hands Jules his helmet, saying 'Tiens, Alien' ('here you are, Alien') (Leclère 1991: 37).

In other words, the film's constant splitting, grounded in the basic split between the worlds of the father and of the mother, is a logical consequence of what one could call an anxious centrifugal mapping of the world on the mother's body first, followed by the father. There is then considerable logic in the film's opening sequences being devoted to the diva rather than to Saporta. The infant and the spectator begin with the mother, centre of the pre-Œdipal world, and the film gradually constructs the splitting paths away from that centre in a process of symbol formation which allows the infant and the spectator to come to grips with 'the outside world and reality in general'.

For this process to work for the spectator of the film, it is vital, I would suggest, that the mother and the father should be strong figures, but that the point of identification, Jules, should be weak, an empty vessel, in Kleinian terms an unformed ego as yet to be formed by the working through constituted by the film. It is clear that the diva, a black American, is sufficiently different and unusual in terms of the French police-thriller genre to which the film belongs, for her to appear strong in the first instance; and it is equally the case that Gorodish, partly because he is presented as an enigmatic and all-powerful figure, also manages to carry the role of good father. The film's problem is Jules: he must be weak for the working through to have effect, but how can such a weak character carry the focalisation necessary for the identification which logically precedes that working through? The answer is less the name, which suggests exemplarity, as Forbes points out (Forbes 1992: 66 and 268, n. 23), if not ordinariness, but the tapes: Jules projects in Kleinian terms by stealing the good voice, and introjects because he is given a harmful voice, Nadia's tape, which belongs to the father's world. Jules, then, is as much the focal point as the diva, or rather, the diva is the point of departure for the splitting mechanisms, while Jules is the point of convergence where they cross. We care about Jules because we recognise in him, and therefore recall it cathartically, the moment of ego development when the paranoid–schizoid position, with its frantic splitting, starts to work towards the depressive position, suffused with guilt, in this case, the guilt of having robbed the diva/mother. The tapes, themselves split into good and bad, are the primal objects of the film; they motivate the narrative (in the strong sense that they move the narrative along), they are a source of confusion, fear and trade. It is fitting that they should contain the voice of the good and bad mothers, both attempted escapes from reality: the diva's voice as a flight into the pre-verbal, and Nadia's a flight from the death-oriented law (quite literally since Saporta is a chief of homicide) of the father.

That flight away from reality, and its gesture towards reintegration with the mother is of course impossible. The film works towards it on two occasions. The first is the Queen of the Night sequence, where Jules and the diva meet in a café and spend the night walking through Paris. By the emphasis on classical statues, the sequence recalls very forcefully the opening shot of the film (the Three Muses), and is clearly meant to signal a space of security (Jules is there because he cannot go home), a lull in the action. During this sequence, the diva is called 'Queen of Africa' by the street-seller, and 'Queen of the Night' by Jules, an exalted status stressed by Jules's respectful holding of the diva's umbrella high above her, a height associated with ceremony. In the middle of the sequence, his respectful distance will change into a timid touching of the diva's shoulder, as he quite literally, moving one chair at a time, draws closer to her. A small detail also emphasises the sequence's move towards integration with the ideal: the street-seller gives the diva a small toy bird, saying that it is a magic bird, and the sequence ends with a close-up of the bird as the diva sleeps and Jules lies awake on the diva's couch, in much the same position as he was in his garage when listening to the tape of the diva. Moreover, the bird is echoed later in the film by the bird at the centre of Gorodish's puzzle, upon which the Taiwanese will leave a wad of banknotes, contrasting the magic bird of the ideal with the bird of commerce. The sequence, by its contrast with the opening of the film, when Jules could only gaze on the diva and record her from afar, emphasises both his respect of her, but also his physical closeness.

A second sequence works towards reintegration with the mother, this time through dramatic resolution of the splitting mechanisms: Gorodish kills the bad father, Saporta, who has earlier killed the bad mother (Nadia), and aspects of the bad father are killed (the two thugs). Alba is reaffirmed as good mother through her caring role during Jules's recovery, and the diva develops affection for Jules who has robbed her: this theft is 'unbelievable' (as the diva herself says; Leclère 1991: 32) in terms of narrative logic, but completely explicable in Kleinian terms of the move towards reintegration.

Final integration, though, is impossible.[37] In this respect, the final shot of the film, where it is unclear whether Jules and the diva make love, is logical: Jules is closer to the diva than either at the beginning of the film (when all he could do was listen to a tape), or during the time he spends with her (when he listens to her practise, has breakfast with her, and manages to touch her shoulder), but at the same time, it is the not complete integration that the metaphor of love making might have signalled. Beineix's film therefore aims for a purity which Delacorta's novel, trapped in its stereotypes, cannot achieve.[38]

Deleuze and the spirituality of the baroque

The Kleinian splits work to establish contrasts and parallels in the film. They work like baroque fragmentation, whose 'infinite replication and differentiated repetitions' gesture to a 'missing centre' (Degli-Esposti 1998: 8), which, I would like to suggest, is co-terminous with Klein's moment of complete integration, always gestured towards in a very baroque fascination with movement, but never realisable.

Degli-Esposti talks about baroque aesthetics as a combination of 'conceit, stupor, marvel, and metaphysical shock' (Degli-Esposti 1998: 8), all of which, I would suggest, are operative in *Diva*. The narrative

---

37 As Klein emphasises on several occasions: 'Complete and permanent integration is ... never possible. For under strain from external or internal sources, even well integrated people may be driven to stronger splitting processes, even though this may be a passing phase' (Klein 1988: 233); 'full and permanent integration is never possible for some polarity between the life and death instincts always persists and remains the deepest source of conflict. Since full integration is never achieved, complete understanding and acceptance of one's own emotions, phantasies and anxieties is not possible' (Klein 1988: 302).

38 The end of the novel does try to suggest purity by its emphasis on pure colour and the dream, but in the end, this is subsumed within sensuous eroticism: 'Jules sentait qu'il n'avait plus de vêtement. Contre lui, impalpable et nuageux, le corps de Cynthia n' était plus séparé du sien. Jules eut l'impression que soudain la salle se renversait. Le ciel n'était qu'une symphonie de couleurs pures sur lequel se détachait parfois le visage, le cou et les épaules de Cynthia qui lui fit l'amour longtemps presque sans bouger, comme dans un rêve qui n'avait pas de fin' (Delacorta 1981: 223) ('Jules' clothes had somehow left him. Cynthia's body, nebulous in the shadows, was no longer separated from him. Suddenly, he had the feeling that the auditorium had turned upside down. The sky was a symphony of pure color, a radiant background against which appeared Cynthia's face, neck and shoulders while she made love with him for a long time, almost without moving, as in an endless dream'; Delacorta 1997: 135–36).

contrasts and parallels are conceits; the film is full of visual conceits whose intention is to cause us to marvel (such as the reflection of the diva in the sunglasses, the overhead shot of Jules, Alba and Gorodish entering the lighthouse); and, as I have just suggested, the film's thrust, both narratively through splitting devices, and visually through the emphasis on blueness, is towards a meta-discourse on an idealised art, separate from commerce, which is itself a metaphor for the spiritual. The excess of the visual, so criticised by reviewers and critics during the 1980s, is, in the postmodern 1990s, an example of the desire for a beyond, but rooted firmly in the world of the senses. As is often said of baroque architecture, *order*, associated with Protestant sobriety, gives way to the Counter-Reformation's *sensation*, in both senses of the word. Classical lines are put under pressure and twisted (the word baroque comes from the Portuguese meaning an irregular pearl) into volutes, curls, spirals, whorls, and matter is shot through with light to reflect God's splendour, or, as Deleuze puts it, 'une forme tourbillonnaire qui se nourrit toujours de nouvelles turbulences' (Deleuze 1988: 7).[39] Similarly, in *Diva* we find an emphasis on circular camera movement, unusual lighting effects (of which the emphasis on blue is but one example), a convoluted narrative.

These effects create a sense of a labyrinth or knot, to take up Calabrese's terms, or, in Deleuze's reworking of baroque movement, a fold. In a previous piece on *Diva*, I suggested that this labyrinth marked the film as 'a traditional narrative of initiation, a rite of passage' (Powrie 1997: 118), with the mother at the centre of the labyrinth. Here, I am more interested in Deleuze's explanation of Leibniz's allegorical baroque house. This house is folded into two distinct parts. There is a lower part, with five openings, representing the world of the senses (and the public world), and an upper part, a *camera obscura*, representing the soul, closed to the outside world, but resonating 'comme un salon musical qui traduirait en sons les mouvements visibles d'en bas' (Deleuze 1988: 6).[40] The point of this relationship is that the one is indissociable from the other: soul and body go together for Leibniz. Deleuze expresses this in a wonderful phrase: the soul discovers in the body 'une animalité qui l'étourdit,

---

39 'A vortical form always put in motion by renewed turbulence' (Deleuze 1993: 4).
40 'As if it were a musical salon translating the visible movements below into sounds up above' (Deleuze 1993: 4).

qui l'empêtre dans les replis de la matière, mais aussi une humanité organique et cérébrale ... qui lui permet de s'élever, et le fera monter sur de tout autres plis' (Deleuze 1988: 17).[41] Music in *Diva* functions as this rising up, the spiralling upwards from the tangled pleats of matter towards the ideal, which I have defined in Kleinian terms as the complete, but impossible integration with the mother. It is easy to forget how startling the opening of the film was for audiences at the time, who would have been expecting a police thriller, but were given a poignant (and then largely unknown) opera aria accompanied by a series of dizzy camera movements.

Similarly, the use of light and other conceits of the *mise en scène* are related to the separation but indissociability of the inside and the outside in Leibnizian metaphysics. Deleuze explains this by alluding to baroque architecture, pointing out the 'cette scission de la façade et du dedans, de l'intérieur et de l'extérieur, l'autonomie de l'intérieur et l'indépendance de l'extérieur, dans de telles conditions que chacun des deux termes relance l'autre' (Deleuze 1988: 40).[42] I would like to extrapolate from this point to say that the criticism of the film as a stereotypical narrative ground onto which are grafted dazzling effects of *mise en scène* points to a dichotomy which, logically, does not exist: spectators take in both narrative and *mise en scène* at one and the same moment; it is criticism which separates the inseparable so as to dissect the work (or body/corpus). A comment made by Deleuze on a painting by Tintoretto, *The Burial of Count Orgaz*, for me at least, inevitably conjures up moments in *Diva* when Jules, in particular, is caught up in the tangled pleats of the real, represented by the law, both 'good' (the good policemen, with Saporta as their chief) and 'bad' (the thugs, also working for Saporta), the two, not coincidentally, brought together in one of the film's more thrilling chases in the labyrinth of the Paris métro:

> Chez le Tintoret, l'étage du bas montre les corps en proie à leur propre pesanteur, les âmes trébuchant, s'inclinant et tombant dans les replis de la matière; au contraire, la moitié supérieure agit comme un

41 'A vertiginous animality that gets it tangled in the pleats of matter, but also an organic or cerebral humanity ... that allows it to rise up' (Deleuze 1993: 11).
42 'Severing of the façade from the inside, of the interior from the exterior, and the autonomy of the interior from the independence of the exterior, but in such conditions that each of the two terms thrusts the other forwards' (Deleuze 1993: 28).

puissant aimant qui les attire, leur fait chevaucher des plis jaunes de
lumière, des plis de feu qui raniment les corps, et leur communique
un vertige, mais 'un vertige du haut'. (Deleuze 1988: 41–42)[43]

As Deleuze says, folds in the baroque, and by extension the various
doublings or splittings in *Diva*, 'prennent autonomie, ampleur, et *ce
n'est pas par simple souci de décoration*, c'est pour exprimer l'intensité
d'une force spirituelle qui s'exerce sur le corps, soit pour le renverser,
soit pour le redresser ou l'élever, mais toujours le retourner et en
mouler l'intérieur' (Deleuze 1988: 166–67; his emphasis).[44] He is
here referring specifically to folds of clothing in baroque paintings,
but the general point holds: lighting effects, which are one of the most
commented on aspects of the film, *are not just decorative*, but are an
essential part of the way in which the film tries to construct an
idealised world folded in and over the world of the senses, an ideal
which I have also defined as the integration with the complete object,
what one might wish to call the primal fold, the mother, here represented by the diva, the godlike voice which precedes individuation.

I have been using Deleuze's distinction between the upper and
lower floors of the baroque house as an abstract schema to explain the
relationship between what we see and hear in the film, and the film's
working through splittings/doublings/folds in the attempt to reach
the unreachable and the unarticulable. However, one could also work
with this allegory in a more literal fashion, since the *camera obscura*,
the private world of the soul, which I have suggested is the same as
the position of complete integration, is figured in the film by the
opening space, the opera. A first point is the type of space that the
opera represents. It is, etymologically, a space where a multiplicity of
works are brought together and performed; 'opera', then, arguably
represents the working through of a multiplicity of splittings, as I
have tried to suggest using Klein (and it is worth remembering, as I

---

43 'In Tintoretto the lower level shows bodies tormented by their own weight, their
souls stumbling, bending and falling into the meanders of matter; the upper
half acts like a powerful magnet that attracts them, makes them ride astride the
yellow folds of light, folds of fire bringing their bodies alive, dizzying them, but
with a "dizziness from on high"' (Deleuze 1993: 30).

44 'Acquire an autonomy and a fullness *that are not simply decorative effects*. They
convey the intensity of a spiritual force exerted on the body, either to turn it
upside down or to stand or raise it up over and again, but in every event to turn
it inside out and to mould its inner surfaces' (Deleuze 1993: 122).

have pointed out already, that the 'opera' is in fact two separate Parisian locations; it is therefore always already split). It is also, with its emphasis on the womb-like dome, as well as by its emphasis on the diva at its centre, the uterine space where Jules as Every(wo)man tries to integrate with the mother. At the beginning of the film, that space is a very public space, with a strong emphasis on the audience, scanned by the camera on several occasions, and shot through with acquisitiveness: Jules records the diva's voice, the Taiwanese want to buy it, and the audience has paid to listen. By the end of the film, that public space, or in Deleuze's terms, the lower part of the house representing the senses, or the 'pièces communes' (Deleuze 1988: 161)[45] in the sense of rooms which are common or public, has been folded, by the plot's multiple twists and turns, by the volutes of lighting and *mise en scène*, into the upper part of the house: there is no audience, just Every(wo)man and the mother, transfixed by the voice.

The world of the senses, the law of the father, the scopic, has been folded into the mother's body, in a process of dazzling and excessive melodrama, creating a 'memory in feeling' activated by the invocatory. But as the aria says, although we may not understand it the first time we hear it: 'Je vais m'en aller au loin, très loin, là-bas où les nuages sont dorés, là-bas où la neige est blanche ... Sans doute ne me reverras-tu plus, plus jamais' (Leclère 1991: 25).[46]

45 'Common rooms' (Deleuze 1993: 119).
46 'I will go far away, very far, where the clouds are golden, where the snow is white ... No doubt you will never see me again, never again.'

References

Anon. (1981a), 'Une histoire farfelue, ou les aventures d'un jeune postier', *L'Humanité*, 3 March.
Anon. (1981b), '*Diva* , *Nouvelles Littéraires*, 13 March.
Anon. (1981c), '*Diva*', *Minute*, 18 March.
Austin, Guy (1996), *Contemporary French Cinema*, Manchester and New York, Manchester University Press.
Auty, Martyn (1982), 'Breathless: *Diva*', *Sight and Sound* 51: 302.
Baignères, Claude (1981), 'La quête de l'absurde', *L'Aurore*, 17 March.
Baudin, Brigitte (1981), 'Beineix: un opéra policier', *Le Figaro*, 11 March.
Beineix, Jean-Jacques (1981), 'Réalisation', *Le Film Français* 1855: 26–27.
Beineix, Jean-Jacques (1983), 'Les confessions d'un enfant du siècle et du cinéma', *Première* 75: 119–21, 130–35.

Beineix, Jean-Jacques (1989), 'Jean-Jacques Beineix', in *L'Aventure du premier film*, edited by Samra Bonvoisin and Mary-Anne Brault-Wiart, Paris, Barrault, 148–59.

Beineix, Jean-Jacques (2001), 'Autant en emporte le divan: Jean-Jacques Beineix et Jean-Hugues Anglade', *Ciné-Livre* 4: 54–59.

Bescos, José-Marie (1981), *Diva*', *Pariscope*, 25 March.

Billard, Pierre (1981), 'Ne ratons pas le premier métro', *Le Point* 444, 23 March, 23.

Bosséno, Christian (1981), '*Diva*', *Image et Son*, 361: 30.

Carcassone, Philippe (1981), '*Diva*', *Cinématographe* 66: 76.

Chazal, Robert (1981), '*Diva*: amour et bel canto', *France-Soir*, 16 March.

Coppermann, Annie (1981), 'La Diva', *Les Echos* 13333, 17 March.

Cuel, François (1981), '*Diva*', *Cinématographe* 66: 76.

Dagle, Joan (1991), 'Effacing race: the discourse on gender in *Diva*', *Post Script* 10/2: 26–35.

Degli-Esposti, Cristina (1998), 'Postmodernism(s)', in *Postmodernism in the Cinema*, edited by Cristina Degli-Esposti, New York and Oxford, Berghahn, 3–18.

Delacorta (1981), *Diva*, Paris, Marabout. First published by Paris, Seghers 1979.

Delacorta (1997), *Diva*, translated by Lowell Blair, London, Bloomsbury Film Classics (translation first published by New York, Summit Books, 1983).

Deleuze, Gilles (1988), *Le Pli: Leibniz et le Baroque*, Paris, Editions de Minuit.

Deleuze, Gilles (1993) *The Fold: Leibniz and the Baroque*, translated by Tom Conley, London, Athlone.

Doane, Mary Ann (1980), 'The voice in the cinema: the articulation of body and space', *Yale French Studies* 60: 33–50.

Forbes, Jill (1992), *The Cinema in France: After the New Wave*, London, BFI/Macmillan.

Greene, Naomi (1999), *Landscapes of Loss: The National Past in Postwar French Cinema*, Princeton, New Jersey, Princeton University Press.

Hagen, W.M. (1988), 'Performance space in *Diva*', *Film/Literature Quarterly* 16: 155–58.

Halimi, André (1981), *Diva*', *Pariscope*, 18 March.

Hayward, Susan (1993), *French National Cinema*, London and New York, Routledge.

Jameson, Fredric (1992), '*Diva* and French socialism', in *Signatures of the Visible*, New York and London, Routledge, 55–62. Originally published in *Social Text* 6 (1982): 114–19.

Kelly, Ernece (1984), '*Diva*: high-tech sexual politics', *Jump Cut* 29: 39–40.

Klein, Melanie (1986), *The Selected Melanie Klein*, edited by Juliet Mitchell, Harmondsworth, Middlesex, Penguin Books.

Klein, Melanie (1988), *Envy and Gratitude and Other Works 1946–1963*, London, Virago Press.

Lang, Robert (1984), 'Carnal stereophony: a reading of *Diva*', *Screen* 25: 70–77.

Leclère, François (1991), *Diva* (découpage), Paris, L'Avant-Scène Cinéma, 407.

Leirens, Jean (1982), 'Thriller à la française', *Amis du Film Cinéma et TV* 312–13: 4.

Milne, Tom (1982), '*Diva*', *Monthly Film Bulletin* 584:190–91.

Parent, Denis (1989), *Jean-Jacques Beineix: Version originale*, Paris, Barrault.

Pérez, Michel (1981), '*Diva*', *Le Matin*, 14 March.

Powrie, Phil (1990), *Contemporary French Fiction by Women: Feminist Perspectives*, Manchester, Manchester University Press.

Powrie, Phil (1997), *French Cinema in the 1980s: Nostalgia and the Crisis of Masculinity*, Oxford, Clarendon Press.

Ramasse, F. (1981), '*Diva*', *Positif*, 243: 68.

Revie, Ian (1994), 'Paris remythologised in *Diva* and *Subway*: *Nanas népolarisées* and *Orphées aux enfers*', in *Mythologies of Paris*, Stirling, Stirling French Publications 2: 28–43.

Rochereau, Jean (1981), 'La Cantatrice et le postier', *La Croix*, 14 March.

Rodowick, David Norman (1992), *The Difficulty of Difference: Psychoanalysis, Sexual Difference, and Film Theory*, London, Routledge.

Rolin, Gabrielle (1981), 'Rififi et bel canto', *Combat socialiste*, 24 March.

Rouchy, Mare-Elizabeth (1981), 'Irène Silberman: priorité au spectacle', *Le Matin*, 11 March.

Rowe, Kathleen (1991), 'Class and allegory in Jameson's film criticism', *Quarterly Review of Film and Video* 12/4: 1–18.

Sainderichain, Guy-Patrick (1981), '*Diva*', *Cahiers du cinéma* 322: 66.

Saint Bris, Gonzague (1983), 'France Etats-Unis: une nouvelle alliance', *Quotidien de Paris*, 11 August.

Sarran, Patrice de (1981), '*Diva*: belles images sur un écran glacé', *La Nouvelle République du Centre-Ouest*, 12 June.

Schidlow, Joshka (1981), '*Diva*', *Télérama* 1627, 18 March, 31.

Siclier, Jacques (1981), '*Diva*', *Le Monde*, 18 March.

Siclier, Jacques (1991), *Le Cinéma français, 2: de Baisers volés à Cyrano de Bergerac 1968–90*, Paris, Ramsay Cinéma.

Silverman, Kaja (1980), 'Masochism and subjectivity', *Framework* 12: 2–9.

Silverman, Kaja (1988), *The Acoustic Mirror: the Female Voice in Psychoanalysis and Cinema*, Bloomington, Indiana University Press.

Studlar, Gaylyn (1985), 'Masochism and the perverse pleasures of the cinema', in *Movies and Methods*, vol. 2, edited by B. Nichols, Berkeley, University of California Press, 602–21.

Tranchant, Marie-Noëlle (1982), 'La passion du cinéma selon Jean-Jacques Beineix', *Le Figaro*, 8 March.

Vaugeois, Gérard (1981), '*Diva*', *L'Humanité*, 20 March.

White, Mimi (1988), 'They all sing ... voice, body and representation in *Diva*', *Literature and Psychology* 34/4: 33–43.

Yervasi, Carina L. (1993), 'Capturing the elusive representations in Beineix's *Diva*', *Literature/Film Quarterly* 21/1: 38–46.

Zavarzadeh, Mas'ud (1983), '*Diva*', *Film Quarterly* 36: 54–59. Reprinted with minor changes in Mas'ud Zavarzadeh, *Seeing Films Politically*, Albany, State University of New York Press, 1991, 216–27.

1 Monsieur Michel practises howling like a dog (*Le Chien de Monsieur Michel*)

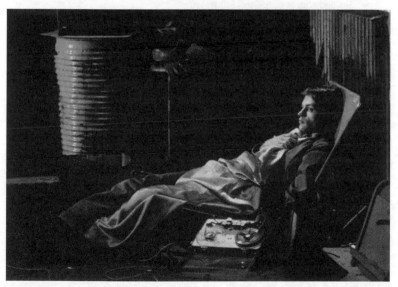

2 Jules listens to the stolen voice (*Diva*)

3 Jules and Alba in Gorodish's loft (*Diva*)

4 Le Curé and L'Antillais (*Diva*)

5 Jules in the métro (*Diva*)

6 Beineix, Depardieu and some of the crew of *La Lune dans le caniveau*

7 Loretta visits Gérard, tempting him to 'Try another world' (*La Lune dans le caniveau*)

8 Gérard fights off Bella's hired guns among the bananas (*La Lune dans le caniveau*)

9 The phallic Virgin (*La Lune dans le caniveau*)

4

La Lune dans le caniveau (1983)

Synopsis

Gérard Delmas, the docker, supports and lives with his father, an out-of-work ambulance driver, his stepmother, Lola, and her daughter, Bella, with whom he has a relationship. Every night he returns to the spot where his sister, Catherine, to whom he was very close, committed suicide after being raped. He suspects everyone, even his own brother, Frank, a down-and-out who will do anything for a drink.

In The Mikado Bar Gérard picks up a wager set up by playboy Newton Channing, to eat through a large block of ice. He suspects Channing of his sister's rape, and talks to him as the bar closes. Channing's sister, Loretta, comes to collect her brother from the bar. Gérard gives her his address. He returns home, and gives a violin to his father. Bella, who wants to marry him, throws a fit of jealousy. Loretta arrives. She and Gérard drive to the docks, where she asks him to take her away; he refuses. He returns to the gutter where his sister died, and meets a painter who painted her portrait. He goes to see the portrait and sleeps at the painter's. During the night he dreams of his sister's visit to him in hospital after an accident at work.

Loretta visits him at work the next day, and takes photographs of him. He tries to take the camera, and fights with the foreman. Loretta apologises and gives him the camera. He returns home and dresses in his Sunday best to return the camera. Bella tells him that it is obvious that he has fallen in love with Loretta. He stops at The Mikado Bar for a drink. Loretta arrives, and they drive to her house before going to a cathedral where they are married. Gérard wakes up in his stepmother's bed. She throws him out, and he dreams drunkenly of seeing his sister lying in the morgue. When he looks at her face, it is Loretta's. He wakes up again, this time in Bella's bed. He tells Bella that he is married.

The next day, he is attacked by two thugs in a banana warehouse. He gets the better of them, and discovers that Bella has paid them to teach him a lesson. He suspects that the rapist has given Bella the money, and finds out from her that it is Frank who paid her. He goes to The Mikado Bar where Newton Channing announces that he is engaged to one of the ageing prostitutes. Gérard tries to kill his brother, but the painter stops him. Loretta arrives, but he returns to Bella.

Background

Beineix proposed an adaptation of David Goodis's 1953 novel *The Moon in the Gutter* to the producer Lisa Fayolle, who had been enthused by *Diva*. He was attracted to the novel's darkness:

> Une histoire totalement négative, très noire, c'était un périple sombre avec des brillances, des chatoiements, des rougeoiements ... Il y avait aussi ce jaillissement d'une certaine émanation de la femme, cette fille qui arrivait dans cette voiture, c'était vraiment le mythe de la femme fatale à l'état pur ... Et puis il y avait ces sourdes vibrations du doute, de la jalousie ... Enfin, plein de choses qui touchent l'inconscient. (Beineix 1983b: 49)[1]

He worked on an adaptation with Olivier Mergeault for six months. Eighty per cent of the film takes place at night, which required a studio (the Cinecittá studios; the remainder of the film was shot in Marseilles), and has for that reason been likened to Coppola's *One From the Heart* (1982). Beineix insists, however, that the only thing the two films 'have in common is Nastassia Kinski and studio sets' (Buckley 1984: 31), and that, according to him, 'the only thing I owe to Coppola is Nastassia Kinski. I knew her from the Polanski film (*Tess*)

---

1 'A totally negative story, very black, it was a dark journey with flashes of light, shimmers, glows ... There was also the eruption of a particular embodiment of woman, that girl who arrives in that car, it really was the myth of the femme fatale at its purest ... And then there was gnawing doubt, jealousy ... In short, lots of things which affect the unconscious.'

[1982], but when I saw her in *One From the Heart*, I had a stroke in the heart' (Buckley 1984: 31). Depardieu's character is based on Stanley Kowalski (Marlon Brando), although Beineix claims never to have seen *A Streetcar Named Desire* (1951), although he 'did study the photographs' (Buckley 1984: 31).

Not only was the street reconstituted in the studio, but Hilton McConnico created designs for all elements of the decor, right down to the bottles in the bar (Red Devil's gin, Finner beer) and packets of Box Car Special cigarettes. Beineix decided to use only the very mobile Louma camera. As with *Diva*, he paid particular attention to colour. In the same way that *Diva* is a 'blue' film, so *La Lune dans le caniveau* is a 'green' film, and, as was the case with *Diva*, the decision to use a particular colour scheme led to constraints and, according to Beineix, even more difficulties: 'Blue is easy, green is less easier [*sic*] – because of the skin. Green makes the skin reddish or yellow; blue makes your face paler, but you don't have the same problems' (Buckley 1984: 31). His perfectionism extended to insisting on exact colour matches between Loretta's red dress and the red Ferrari.

Unsurprisingly, the film took sixteen weeks to make instead of the twelve weeks which had been intended, and cost 24 m. francs instead of the estimated 19 m., a relatively high amount in French film-making terms. There were difficulties on the set, with reported disagreement between Beineix and Depardieu, who had been imposed on Beineix because he was a more 'bankable' star (Beineix 2001: 109); Beineix would have preferred Bernard Giraudeau or Gérard Lanvin. Depardieu subsequently labelled the film 'La lune dans les égouts' ('The Moon in the sewer') on French radio, claiming, the day before the press conference in Cannes, that Beineix refused to have a public preview so as to make the film more watchable, and more generally refused to listen to anyone on set (Rouergue 1983). Beineix was much more generous in his evaluation of Depardieu. Admitting that the problem with great actors is that they are highly strung, and that his relations with Depardieu 'n'ont pas toujours été faciles, pas toujours tendres' (Beineix 1983a: 52),[2] he nevertheless emphasises the fascination which Depardieu had for him:

> Je peux rester des heures rien qu'à le regarder! Et au fond le seul reproche que je lui ferai, c'est de ne pas avoir toujours senti le regard

---

2 'Were not always easy, not always gentle.'

qui était sur lui et l'intérêt profond que je lui portais.... Cette sensation d'énormité, de puissance, mais aussi, à d'autres moments, une certaine force de l'impuissance ... Il apporte au film toute une subtilité qui est bien au-delà des mots ... Cela tient à la nature même de sa morphologie que j'ai prise en compte en tant qu'être, dans la moindre de ses attitudes. (Beineix 1983a: 52)[3]

There are key themes here which I shall return to: potency and impotence, the fascinated gaze, the body without a voice.

At the end of production, Beineix had four hours of film, which was initially edited down to an overlong three hours and ten minutes; Beineix cut a further ten minutes in the four months between Cannes and the film's opening in New York. The final cut, lasting two hours and seventeen minutes, required cutting two entire sequences.

Adaptation

As was the case with *Diva*, Beineix and Mergeault did not change much of the story-line, and much of the dialogue is taken straight from the novel. This makes the often small changes that much more significant. There are, for example, hardly any instances of the kind of narrative compression which a longer novel might have required. The only example is in Chapter 6, where William Kerrigan, as the Depardieu character is called in the novel, having met Loretta for the first time, bumps into a prostitute, Rita, before talking to the painter. The purpose of this encounter is mainly to stress Kerrigan's feeling of guilt, which is returned to in the encounter with the painter. More interesting, though, in the same chapter, is Kerrigan's flashback while with the painter. In the film, his sister visits him after he has had an accident at work, and he berates her for wearing a skimpy dress and high heels, thus drawing attention to her erotic potential. This is underlined by the fact that the sequence is close narratively to Truffaut's *L'Homme qui aimait les femmes* (1977), except that Bertrand's

---

3 'I can spend hours just looking at him! And in the end the only reproach I would have is that he did not always feel my gaze on him and the close attention I was devoting to him. A feeling of enormity, of strength, but at the same time, a kind of strength of impotence. He brings all kinds of subtleties to the film which are beyond words. It is connected to the way he appears, which I took close account of, in the smallest detail of a pose.'

(Charles Denner) lunge to touch the nurse kills him. In the novel, the flashback is quite different and avoids any notion of eroticism. Catherine is presented to the reader as very demure: 'she always wore low-heeled shoes and loose-waisted schoolgirl dresses and looked much younger than eighteen' (Goodis 1983: 440). She is followed to a drugstore by three young men, meeting Kerrigan on the way, but she defuses the potentially explosive situation by politeness: 'her voice was like a soothing touch' (Goodis 1983: 442). The film, as can be seen from this example, stresses the erotic allure of both Catherine and Loretta, the two ideal women in an otherwise sordid world. This partly explains why Loretta drives a red Ferrari in the film, rather than the grey MG with yellow upholstery of the novel (Goodis 1983: 428), since the car is iconically sensual, not only in form but also in colour. The way out of the sordidness of Vernon Street in the novel is through an idealised virginal woman, whereas the film complicates this ideal by eroticising it.

At least one other small detail suggests this shift of emphasis to the erotic. Bella and Kerrigan talk on the verandah of the house in the novel, whereas in the film, we are first introduced to Bella as she swings in the yard, banging her feet relentlessly against a broken-down ambulance, the camera placed, like the eye of the voyeur, in the position of the ambulance door, with a view of her open legs as she swings towards it. The accompanying music – with a Caribbean flavour as she swings forwards and backwards, changing to a more distinctly Arab music as she swings from side to side – is clearly intended to emphasise her sensuality, although it also functions to compensate for something the novel insists on, but which the film's dialogue cannot easily convey, namely her mix of ethnic origins inherited from her mother, who is said to be 'Cherokee ... mixed with French and Irish, with accent on the more explosive traits of each' (Goodis 1983: 420). Bella's mother, Lola, is in fact played by an Afro-American actress Bertice Reading, and Victoria Abril who plays Bella is Spanish; this has the virtue of retaining the idea of ethnic mix presented in the novel, although it sets up a curious ethnic discontinuity between mother and daughter.

The Depardieu character corresponds to the well-built docker of the novel, except that Kerrigan has two striking scars, which mark him as belonging to a particular area and class, 'just a couple of badges that signified he lived on Vernon Street and worked on the docks' (Goodis 1983: 404). Depardieu does not have the physical marks of entrapment in his milieu, but, as I shall be arguing, his voice is 'scarred' in much the same way as Kerrigan's face.

There is a second major narrative change, this time not a compression but a displacement, which affects our view of Gérard. The film derisively underlines his refusal of the ideal, first with a voice-over at the end of the film which makes explicit something which is only implied in the novel, that he is afraid of leaving home, and afraid of Loretta; and, second, by having the contrast of Newton's engagement at the moment when he is breaking off with Loretta, whereas in the novel, the ageing prostitute recovers a certain dignity by insisting on her independence ('this pussycat's a self-supporting individual'; Goodis 1983: 512) and on the impossible chasm of class ('it's every cat to his own alley'; Goodis 1983: 512), a sentiment which Kerrigan echoes, and which convinces him that he should stay in Vernon Street.

The sense of derision is also there in a small change, a change of name for the major location of the narrative in both novel and film, Dugan's Den, which in the film is called The Mikado Bar. The latter signals exotic otherness; life on Vernon Street is certainly 'other', but exotic only in the ironic sense that it is sordid.

The film, then, with the exception of a heightened eroticism, is considerably more faithful to the novel than many reviewers' comments might have suggested in 1983, as we shall see below. Indeed, the film is, arguably, despite the reticence of reviewers, very close to the novel's flavour. Reviewers criticised the disparity between the novel's sordidness and the brilliance of Beineix's images, whereas this corresponds very much to Goodis's style, as the following comment by Mike Wallington, who wrote the introduction to the British edition of the novel, suggests:

> The Goodis signature adds up to a calculated excess of style. *Noir* shorthand of tone and motif is amplified – it's never hot but treacly, or always far below zero, and grey gives way to Œdipal yellows, pinks and lavenders; the street, the moon, the gutter, all have become fetish, and their meanings expand. Most of all, the Goodis signature is the sudden and disorientating image that creeps up on you, and tatoos itself into the narrative. (Goodis 1983: ix)

Beineix's version of Goodis's world depends to a large extent on striking images, some of which are changes to the novel. For example,

Gérard gives his father a violin for his birthday, although Tom cannot play it, thereby reinforcing the sense of hopelessness; the fight in the warehouse is made the more dramatic by it being a warehouse full of bananas (the novel focuses less on the location than on details of the fight). Similarly, Gérard and Loretta are married not in the dingy house of Vernon Street belonging to an old Greek man, but in a cathedral on a hill, reminiscent of *Diva*'s secluded lighthouse. Apart from the magical nature of the location, this will allow Beineix to elaborate one of the more startling images of the film. The wedding ring in the novel is 'the ring from a loose-leaf notebook' (Goodis 1983: 481). In the film, however, this prosaic detail becomes the more highly charged image of the plastic halo from a statuette of the Virgin Mary, an image I shall return to.

Other images are familiar from *Diva*. There is, for example, a play with distorted mirror images. In *Diva*, the singer was mirrored in the sunglasses of the Taiwanese businessman; in *La Lune dans le caniveau*, Loretta is mirrored in the lens of her camera, suggesting 'woman' as impossible ideal; or, in a similar vein, the frequent billboard image of a bottle of alcohol called Stromboli with its derisive 'Try another world' caption, which stresses the allure of the ideal, but its impossibility; or, finally, the striking use of colour, such as the play on red and blue at different points during the film. Beineix has made it clear that the use of colour was in part an attempt to suggest a state in between dream and reality: 'J'ai cherché à rendre le vrai un peu faux et inversement de façon à ramener le tout à mi-chemin du rêve et de la réalité. Pour prendre un exemple nous avons coloré les fumées d'une cokerie' (Beineix 1983b: 25).[4]

Both novel and film have a dreamy, if not nightmarish atmosphere which suggests the impossibility of escaping one's past. As Wallington says, 'the dreadful gloom – the foreboding that hangs like a pall over every page of Goodis – is a fear of remembrance. But there's nothing that will heal the wounds – a chance encounter, like a *déjà vu*, can re-open cracks in the past, so can a stain in the street, or a glimpse of moonlight through shutters' (Goodis 1983: ix). The sense of being giddily trapped is frequently conveyed in the novel by Kerrigan's sense of impotence combined with disorientation:

4 'I sought to make the real a bit unreal and vice versa so as to place the whole thing half-way between dream and reality. To take an example we coloured the smoke coming out of a chimney-stack.'

The floor seemed to slide under his feet, taking him away from the bar. The ceiling moved backward and the walls moved and the door came closer. (Goodis 1983: 471)

He wanted to open the door and get out. He wondered why he couldn't get out. (Goodis 1983: 472)

It wasn't her words that he heard. It was like soft music drifting through the dream. And the dream was taking him away from everything he'd known, every tangible segment of the world he lived in. (Goodis 1983: 474)

He had a feeling the room was moving. It was like a chamber on wheels going away from everything, falling off the edge of the world. (Goodis 1983: 504)

The film achieves the same end by a combination of two elements. The first is the disquieting flashbacks which do not occur in the novel (Gérard in hospital visited by his sister; Gérard visiting the morgue, where his sister turns into Loretta). The second is the use of the camera. This can be obsessively mobile; a good example of this is Gérard and Loretta's first meeting in The Mikado Bar. The camera twice sweeps around Newton and Gérard as they speak (tracking left and panning right as it keeps the pair in focus), a movement which is repeated once Loretta enters the bar, this time with the non-diegetic love theme (sweeping romantic strings and piano) and the irregularly flashing lights of the last tram. As Beineix said in interview, 'la caméra doit traduire l'agitation interne, le stress, l'attente ... . Elle doit ... être sensible aux ondulations de la musique ... C'est comme un serpent' (Beineix 1983a: 49).[5] Or the camera can be placed in unusually stark angles. Both procedures disorientate, evoking the disorientation and entrapment of the protagonist. Interestingly, a similar use of the camera can be found in Yolande Zauberman's *Clubbed to death* (1997), where it serves to convey the disorientation of the main protagonist Lola (Elodie Bouchez), sucked into the heady combination of passionate love and drugs, thus translating the alienation of 1990s youth, just as Beineix's film translates a similar alienation in the 1980s and the desire to transcend it.

5 'the camera should convey internal agitation, stress, expectation. It should be sensitive to the undulations of the music'.

The repetitive slowness of the camera is in fact a key to what Beineix was trying to achieve, which is the exploration of intensity in an attitude of, to use a phrase familiar in film studies, passionate detachment: 'The entire film is an attempt to stop time. Man is an eternal moment in time, and the way one experiences the intensity of life makes time pass either quickly or slowly. This is what an artist does – freezes a moment in time and explores it' (Beineix 1983c: 18).

Reception

Despite Beineix's plea, that he was merely echoing Goodis's tragic vision with a language appropriate to it, even a periodical which had been pro-Beineix, *Première*, found the camera hard to take. There was a persistent assumption that Beineix had overused the very mobile Louma, and that its use, according to Esposito:

> Finit par rendre la mise en scène répétitive, surchargée de temps vides (le chemin de la Louma d'un centre d'intérêt à un autre n'est pas toujours passionnant), et elle imprime au film un rythme, une démarche trop grandiloquente. Dans *La Lune dans le caniveau*, tout, absolument tout, a l'air capital, dramatique, tragique: le moindre geste, le moindre regard, la moindre mouvement de la caméra. C'est trop. (Esposito 1983: 95)[6]

When it was shown at the Festival de Cannes, the film was booed by some critics in the auditorium even before it had started, and the ensuing press conference was tense. The first question put to Beineix, calculatingly aggressive, was 'Pourquoi les dialogues de vos films sont-ils si légers?', to which Beineix responded equally aggressively: 'Pour qu'ils ne soient pas lourds' (Esposito 1983: 95).[7] Although the conference was tense, Beineix was able to expound his view of the new cinema, based on the image, pointing out that his main interest was 'le langage universel des images et de la musique', that 'le lieu

6 'Ends up by making the *mise en scène* repetitive, weighed down with empty moments (the tracking of the Louma from one centre of interest to another is not always interesting), and it gives the film a rhythm, a pace, which is overly grandiloquent. In *La Lune dans le caniveau*, everything, absolutely everything, appears crucial, dramatic, tragic: the smallest gesture, the slightest look, the smallest movement of the camera. It's too much.'

7 'Why are your dialogues so light?' 'To avoid being heavy.'

géométrique du cinéma, c'est l'image et pas le dialogue' (Cartier 1983).[8]

The aggressive flavour of the encounter is well conveyed in the pages of *Cahiers du cinéma* a few months after Cannes:

> Quand Beineix déclarait à qui voulait l'entendre, à Cannes, qu'il 'n'en a rien à foutre de la vérité' et qu'il veut faire un cinéma de l'Image, enfin synchrone avec 'l'éclatement de la morale et des dogmes', c'est bien de cela qu'il s'agit, d'en avoir fini une fois pour toutes avec le vieux cinéma moderne – dont il ne veut rien savoir – et d'annoncer le nouveau cinéma dont il rêve, le cinéma de l'époque des spots publicitaires et des vidéo-clips, un art de l'Image comme séduction et magie, une écriture toute de surface. (Bergala 1983: 5)[9]

Bergala is criticising what he sees as the evacuation of the real from Beineix's images. The images are no longer fake in the way in which a theatrical decor is fake but nevertheless gestures towards a reality; they are artificial and contrived, gesturing only to themselves as image. He cites the Stromboli advert in *La Lune dans le caniveau* and the limousine murals in *Diva*, which for him exemplify Beineix's style: 'filmer en tant que tel un décor peint en trompe-l'œil, c'est-à-dire filmer quelque chose qui est déjà entièrement, avant filmage, du côté de l'illusion et de l'artefact' (Bergala 1983: 8).[10]

The same number of *Cahiers du cinéma* carried an article by the film-maker Olivier Assayas on advertising. While recognising something which Beineix has always said, that advertising had recognised the potential of new technologies and had pushed research into visual style forwards, and while being prepared to admire the way in which a film-maker such as Ridley Scott had used advertising techniques but put them at the service of a renewal of film genre, Assayas is vituperative about what he sees as Beineix's capitulation to the image for its own sake:

8 'The universal language of images and music', 'the locus of the cinema is the image and not dialogue.'

9 'When Beineix declared to whoever was prepared to listen that he "couldn't give a shit about truth" and that he wanted to create a cinema of the image, which would at last correspond to "the exploding of morality and dogma", he couldn't have made it clearer that he wants to put an end, once and for all, to the old modern cinema – which he wants nothing to do with – and wants to announce the new cinema of his dreams, the cinema of advertising commercials and videoclips, an art of the image as seduction and magic, all surface.'

10 'Filming as it is décor which is painted as trompe-l'œil, that is to say filming something which is already totally, before you film it, illusion and artefact.'

Il organise ... des éléments piochés partout ailleurs, vaguement inédits au cinéma, ce qui suffit en effet à faire un *look*. *Look* hideux mais *look* tout de même. Seulement il n'y pas de film. Rien qui ressemble de près ou de loin à du cinéma dans cette mise en scène tonitruante du vide où la pure misère du propos ou des idées est travestie de machinerie tarabiscotée, de décoration de souk, et de rhétorique visuelle attrape-gogo. ... *La Lune dans le caniveau* est conçu comme une sorte d'apothéose de l'emballage au service de l'emballage qui n'emballe rien. (Assayas 1983: 26)[11]

The aggressiveness shown by *Cahiers du cinéma* tells us as much about the way in which those the *Cahiers* represented felt threatened by technological change, changes in audiences, and therefore in their own position, as it does about Beineix. The key issue to retain is the new language which *Cahiers* acknowledged while criticising, and this, often less vituperatively, was the position taken by most reviewers.

Devarrieux, in *Le Monde*, for example, says: 'Il casse le roman pour approcher un nouveau langage cinématographique. Ce langage, tout à fait malhabile, est probablement fondé sur une modernité qui nous entoure, mais dont on ne connaît pas encore les termes' (Devarrieux 1983).[12] Beineix himself suggested that the search for a new language was one of the major motivating factors behind the film: 'Je me suis posé la question de l'essence du cinéma, du langage de l'image. J'ai recherché une autre dimension à ce langage ... . Le cinéma n'est pas forcément au service de l'histoire, c'est-à-dire de la chronologie et de la réalité; il est peut-être aussi au service de la matière' (Beineix 1983b: 24).[13] Reviewers were on the whole happy to accept this view. The film

11 'He organises elements he has dug up from all over the place, things you might not have seen before in the cinema, which is all you need to create a look. It's a hideous look, but it's a look all the same. The only thing is, there is no film. Nothing which remotely ressembles the cinema in this resoundingly empty *mise en scène* whose sheer vacuity is dressed up with over-elaborate machinery, gaudy decoration, and visual rhetoric for suckers. ... *La Lune dans le caniveau* is conceived as a kind of apotheosis of wrapping at the service of wrapping which wraps nothing.'

12 'He denatures the novel so as to create a new film language. That language, very clumsy, is probably based in a modernity which surrounds us, but whose terms we do not yet know.'

13 'I asked myself what the essence of cinema was, what was the language of the image. I sought another dimension of this language. The cinema is not necessarily at the service of a story, in other words chronology and reality; it is perhaps also at the service of matter.'

was 'un poème visuel' (Anon. 1983),[14] 'un opéra d'images' (Billard 1983),[15] sumptuous perhaps, but certainly pretentious (Klotz 1983). The major problem, according to most, was that the attempt at a new language left the spectator cold. It is a term frequently used; the reviewer of the *Revue du cinéma* speaks of the film's 'esthétisme glacial' (Ross 1983: 22),[16] and *L'Express*'s reviewer formulates the same point more vulgarly: 'On s'en fout, voilà le vrai drame de ce drame. On reste là, glacé, cloué à son fauteuil, balançant entre ironie et ennui' (Heymann 1983).[17] A little more charitably, *Télérama*'s reviewer thought it a better film than *Diva*, labelling it 'une énorme boursouflure, gonflée d'âme et de passion' (Carrère 1983).[18] The term 'boursouflure' (originally meaning a blister, but meaning figuratively a bombastic or bloated work) is used by others (for example, Logette 1983: 48, who uses it considerably less charitably), but as I shall argue, the term is useful in thinking about the film theoretically. Finally, I shall close this brief review of the film's reception by quoting a reasonably balanced view of the film's strengths and weaknesses as they have appeared in these few comments: 'Mise en scène insolente et insolite, tortueuse et torturée ... Cela dérange, presque inquiète, ce mal, cette folie de filmer ... Rendez-vous à la cinémathèque. Dans quelques années' (Bescos 1983).[19] Towards the end of the decade, Beineix himself reiterated the long-term view: 'Le destin de *la Lune* s'est joué en une seule projection. Ce film a été un échec, mais il y a des échecs dont on parle longtemps. Et peut-être qu'à la longue ce ne sont plus des échecs' (Parent 1989: 196).[20]

The reaction by critics at Cannes no doubt contributed to the film's lack of success; it attracted some 616,940 spectators in France, representing only about a quarter of *Diva*'s total. Time does not seem

---

14 'a visual poem.'
15 'an opera of images.'
16 'icy aestheticism.'
17 'You couldn't give a shit, that's the real drama of this drama. You sit there, ice-cold, nailed to your seat, oscillating between irony and boredom.'
18 'hugely inflated, puffed up with spirit and passion.'
19 'The mise en scène is insolent and unusual, tortuous and tortured ... . The mad urge to film is disturbing, almost worrying. Rendez-vous in the cinemathèque. In a few years time.'
20 '*La Lune*'s fate was decided in one showing. It was a failure, but there are failures which people talk about for a long time. And perhaps in the end they are no longer failures.'

to have changed many critics' views of the film. Frodon, in his monumental history of post-new wave cinema written for the centenary of the cinema, is if anything just as scathing in his judgement of what critics then and now see as the archetypal film of the *cinéma du look*, or 'le Visuel' as Frodon calls it, reminding us in the following comment that the film was disavowed very publicly by its star, Depardieu:

> Le travail de Beineix ... ne consiste pas à illustrer une trame de fiction très conventionnelle, mais à la faire disparaître dans des jeux d'artifices visuels, à la consumer. C'est sans doute ainsi qu'il faut entendre l'éclat de Gérard Depardieu ... désavouant publiquement celui-ci: sa mauvaise humeur publique traduit le sentiment que ce film-là s'est fait contre lui, contre les comédiens, contre les histoires auxquelles ceux-ci ont vocation de donner chair. *La Lune dans le caniveau*, et le cinéma qu'il annonce, est d'une autre matière, une matière de synthèse. (Frodon 1995: 576)[21]

The characteristics of the film which promote its synthetic visual nature are, according to Frodon, the use of the ultra-mobile Louma camera, the use of video remote control, and the steadycam camera, all of which in his view represent forms of 'interposition supplémentaire technique entre la réalité et son enregistrement', leading increasingly to the 'fétichisme de l'image et à son abstraction de la réalité' (Frodon 1995: 576–77).[22]

Since Frodon's volume is likely to remain a standard text for some years, it may be worth pointing out basic errors in Frodon's analysis, not least the assumption, made by others as well, that Beineix had used the Louma:

> Frodon parle de l'usage de la vidéo control. Je me dois de dire que je n'ai jamais utilisé ce type de matériel sur aucun de mes films. Il n'y a jamais eu non plus de moniteur sur mon plateau. Je déteste ce type d'appareil qui éloigne le metteur en scène des acteurs. D'autre part,

21 'Beineix does not try to illustrate a conventional story, but makes it disappear in visual pyrotechnics, which consume it. That is no doubt the explanation for Gérard Depardieu's public outburst against the film. His ill-tempered public outburst suggests that he realised that the film had been made against him, against the actors, against the stories which it is an actor's vocation to embody. *La Lune dans le caniveau*, and the cinema which it announces, is made of something else, something synthetic.'

22 'Something else which is placed between reality and the recording of reality'; 'fetishism of the image and its abstraction from reality.'

Frodon parle du Steadycam. Or, dans *La Lune dans le caniveau* pas un seul plan n'a été filmé au Steadycam; je n'ai d'ailleurs jamais utilisé ce procédé. En revanche, je cadre moi-même mes films, je suis donc le premier à voir mes comédiens dans leur travail; d'autre part, je travaille souvent à l'épaule. Enfin, Frodon cite encore la caméra Louma ultra-mobile; c'est tout le contraire, la Louma est une grue, et la lourdeur de son emploi la rend très difficile à utiliser.[23]

Some critics were more generous. Siclier, for example, criticises the film, as he did *Diva*, for its visual excess, but is prepared to see qualities in it: 'la création d'un nouveau "réalisme poétique" et ... la transformation du monde de Goodis en cauchemar esthétique' (Siclier 1991: 258).[24] Others have espoused Bassan's revisionist view of the *cinéma du look* as neo-baroque (see Prédal 1991: 462–64). Arguably, more than any of the films of the *cinéma du look*, *La Lune dans le caniveau* exemplifies the characteristics Bassan enumerates: a *mise en scène* which privileges exuberance, light, movement, especially the curves and curls of the camera, and an emphasis on sensation. And yet, the film should be seen less perhaps as the archetypal film of the *cinéma du look* than as an attempt to work on a new film language. In the remainder of this chapter I shall be exploring that language and the way it generates a particular type of nostalgia unanchored in the real, unlike, say, heritage cinema. I shall then locate the film's visual style and its narrative concerns in a genre which reviewers have on the whole not mentioned in relation to *La Lune dans le caniveau*. And yet, with its plot of the hero seduced away from his family by a *femme fatale*, its excessive stylisation, its claustrophobic small-town atmosphere, its emphasis on the family, its constant recourse to aggression as a form of displacement for alienation, *La Lune dans le caniveau* is

23 'Frodon speaks of the use of video control. I have to say that I have never used this type of technology in any of my films. I have had a monitor on set, and I detest this type of technology which distances the film-maker from the actors. Moreover, Frodon speaks of the Steadycam, but in *La Lune dans le caniveau* not a single shot was taken using the Steadycam. In fact I have never used it. On the other hand, I set up the camera for my films myself, and am therefore the first to see my actors at work, and I often work with the camera on my shoulder. Finally, Frodon talks about the ultra-mobile Louma, but it's quite the opposite, the Louma is a crane camera, and its heaviness makes it quite difficult to use' (e-mail correspondence, 29 November 1999).

24 'The creation of a new "poetic realism" and the transformation of Goodis's world into an aesthetic nightmare.'

less a film in the French art-house tradition, despite many references to Carné in particular, than a distant relative of Hollywood melodrama. And, finally, I shall explain why the main interest of the film beyond its re-articulation of melodrama is the way in which Depardieu-as-star is reconfigured in the film, his iconicity questioned: he is de-iconised and re-iconised by the film in a gesture towards an impossible authenticity.

The film language of the unconscious

The constant movement of the camera, which infuriated so many reviewers, who, in line with Frodon's view summarised above, saw in it nothing more than a fetishisation of the technically possible with no meaning but itself, forms part not just of a distinct visual style, but, arguably, of a set of significations which have to do with the fascination for the body and its misrepresentation in the film image. It is instructive to compare the mobile camera in *La Lune dans le caniveau* with its use in Tavernier's *Un dimanche à la campagne*, which appeared a year later. The extreme mobility of the Steadycam in the opening sequences of *Un dimanche à la campagne*, harshly commented on by many reviewers, was, according to Tavernier, an attempt to avoid the immobility of painterly composition (see Powrie 1997: 39, 48), and by extension a ploy to anchor the spectator in the flux of the real. In *La Lune dans le caniveau*, I would argue, the mobile camera denotes desire rather than an uncovering of the real, and not even a desire for the real, but a desire for desire in its most abstract sense, an attraction to desire as flux and constant deferral. That desire is nevertheless anchored in actors' bodies; indeed, one of the more interesting features of the film is the sweat which drips on and from the principal protagonists' bodies, with the exception of Loretta. That is one reason why I cannot agree with Frodon's view of de-realisation and the evacuation of the actor's body.

Nor am I entirely happy with Austin's view of the film. Broadly speaking, Austin's interpretation of *La Lune dans le caniveau* is predicated on the dichotomy between naturalism and fantasy, represented over determinedly by the film's title: the moon as ideal, as fantasy, versus the sordid reality of the gutter (Austin 1996: 122–24). Certainly, this is what Goodis intends in the source novel, the distance between the reality of low life and the impossibility of escape, and his novel is darkly negative, a pessimistic social comment. But this view depends on seeing the world of work in the film (as well as the world of the low-lifes in the bar) as part of the sordid 'reality', whereas in fact the world of work is spectacularised. This is especially the case in the warehouse fight sequence, where Gérard fights for his life among clumps of bananas; but it also applies to the other shots of the docks, to such an extent indeed that one reviewer, commenting ironically, indeed vituperatively, on the long-distance shot of Depardieu and his workmates on a container just prior to the storm which drives Depardieu to the warehouse, sees the shot less as a naturalist representation of the real than as an advertising clip, a 'spot clandestin' as he calls it, indicating in the following comment the possible advertising themes that the shot reminds him of:

> Quatre silhouettes de travailleurs (les Dockers sont sympas), découpées ... sur un ciel couchant (Soif d'aujourd'hui) et juchées sur des containers titanesques (1500 litres de Guerlain? 15 tonnes de camembert? La dernière collection Saint-Laurent?). Va et vient des grues (Souscrivez à l'emprunt Chantiers de l'Atlantique), aller et retour des containers (Votre banque est exportatrice). (Lefort 1983)[25]

One could argue that the topos of 'work' is midway between the gutter of Vernon Street and the ideal of uptown, a first step out of mire, narratively speaking. But in fact the work shots are more complex than such a simple schematisation allows; 'work' shots not mentioned by Lefort, where Depardieu is, arguably, pictured as the tortured and romantic working-class hero, throw yet another light on this use of the docks, as I shall explain below.

Beineix, to return to Austin's dichotomy between naturalism and fantasy, is not interested in the social, insofar as this could be represented by naturalism. As he puts it in an interview, 'les démonstrations politiques ou philosophiques ne m'intéressent pas, elles restent trop simplistes. Il y a dans *La Lune dans le caniveau* une opposition entre pauvreté et richesse, mais elle se résout dans la détresse commune, qui est un mal métaphysique où les clivages

---

25 'Four silhouetted workermen (Dockers are Wonderful), against the setting sun (Today's thirst) and perched on gigantic containers (1500 litres of Guerlain? 15 tons of camembert? Yves Saint-Laurent's latest collection?). Toing and froing of the cranes (Subscribe to an Atlantic Shipyards' loan), comings and goings of the containers (Your bank is a key exporter).'

sociaux n'ont plus cours' (Tranchant 1983).[26] He is attempting, in his view, to find the visual equivalent for alienation: 'trouver au malaise, au mal d'être contemporain des équivalents visuels, parce que l'image est le langage de notre siècle' (Tranchant 1983).[27] Beineix's excessively stylised *mise en scène* functions in this respect according to the typical view of the postmodern image as hyper-real, a term used by Beineix himself to explain stylistic excess in *La Lune dans le caniveau*: 'en accumulant les éléments réalistes, et même hyperréalistes, on finit par échapper à la réalité' (L. 1983).[28]

One could argue, along with Beineix, that he is attempting to locate a style which could act as the unconscious of an epoch: 'I wanted to make the subconscious materialize on the screen. I didn't want to be in the service of logic, of reality' (Beineix 1983c: 17). Certainly, this is to be contrasted with the literalist or manifest reading suggested by Chion, who complains that camerawork in the film is empty of signification. Whereas strong camera movements, says Chion, usually assume the function of punctuation or dramatisation, in *La Lune dans le caniveau* 'elles se retrouvent accumulées, mais déboussolées, indécises, comme "désaffectées". On ressent une arythmie générale, un parasitage et une annulation mutuelle des effets techniques dans un ensemble dont la logique, la courbe, a été perdue' (Chion 1983).[29] This view demands a literalist reading of camerawork at the service of narrative, whereas Beineix is clearly aiming for meta-narrative camerawork, as far from the real as the dream is from quotidian reality. For example, responding to a comment on the fact that the film is mostly shot at night, he said that 'les profondeurs de la nuit correspondent aussi aux profondeurs de l'inconscient' (Beineix 1983b: 24).[30] And in another interview, he said: 'Le mystère de la femme est l'inconnu. Sa

26 'I am not interested in political or philosophical demonstrations, they are too simplistic. In *La Lune dans le caniveau* there is a contrast between poverty and wealth, but it is resolved in a common distress, which is a metaphysical distress where the social divide is no longer operable.'
27 'Find visual equivalents for the contemporary malaise, because the image is the language of our century.'
28 'By accumulating realist, even hyperrealist elements, you end up escaping from reality.'
29 'There is an accumulation of them, but they are confused, uncertain, "disused", as it were. You feel a general lack of rhythm, a kind of image interference and a cancelling out of technical effects in a whole whose logic has been lost.'
30 'The depths of the night correspond to the depths of the unconscious.'

lecture en est psychanalytique, parce que, après tout, je m'interroge sur le malaise de l'homme qui ne sait pas très bien où la situer. Un homme n'est pas un homme quand il ne se reconnaît pas une certaine fragilité' (Gasperi 1983).[31] In other words, the film's language is an attempt to approximate a psychoanalytic interrogation of a malaise, which is here defined as both a general malaise, and the specific malaise of the contemporary male. Both of these types of malaise are collapsed in 'Depardieu'. The fascination of the film is Depardieu's fragility: he is caught midway between character (Gérard) and star ('Gérard'), and as is fitting, this fragility is located in Depardieu's body, which is the key for reading the film as melodrama.

Melodrama

The dysfunctional family

La Lune dans le caniveau's emphasis on the body is mentioned by several reviewers, who see it as part of the film's sordidness, not so much hyper-real as far too real, it would seem: the characters are 'mannequins inexpressifs au débit monocorde dont la passion et la flamme semblent se réduire aux gouttes de transpiration qui suintent de leurs corps' (Ross 1983: 23).[32] Victoria Abril also stressed the impact of the body in an apparently disingenuous comment justifying her excessive sexualisation and nudity in the film, which she refers to as 'un jeu charnel si puissant que j'ai l'impression d'y avoir laissé un morceau de mon corps' (Seguret 1983).[33] Beineix is not interested in the real, nor necessarily in fantasy as an escape from the real, I would argue, despite the comment on the hyper-real. He is more interested in locating desire, metaphorised in the film's fascination with the eroticised body, a desire caught in social structures, signified here by the insistence on the family, typical of melodrama; as Beineix points

---

31 'The mystery of woman is the unknown. You need psychoanalysis to interpret it/her, because after all I am asking questions about the malaise of man who does not quite know where to situate it/her. A man is not a man if he does not recognise a certain fragility in himself.'

32 'Inexpressive dummies who speak monotonously and whose passion seems to be reduced to the beads of sweat coming from their bodies.'

33 'A carnality so strong that I had the impression of leaving part of my body in the film.'

out, 'Goodis's story was Œdipal; it had the triangle of the mother, father, and the boy-in-between' (Beineix 1983c: 17). My emphasis on the erotic may seem an unlikely point, given the film's alleged coldness; but Beineix's response to this point is even more instructive than Abril's emphasis on the film as a vehicle for the eroticised body: 'la frigidité ... c'est la volonté d'éterniser le désir' (Gasperi 1983).[34] The film, in other words (and here we can recall Beineix's suggestion above that he was trying to stop time), attempts to capture and freeze-frame desire in its raw state, and tries to achieve this by a disarticulation of the normal film language, 'faire d'une enquête une quête', as he says of the film's subversion of the *polar* (Anon. 1982).[35] Reviewers interpreted this as ponderousness or portentousness, much as they did for Carax's *Mauvais Sang* three years later.

Unlike *Mauvais Sang*, however, *La Lune dans le caniveau* is not just a disarticulated *film noir*, but also a melodrama, and has melodrama's typical preoccupations with excess and repressed sexuality. Just as the claustrophobic *mise en scène* figures the claustrophobia of the dysfunctional family structure, and the excessively stylised *mise en scène* figures the repression that that structure brings about, as Nowell-Smith, among others, has argued (Nowell-Smith 1977), so too, and more importantly, repressed sexuality is mapped onto the bodies of the characters. These bodies, with the exception of the two enigmatic women (the hero's raped sister Catherine and Loretta, the woman from uptown who resembles her), sweat constantly, reminding the spectator of the immediacy of bodily functions in general and, through the connotations of body heat, of sexuality in particular.

That sexuality is guiltily nostalgic. Melodrama looks back, as Susan Hayward reminds us, 'at what is dreamt of as an ideal time of respectability and no anti-social behaviour. It dreams of the unobtainable ... . (It) plays out forbidden longings, symptomatic illness and renunciation' (Hayward 1996: 205). Clearly, Gérard's longings in the film correspond to this description. He longs for something better, which had been incorporated for him in his sister, and which he projects onto Loretta, the typically unobtainable *femme fatale*, whom he will have to renounce when he realises that he can never be part of her world. But that projection is complicated by his fascination for his

34 'Frigidity is the wish to make desire last forever.'
35 'To turn an investigation into a quest.'

dead sister, and indeed his feelings of guilt for his incestuous longing for her, a problematically displaced eroticisation, I would argue, of the longing for the purity of the maternal origin.

Gérard's mother is dead, just as the Channings' parents are, and the structure of relationships in *La Lune dans le caniveau* emphasises the quest for the lost mother patterned onto the incestuous desire for the sister. Newton Channing lives in a quasi-incestuous relationship with his sister who acts like his mother; he marries a mother substitute, one of the low-lifes in the ironically named Mikado Bar. Similarly, Gérard is destined for Bella, his half-sister, although he yearns for Loretta, who is a sister-substitute, and will end up mistakenly in his stepmother's bed after the non-consummmation of the marriage with Loretta. All three are linked in the film by the *mise en scène* of the hospital (which is not part of the original novel, thus allowing us to read the codes symptomatically), and by extension by Gérard's attraction to them. Catherine visits Gérard in hospital as he lies after his accident at work, and the sequence will be recalled in his drunken fantasy after the marriage, only the dead Catherine will be replaced by a dead Loretta; and, finally, Bella is first seen swinging lasciviously against a broken-down ambulance.

The two sons feel guilt, Newton because he was responsible for his parents' death in a car accident, and, since he hated them, we assume that he may have killed them on purpose, and is now consumed with guilt. Similarly, Gérard feels guilt for his sister's death. The reasons for this are obscure, but are clearly linked to incestuous desires, which are articulated by his brother Frank more clearly than Gérard can articulate them himself. One of the major differences between the novel and the film makes this incestuous desire and the ensuing guilt clearer. It is the hospital sequence, where Catherine visits Gérard who has suffered an accident in the docks, his hand pierced by an acetelyne beam when helping a fellow worker caught underneath a pile of fallen pipes. Quite apart from the obvious indications of castration, which I shall return to, this sequence is remarkable for its highly organised, indeed fetishised *mise en scène*, as well as for the exchange between brother and sister. Gérard berates Catherine for being dressed in a revealing white dress. 'Tu mets des robes de pute maintenant', he says.[36] She responds that she did so for him, and leaves upset, only to

36 'You're wearing tarts' dresses now.'

be raped by a stranger and to commit suicide. The focus on a highly erotic incestuous brother–sister relationship, associated with the dead mother, seems to me to be a clear indication of the Kleinian depressive position, where the infant 'rage(s) against the mother for the frustrations she causes [by withdrawing her breast], but now, instead of fearing retaliation, it feels guilt and anxiety for the damage it itself has done in phantasy' (Klein 1986: 20).

Gérard's mother has been replaced by the threatening 'bad' mother Lola who is contrasted with the 'good' mother substitute, Loretta. Although both women are 'other', they are stereotypically coded: Lola is unpleasantly coded as 'bad' by her blackness (in the original novel, she is Cherokee rather than Afro-American), and her constant shouting at her apparently henpecked husband. Like most of the characters she sweats profusely, and is thus triply contrasted with Loretta, who is soft-spoken, and appears mostly in a white dress, her hair ruffled in the Mikado Bar by the fan, suggesting coolness. Moreover, Loretta's appearances are almost magical; she materialises as if on a wave of inflated music and sweeping camerawork.

Music

Maternal loss is thus figured by music, which is a crucial component of melodrama. Work on music by Barthes and Kristeva during the 1970s laid an emphasis both on the body, and on music as maternal. Psychoanalytic accounts of film music suggest that it gratifies the spectator by the pleasure of reunion with the mother, while paradoxically reminding the spectator of that loss: 'Coinciding with its ability to reconstitute the maternal object and to simulate the primordial pleasure of the subject's unity with her, music simultaneously reminds the subject of its present separation from her' (Flinn 1992: 63). This reminder occurs in a small detail, which is nevertheless significant for being an addition to the novel, namely the father's violin.

The violin is given by Gérard to his father on his birthday. His father has never learned how to play, however, and it will later be smashed over his head by his irate wife. The violin could then be taken to signify the impotence of the father, unable to struggle out of mourning for his daughter who has committed suicide. The violin is also, I would argue, an excessive diegetic codification for the inflated non-diegetic music, based on the stereotypical sweeping strings and piano arpeggios, associated with Loretta.

The sweeping music associated with Loretta is, like many other elements of the film, overdetermined. It is intrusively obvious, both quantitatively, since it seems too loud in comparison with the rest of the soundtrack, and qualitatively, since it is associated with sweeping camera movements. This excessive coding is further aggravated as it rapidly becomes associated with Loretta, and, by extension, with the unattainable, its tenor therefore being a depressive melancholy in keeping with the regressive nostalgia of melodrama signalled above by Hayward.

The intensity of the music in the film draws attention to the body, as much as it might do to some sense of loss. This association of music and the body has been addressed by Kivy. Melodrama in the theatre, defined as 'a form of drama in which the words are spoken, with musical accompaniment' (Kivy 1997: 320) did not survive. It did, however, survive in film, even after the advent of the talkies when one might plausibly have assumed that it was no longer necessary to fill the gap of speech. To account for this, Kivy suggests that music in some sense 'stands in' for the loss of the real (theatrical) presence of human beings in a film. In the case of Loretta, the body is always presented as 'cool'. When she first appears, she is dressed in white, and ruffled by a breeze which up until that point had been conspicuous by its absence in the torrid heat of the night. The distant, nostalgically coded 'maternal' body is contrasted with the body of Gérard, which is nevertheless grounded in nostalgia, as I shall explain in the following section.

Gérard/'Gérard'

The intertexts as ground

The regressive melancholy of melodrama is one form of nostalgia. There is another apparent nostalgia at work in the film, intertextuality. Intertextual elements might have been seen as typical of the postmodern film, but I would like to characterise them as melancholic ciphers rather than the intertextual collage of recycled cinematographic commodities often viewed as pastiche in postmodern films.

Austin points out how Nastassia Kinski's character Loretta is informed by her roles as the fantasy figure in Coppola's studio musical *One From the Heart* (1982) and the romantic heroine in Polanski's *Tess* (1979) (Austin 1996: 123). While these echoes undoubtedly affected spectators' views of Loretta, they are no more telling than the usual connotations attached to stars. More obvious is the reference to Truffaut's *Tirez sur le pianiste* (1960) which was also based on a Goodis novel. But more systematic, and indeed more interesting in relation to the use of Depardieu's body, are the echoes which most French reviewers pointed to, namely echoes of Carné's films. To some extent this was motivated by Beineix's statement at the press conference in Cannes that *La Lune dans le caniveau* represented his *Les Enfants du paradis* (1945; Cartier 1983), and one can see how this studio-set story of unattainable love bears a strong resemblance to the narrative of *La Lune dans le caniveau*. But then there are many other echoes of Carné's films, noted by reviewers: the studio set reminded many of *Les Portes de la nuit* (1946; Bescos 1983; Pérez 1983), another story of unattainable love, to which *La Lune dans le caniveau* is much closer in both tone and narrative, as Jean Diego (Yves Montand) falls in love with the high-society wife, Malou (Nathalie Nattier) returning to her working-class roots downtown. Their waltz in her father's store-yard is uncannily close in its *mise en scène* and fantastical atmosphere to the marriage sequence in *La Lune dans le caniveau*. But then again, there are obvious parallels with *Quai des brumes* (1938) through the port setting (Heymann 1983; Jamet 1983; Greene 1999: 163), and with *Le Jour se lève* (1939; the *quartier populaire* and its marginalised working-class hero; Jamet 1983). Nor is Carné the only classical director alluded to, for, as Austin points out (Austin 1996: 124), one of the early sequences of *La Lune dans le caniveau* where Gérard munches his way through a block of ice as a wager, recalls Jean (interestingly, as is the case for Gérard in *La Lune dans le caniveau*, Jean is also the name of the actor concerned, Jean Dasté) moping for Juliette (Dita Parlo) on an even bigger block of ice in Vigo's *L'Atalante* (1934).

Remembering that *L'Atalante* is a key intertext for Carax's *Les Amants du Pont-Neuf* (1991; see Hayes 1999), we might well think that *La Lune dans le caniveau*'s references to the same film could suggest a Caraxian nostalgia for pre-World War II cinema (see Powrie 1997: 132). The reference to *L'Atalante*, however, is purely fortuitous. The eating of a block of ice occurs in the Goodis novel, although it is not Kerrigan who eats it, and the eating is not for a wager, but because of the heat. References to the films of Carné, on the other hand, seem considerably less fortuitous, and it is worth outlining their function. They are overdetermined, and this makes them spill over into postmodern parody whose impact is to cancel each other out as the spectator is batted from one Carné intertext to another. The films thus shade off into each other forming a vague but paradoxically located pastness. The films gestured at are ciphers in the literal sense that they are zeros, or emptiness,[37] the degree zeros of a diffuse but at the same time specific desire which is not nostalgia, but a desire for nostalgia, a longing for locatedness not in the pre-war period, but in the specific world of Carné with his doomed working-class heros.[38]

The result of this almost abstract longing is to create an emptiness, a blank ground upon which Depardieu inscribes his body. The problem for Depardieu is that his acting style relies heavily on being located within a context against which he usually rebels. When the context is as vague as a desire for nostalgia, Depardieu cannot even rage, as he usually does. The sequence where he loses his temper, for example, when he has dressed in his Sunday best to return the camera to Loretta, is one of the least convincing sequences in the film.

Reviewers who pointed to the many Carné echoes tended to make the obvious point that if the visual style and some of the narrative elements ressembled Carné's work, Beineix did not have the benefit of Prévert's scriptwriting: 'Je lui souhaite de se trouver quelqu'un à l'image de celui qui fut pour beaucoup dans la réussite de Carné. En somme, J-J Beineix a presque tout pour lui. Mais il lui manque un Prévert' (Favre 1983);[39] the film 'sue pour évoquer son Carné sans son Prévert' (Lardeau 1983: 36).[40] But this is to miss the point, and to

37 The word *cipher*, or *chiffre* in French, derives from the Arabic *çifr* (*zero*), a substantivisation of *empty* or *void*.

38 This analysis is very similar to Greene's, who also uses the term 'cipher', applied to Depardieu, whom she sees as 'hollow' (Greene 1999: 176), a melancholic mask of Gabin (Greene 1999: 177). The difference in our analyses lies in the fact that Greene sees *Quai des brumes* as the only intertext.

39 'I hope for his sake that he will find someone in the image of the person who played a large part in Carné's success. In short, Beineix has nearly everything going for him. But he is missing a Prévert.'

40 'The film tries desperately hard [literally: sweats] to evoke Carné without Prévert.'

reduce film to precisely the kind of palimpsestic recycling which often features in critiques of postmodernism. It is essential that the dialogue in *La Lune dans le caniveau* should not overwhelm the spectator with its poeticity; it is essential that the characters should not be articulate, because they would then transcend their destiny by articulating its trajectory; it is essential that they should be without real voice, reduced to their body, the immediacy of the body being constrained by the artifice of image, because Beineix is trying to articulate a loss and alienation appropriate to the 1980s, and not to the 1930s or 1940s. Carné's heros are also alienated, but they have a voice, whereas French youth of the 1980s is without a voice, not just alienated but anomic. Depardieu might well be an avatar of the Gabin in Carné's films of the 1930s, but Beineix's Depardieu is far from the articulate revolt of *Le Jour se lève*'s speech of revolt to an assembled community.

Depardieu's voice

Depardieu's voice is the key to the film. Put simply, his ever threatened loss of voice and reduction to body is a feminisation, a loss of authority, which corresponds to the directionlessness of 1980s youth. Depardieu's very public criticisms of the film are understandable in this light. He criticised the film very vocally on José Artur's *Pop-Club*, notoriously calling it 'la lune dans l'égout' (Dupré 1983). The *Pop-Club* was a radio programme, which thus emphasised the voice, and one of Depardieu's major criticisms was that Beineix 'n'écoute personne',[41] Depardieu being the implicit no one to whom Beineix did not listen. When one adds to this the various comments made by reviewers concerning the delivery of the actors – Pérez, for example, considers that the dialogue is both derisory and 'marmonné' (Pérez 1983),[42] and I have already quoted the *Revue du cinéma* reviewer who considers the actors nothing more than 'mannequins inexpressifs au débit monocorde' (Ross 1983: 23)[43] – a pattern emerges which is located in the problematics of the voice. Serge Daney, perhaps the most articulate reviewer of the film, related what he calls the film's aphasia to the actors' fragmented bodies:

41 'doesn't listen to anyone.'
42 'mumbled.'
43 'inexpressive dummies who speak monotonously.'

La Lune dans le caniveau est au fond un film muet, aphasique, et le dialogue – même murmuré – y est indigne d'un mauvais Delannoy des années quarante. Mais le film réduit à sa seule image fonctionnerait-il ? Oui, mais à la façon d'un film muet vu du coin de l'œil, d'un vidéo-clip mode, d'une logorrhée d'images greffées au hasard sur un squelette de récit et des ébauches de corps (Depardieu n'y est pas mauvais, mais il joue déjà 'électronique', comme les acteurs de *Tron*, il ne voit pas le reste de l'image où il est plongé). (Daney 1983)[44]

It is no accident that Daney, making a general point about the way in which the actors are subordinated to the play of the image, singles out Depardieu; nor is it accidental that Depardieu was so vociferous in his criticism of the film; nor, finally, is it accidental that all the characters in the film have the names given to them in the novel, with one exception, Depardieu, who is called by his real first name Gérard instead of William, as in the novel.

This blurs the distinction between reality and fiction, drawing attention to the reality of Depardieu as actor rather than character. What Silverman says when commenting the use of a real amputee in Wyler's *The Best Years of Our Lives* (1946) can be extended to the use of Depardieu's real Christian name, which 'exercises a strong referential pull, seeming to point beyond the text and [Depardieu's] acting to his body' (Silverman 1990: 122). Beineix is using Depardieu, as Depardieu must no doubt have felt most acutely, just as he did when Ferreri used him as the iconic macho who literally castrates himself in *La Dernière femme* (1976), leading to a similar unusually vituperative attack on the director, Marco Ferreri (Depardieu 1988: 65–70). Depardieu, the normally articulate icon of French maleness, is in *La Lune dans le caniveau* refused articulacy; he is reduced to his inarticulate working-class body, 'une ébauche de corps' as Daney dismissively puts it (Daney 1983),[45] since for Daney the body, presumably, can only be fully realised through narrative and voice.

44 '*La Lune dans le caniveau* is really a silent film, aphasic, and the mumbled dialogue is unworthy of a bad 1940s film by Delannoy. But if the film were reduced to its images would it still work? Yes, but like a silent film you watch in the corner of your eye, like a fashionable video-clip, like images spewing forth, grafted haphazardly on a narrative outline and sketches of bodies (Depardieu is not bad in the film, but he is already acting electronic, like the actors in *Tron*, he cannot see the rest of the image in which he is lost).'

45 'a sketch of a body.'

The story of an unattainable love might well be much the same as in *Cyrano de Bergerac* (Rappeneau, 1990), but the difference between the two films is that Depardieu is supremely articulate in Rappeneau's version of Rostand's stage play; indeed, nostalgia is created by the verbal excess which fills the gap between those who could have been sexually close, and that verbal excess is felt as melancholic sublimation. In *La Lune dans le caniveau*, it is the opposite that occurs. Melancholy is generated by the loss of Depardieu's authoritative voice.

The film was criticised for its stylistic inflation and concomitant meaningless. My general point has been that the film evidently conveys meaning, and I have located that general meaning in a social interpretation, youth alienation. Mapped onto this interpretation is the way the film functions as a mediator of the unstable, indeed fragile sign 'Depardieu', whose threatened loss of voice I have said is the key to the film. These two points can be brought together by the following statement by Kristeva (from a volume edited by William Kerrigan, which appeared in the same year as the film, for those who like coincidences). Although she is talking about the relationship between the analysand and the psychotherapist, it seems to me that a more general application can be envisaged:

> The repressed has meaning but no signification .... Signification is what subjective meaning has and this meaning fits into the subject's universe, incorporates his affects and experiences; it 'means' something to him. If it 'means' nothing to him, this indicates that no other has played the role of authenticator of his symbolic experience. Here ... we see the absence of the paternal function through a chain reaction of symbolic deficiencies. (Kristeva 1983: 45)

The emptiness of signification which Chion reads into stylistic camera flourishes is clearly meaningful. Alienation equates to loss of voice which equates to loss of the paternal signifier. Depardieu is, to play on a name which is already played with in the film, lost to God the Father (*départir de Dieu*), disarticulated (*départagé*) between his feminised body and compensatory machismo.

The film thus enacts excessive melodramatic procedures (excessive colour coding, excessive camerawork, excessive music), what reviewers aptly described (although for them it was merely a term of disparagement) as 'boursouflure' or swelling, a hyperinflation of the normal melodramatic procedures, style acting as a metonym for what is a metaphor for alienation; this is less melodrama, then, than *hyper-drama*. This inflation is combined with excessive deflation, the derision which is typical of Beineix, whether it be the taunting of Gérard and the spectator by the 'Try Another World' poster,[46] or the derisive use of the voice-over.

Before concluding on the voice-over which frames the film, it is worth investigating the most intriguing sequence of the film, mainly because it is so different from anything in the novel, and incorporates many of the excessive stylistic features referred to above. Emerging from his stepmother's bedroom clutching a statuette of the Virgin Mary, Gérard collapses to the floor. One of the more interesting features of the sequence is the lighting up of the Virgin as it hits the floor, and the fortuitous positioning of Gérard's eye over a hole in the floor through which he can see his brother Frank playing with a toy bird and mumbling to himself. This extraordinary *mise en scène* manages to encapsulate not just baroque excess (the lighting-up of the Virgin, the eye framed in the hole in the floor), but also an excess of meaning: the Virgin is the statuette from which the plastic halo was taken to serve as a ring for his marriage to Loretta, the tackiness of both the ring and the statuette functioning as derisive reminders of lost dreams. But the statuette is also a reminder of his virginal dead sister, ignominiously raped in a backstreet.[47] And, finally, but not least, the Virgin functions as the phallus which Gérard has lost, the absence of voice, the absence of authority, castrated by the removal of the halo, and yet still brilliantly tumescent. As he clutches this impossible object, Gérard gazes like God the Father ([Depard]Dieu) on his alter ego, his other part (Depard[dieu]) Frank below,[48] his eye framed, his gaze mutilated, the camera vertiginously sweeping down

46 Beineix has said of this poster that 'c'est le message publicitaire, seule alternative à la pauvreté. C'est aussi un appel à la drogue'. ('It's the advertising message, the only alternative to poverty. It's also an appeal to drugs.') (e-mail correspondence, 29 November 1999).

47 The combination of the two figures, Catherine and Loretta, is made clear in what follows. As he lies on the floor, there is a fantasy sequence recalling the earlier hospital sequence; this combines the sister, who walks away from him, as she did in the earlier sequence, and the dead Loretta, her blood dripping from her neck, as Gérard uncovers her.

48 This doubling is even more pronounced in the novel, when Kerrigan tries to strangle his brother: 'There was a gurgling noise. But it wasn't coming from Frank. It came from his own throat, as though he was crushing his own flesh, stopping the flow of his own blood' (Goodis 1983: 509).

to an extreme low angle, in expressionist excess as it signals his fall from grace, God to fallen angel, from virility to castrated and silent male. The voice-over, which is the penultimate sequence, is part of this complex derision.

Conclusion: voice, voice-over and voice over

The voice-over frames the film at beginning and end. Its derisive nature is manifested partly by its occurrence, and partly by its content. To deal with content first, the opening voice-over reads as follows:

> Dans un port de nulle part, au milieu du quartier des docks, un homme venait tous les soirs pour échapper à sa mémoire. [Long sequence of Catherine pursued by rapist] Sept ans s'étaient écoulés, et bien des lunes s'étaient levées dans le ciel noir. On n'avait jamais retrouvé le violeur, l'affaire avait été classée et plus personne s'en souvenait. Pourtant ... Il pensait à cette nuit où sa sœur Catherine était venue mourir là. Il pensait à l'innocence. On l'avait violée. Elle s'était suicidée. Et lui, soir après soir, sans qu'aucune force ne puisse l'en empêcher, il revenait là. Il n'avait qu'une seule idée, retrouver le violeur, arrêter ce manège qui lui prenait sa liberté.[49]

The extraordinary thing about the voice-over is its overwhelming redundancy. We might not have gathered that the pursued woman was Gérard's sister, but the rest of the text is redundant in relation to the images it accompanies, which speak for themselves. The opening voice-over therefore functions as an empty statement, a purely lyrical gesture, unlike, say, the voice-over at the beginning of another melo-drama, *Duel in the Sun* (Vidor, 1946), whose effectiveness relies less on the fact that it positions what follows as legend than it does on its excessive reliance on metaphor, the metaphor of the wild flower blooming in a desert. There is no such metaphor in the voice-over in

---

49 'In a port which could be anywhere, in the middle of docks, a man would come every night to escape from his memories. Seven years had passed, and many moons had risen in the dark sky. The rapist had never been found, the case had been closed and no one remembered it. And yet ... He thought of that night when his sister Catherine had come to die here. He thought of innocence. She had been raped. She had committed suicide. And night after night, no force being able to prevent him, he came here. He had only one idea, to find the rapist, to stop this carry-on which was taking his freedom from him.'

La Lune dans le caniveau (although there is the very strong visual metaphor of the blood),[50] only the tired voice of time passing but not releasing pain from the memory.

The voice-over as a procedure connotes paternal authority. As Silverman says, 'the capacity of the male subject to be cinematically represented in this dis-embodied form aligns him with transcendence, authoritative knowledge, potency and the law – in short, with the symbolic father' (Silverman 1984: 134). *La Lune dans le caniveau* begins with a voice-over, which does not return until the penultimate scene. The voice-over therefore functions as a derisory reminder of what has in fact been lost, the paternal signifier. The fact that the voice-over is delivered by Yves-Marie Maurin (who, you might well ask?), merely underlines the derision. Maurin's only claim to fame is as a minor actor in an all-but-forgotten comedy starring Brigitte Bardot, *En effeuillant la marguerite* (Allégret, 1956). It seems fitting in a chapter devoted to loss and rage against the dying of the paternal signifier that we should conclude on the paradoxical note of a forgotten actor in a forgotten comedy, as the actor of *La Lune dans le caniveau* sweats and disintegrates before our eyes, victim to his incest-ridden fantasies, clutching, derisively, a phallic Virgin Mary.

This is not the final scene, however. The final scene is a suitably chastened Gérard, who has, literally, come to his senses, as the banal voice-over suggests:

> Gérard rêvait d'une ville blanche, de stores pudiques, d'allées ombragées, de parties de tennis invisibles, et de pelouses douces. Il entendait le bruit des jets d'eau et le chant des oiseaux. Mais il avait peur de cette ville, de s'y sentir mal à l'aise, de cette porte qui s'ouvrirait et de cette femme qui l'attendait.[51]

Like the opening voice-over, this one is redundant; read over long-distance shots of the town, it is immediately followed by Gérard's return. He returns to Bella and 'la belle vie', which in this case means

---

50 Talking of the red Ferrari, Beineix says: 'It's not accidental that it's red. It's the colour of blood that the hero sees everywhere in that dead end. She has red lips and a red dress and she arrives like an echo of the blood of his sister. The symbolism of the sister is in representing a sexual taboo' (Beineix 1983c: 17).

51 'Gérard dreamed of a white town, of discreet blinds, shady drives, invisible tennis games, and soft lawns. He could hear the sound of fountains and bird song. But he was afraid of this town, of feeling uneasy, of the door which would open and of the woman who would be waiting for him.'

the life of the senses: sex and food. 'Everything is back to normal', one might be tempted to say, as he says to Bella: 'j'ai faim'.[52] Food signals the return to potency in what seems like a forced closure, in keeping with the derision of the remainder of the film.

The film therefore functions as a machine to question the star as icon. It reconfigures Depardieu, questioning his iconicity as his much-vaunted amalgam of femininity and working-class machismo, the 'suffering macho' as Vincendeau aptly labels him (Vincendeau 1993: 353). Gérard is excessively feminised by the narrative, as we can see by his transcendence of 'rough' origin by middle-class acculturation ('Faites attention', he says to Loretta in the car as they look over the docks, and just after he has wept, 'vous êtes dans un monde de brutes', to which she responds, 'mais vous n'êtes pas une brute, vous vous êtes souvenu de mon nom').[53] He is also feminised by his delivery, which figures a constantly threatened loss of voice, and therefore of paternal authority. But he is also excessively re-iconised as macho male, partly by his swagger, emphasised by costume and camerawork, partly by displays of aggression, especially the fight in the hangar where the cornucopia of bananas functions derisively and certainly over determinedly to restructure the loss of phallic authority. The two terms which Depardieu likes to suggest are part of his composite star persona, sensitivity and swagger, as I have called them elsewhere (Powrie 1997: 180), are in this film pulled radically apart by their excessive *mise en scène*, leaving a fissure, aptly summarised by the collocation of real name and fictional name. Who is the man we see in the final sequence, perfectly framed and elevated by the camera, Gérard or 'Gérard', whose metaphysical hunger has been replaced by a physical hunger? Even with its derisively tacky closure, the film cannot resolve the enigma of authenticity.

Gérard's crime is to have desired his sister, and therefore his mother. His punishment fits the crime: he will marry his stepsister and be hen-pecked by his stepmother, as his father was before him, the ideal Loretta forever refused so that he can continue to expiate incest and voluntary castration.

52 'I'm hungry.'
53 The dialogue is almost exactly that of the novel: 'Don't get too curious, Miss Channing. You're messing around with rough company'. 'You're not rough', she said lightly. Then more seriously, 'You remembered my name' (Goodis 1983: 429).

References

Anon. (1982), 'Tournage: Beineix comme dans un rêve', *Le Point*, 30 August.
Anon. (1983), *'La Lune dans le caniveau* de Jean-Jacques Beineix', *L'Ecole libératrice*, 4 June.
Assayas, Olivier (1983), 'La publicité, point aveugle du cinéma français', *Cahiers du cinéma* 351: 18–26.
Austin, Guy (1996). *Contemporary French Cinema: An Introduction*, Manchester and New York, Manchester University Press.
Beineix, Jean-Jacques (1983a), 'Au-delà du réel: une interview de Jean-Jacques Beineix', *Première* 74: 47–53, 165–66.
Beineix, Jean-Jacques (1983b), 'Entretien avec Jean-Jacques Beineix', *Revue du cinéma* 385: 23–25.
Beineix, Jean-Jacques (1983c), 'Man in the moon', *Film Comment* 19/4: 16–19.
Beineix, Jean-Jacques (2001), 'Beineix sur le divan', *Première* 286: 104–10.
Bergala, Alain (1983), 'Le vrai, le faux, le factice', *Cahiers du cinéma* 351: 4–9.
Bescos, José-M. (1983), *'La Lune dans le caniveau'*, *Pariscope*, 8 June.
Billard, Pierre (1983), 'Agaçant: *La Lune dans le caniveau* de Jean-Jacques Beineix', *Le Point* 558 (30 May).
Buckley, Michael (1984), 'Jean-Jacques Beineix: An Interview with Michael Buckley', *Film In Review* 35/1: 29–33.
Carrère, E. (1983), 'Les noces rouges', *Télérama* 1740, 18 May.
Cartier, Jacqueline (1983), 'Beineix déclenche la première bataille de Cannes', *France-Soir*, 13 May.
Chion, Michel (1983), 'Parlons technique: la caméra désaffectée comme un loft', *Libération*, 13 May.
Daney, Serge (1983), 'Jean-Jacques Beineix: Objectif Lune ... Tintin!', *Libération*, 13 May.
Depardieu, Gérard (1988), *Lettres volées*, Paris, Livre de Poche.
Devarrieux, Claire (1983), *'La Lune dans le caniveau* de Jean-Jacques Beineix', *Le Monde*, 14 May.
Dupré, Frédéric (1983), 'Beineix contre tous', *Le Matin*, 13 May.
Esposito, Marc (1983), 'Beineix en question', *Première* 75: 95–97.
Favre, Pierre (1983), *'La Lune dans le caniveau*: Les portes de la nuit', *La Nouvelle République du Centre-Ouest*, 20 May.
Flinn, Caryl (1992), *Strains of Utopia: Gender, Nostalgia, and Hollywood Film Music*. Princeton, Princeton University Press.
Frodon, Jean-Michel (1995), *L'Age moderne du cinéma français: De la Nouvelle Vague à nos jours*, Paris, Flammarion.
Gasperi, Anne de (1983), 'Beineix: "qu'ils me haïssent pourvu qu'ils me craignent"', *Le Quotidien de Paris*, 16 May.
Goodis, David (1983), *4 Novels*, London, Zomba.
Greene, Naomi (1999), *Landscapes of Loss: The National Past in Postwar French Cinema*. Princeton, New Jersey, Princeton University Press.
Hayes, Graeme (1999), 'Representation, masculinity, nation: the crises of *Les Amants du Pont-Neuf* (Carax, 1991)', in *Contemporary French Cinema:*

Continuity and Difference, edited by Phil Powrie, Oxford, Oxford University Press, 199–210.

Hayward, Susan (1996), *Key Concepts in Cinema Studies*, London and New York, Routledge.

Heymann, Danièle (1983), 'La misère la plus chic', *L'Express*, 27 May.

Jamet, Dominique (1983), *Quotidien de Paris*, 14 May.

Kivy, Peter (1997), 'Music in the movies: a philosophical enquiry', in *Film Theory and Philosophy*, edited by Richard Allen and Murray Smith, Oxford, Clarendon Press, 308–28.

Klein, Melanie (1986), *The Selected Melanie Klein*, edited by Juliet Mitchell, Harmondsworth, Middlex, Penguin.

Klotz, Claude (1983), '*La Lune dans le caniveau*', *VSD*, 19 May.

Kristeva, Julia (1983), 'Within the microcosm of "the talking cure"', in *Interpreting Lacan* (Psychiatry and the Humanities vol. 6), edited by Joseph H. Smith and William Kerrigan, New Haven, Yale University Press, 33–48.

L., J.C. (1983), 'Beineix: la survie par le danger', *Le Point* 554, 2 May.

Lardeau, Yves (1983), 'Le désir à la chaîne', *Cahiers du cinéma* 348–349: 36–37.

Lefort, Gérard (1983), 'Vos images m'intéressent', *Libération*, 13 May.

Logette, Lucien (1983), '*La Lune dans le caniveau*', *Jeune Cinéma* 152: 48–49.

Nowell-Smith, Geoffrey (1977), 'Minnelli and melodrama', *Screen* 18: 115–18.

Parent, Denis (1989), *Jean-Jacques Beineix: Version originale*, Paris, Barrault Studio.

Pérez, Michel (1983), *Le Matin*, 13 May.

Powrie, Phil (1997), *French Cinema in the 1980s: Nostalgia and the Crisis of Masculinity*, Oxford, Clarendon Press.

Prédal, René (1991), *Le Cinéma des français depuis 1945*, Paris: Nathan.

Ross, Philippe (1983), '*La Lune dans le caniveau*: éclipse partielle', *Revue du cinéma* 385: 22–23.

Rouergue, Sophie (1983), 'Quand Depardieu prend ses distances ...', *Le Matin*, 13 May.

Seguret, Olivier (1983), 'Victoria Abril: au clair de lune ... la chair de son corps', *Libération*, 16 May.

Siclier, Jacques (1991), *Le Cinéma français, 2: de Baisers volés à Cyrano de Bergerac 1968–90*, Paris, Ramsay Cinéma.

Silverman, Kaja (1984), 'Dis-embodying the female voice', in *Re-Vision: Essays in Feminist Film Criticism*, edited by Mary Ann Doane, Patricia Mellencamp and Linda Williams, Los Angeles, The American Film Institute, 131–49.

Silverman, Kaja (1990), 'Historical trauma and male subjectivity', in *Psychoanalysis and Cinema*, edited by E. Ann Kaplan, New York and London, Routledge, 110–27.

Tranchant, Marie-Noëlle (1983), 'Les accents baudelairiens de Jean-Jacques Beineix', *Le Figaro*, 12 May.

Vincendeau, Ginette (1993), 'Gérard Depardieu: the axiom of contemporary French cinema', *Screen* 34: 343–61.

5

37°2 le matin (1986)

Synopsis[1]

Betty quits her job and moves in with Zorg, an odd-job man who looks after beach houses. The owner asks Zorg to paint the beach houses in return for letting Betty stay. When Betty realises that the owner expects them to paint all 500 houses, she throws paint over his car. In the ensuing argument with Zorg, she discovers Zorg's manuscripts and reads his novel. The owner hassles Zorg for getting up late. Betty pushes him off the balcony, throws most of the furniture out of the window, and sets fire to the house. She and Zorg leave for Paris.

They move into a former hotel belonging to Lisa, a friend of Betty's, who lets them have a room. Zorg pays their way by doing odd jobs for Lisa, while Betty types his manuscript. Zorg tries to write, but cannot. Lisa's boyfriend, Eddie, who owns a pizzeria, moves in. Betty and Zorg work in the pizzeria, where Betty attacks a disagreeable customer. Betty sends Zorg's novel to publishers, but it is rejected. After receiving a particularly nasty letter of rejection, Betty attacks the publisher. [Zorg goes to the police station and talks with the superintendent, who is also a failed writer; he advises Zorg to get the publisher to drop the complaint. Zorg forces the publisher to withdraw

---

[1] There are two versions of the film, one released in 1986, and a second, longer version, called *version intégrale*, released in 1991, which restored sequences dropped for the 1986 version. These have been placed in square brackets in the synopsis which follows. However, in the central part of the film, sequences have been moved around; there are therefore two separate paragraphs representing each version for this part of the film.

the complaint.] During their celebrations, Eddie gets a phone call telling him that his mother has died.

[Zorg drives them to the funeral.] Zorg and Betty play a duet on the pianos in the shop which Eddie's mother ran. Zorg and Betty agree to Eddie's suggestion that they should run the shop. That night Betty refuses to sleep in the dead woman's bed. After failing to unfold a sofa-bed, they sleep on cushions, Betty insisting that Zorg should put the mattress outside. [The following morning, the bin-men refuse to take the mattress; one of them slashes it up with the hook he has in place of the arm he lost.]

1986 version

Zorg buys a yellow second-hand Mercedes. Zorg rescues the son of Bob the grocer after he has locked himself in the bathroom. Bob's wife, Annie, tries to seduce Zorg unsuccessfully. Betty and Zorg have an argument while Zorg is demolishing a wall in the house. Betty punches her hand through a glass door, and runs through the town to the church, where two policemen question them. Zorg delivers a piano with Bob in a borrowed lorry, but is unable to concentrate because Betty has told him she is pregnant. He is stopped for speeding by the younger of the two policemen, who lets him off when Zorg tells him he is to be a father. Zorg gives Betty some land on a hill with a small barn for her birthday. He buys her some baby clothes. Betty is too tired to make love, so Zorg writes. Betty receives a letter telling her that her test is negative. Zorg finds her with her hair cut roughly and with excessive make-up; he rubs the tomato sauce from his plate over his face.

1991 version (additional elements are still in square brackets)

Zorg buys a yellow second-hand Mercedes. [They make love in it in the countryside.] Betty and Zorg have an argument while Zorg is demolishing a wall in the house. [Betty drives the Mercedes and storms off when Zorg criticises her driving.] Betty punches her hand through a glass door, and runs through the town to the church, where two policemen question them. [Betty sells their first piano.] Zorg rescues the son of Bob the grocer after he has locked himself in the bathroom. Bob's wife, Annie, tries to seduce Zorg unsuccessfully. Zorg gives Betty some land on a hill with a small barn for her birthday. Zorg delivers a piano with Bob in a borrowed lorry, but is unable to concentrate because Betty has told him she is pregnant. He is stopped for speeding by the younger of the two policemen, who lets him off when Zorg tells him he is to be a father. [Betty and Zorg go to a restaurant, where Zorg buys some cocaine from a man in the toilets. Betty is too tired to make love, so Zorg writes.] He buys her some baby clothes. Betty receives a letter telling her that her test is negative. Zorg finds her with her hair cut roughly and with excessive make-up; he rubs the tomato sauce from his plate over his face.

Eddie and Lisa visit, and the four of them spend the day in the countryside where Betty lets herself fall into the water fully clothed. [Zorg tells Eddie about the pregnancy as they are fishing.] One night, Betty tells Zorg that she is hearing voices. Zorg attacks Bob who has told him that Betty is mad. [Zorg robs a security company's offices dressed as a woman. He and Betty go to the seaside, where Betty abducts a young boy, taking him to the toy section of the local supermarket. She and Zorg escape the crowd pursuing them.] Zorg returns home one day to find that Betty has ripped out her eye and is in hospital. He visits her, but she is asleep. The next day, he receives a phone call from a publisher who will publish his book. He goes to the hospital, where he finds Betty strapped down in her bed. She does not respond to him. He attacks the doctor who tells him that she is mad, and he is thrown out of the hospital. He returns dressed as a woman, and stifles Betty with a pillow. The film closes on him writing in his kitchen.

Background

After *La lune dans le caniveau*, Beineix worked on a script for a vampire film, based on the novel *La Vierge de glace* by Marc Behm. This project, for which Beineix bought the rights, and has continued to pay them annually, was shelved because American producers felt that the budget of $20 million was too high.[2] He returned to France and made two advertisements, both, interestingly, given his fourth film, featuring

2 See Parent 1989: 36–38 for a comical account by Beineix of his meeting with the producer Dino de Laurentiis in relation to this project.

big cats: a tiger for an Esso ad, and a black panther for Valentine
paints (the latter in January 1985 with Jean-François Robin, who was
to become the director of photography for *37°2 le matin*). Beineix took
to heart many of the criticisms levelled at *La Lune dans le caniveau*,
commenting either during the making of *37°2 le matin* or on its
release, on his mistakes: 'J'avais fait l'erreur de trop construire
l'image et pas assez le récit' (Beineix 1985: 58),[3] he said during
production, and on its release: 'Il n'est pas nécessaire de faire durer
un plan pour atteindre l'émotion et un mouvement de caméra, s'il
devient infini, risque d'amener une certaine monotonie, alors que je
croyais que ça amenait l'éternité' (Andreu 1986a: 84).[4] Working
within the constraints of advertising helped Beineix achieve economy
of means, which he put to good use in *37°2 le matin*: 'J'ai appris une
certaine discipline du récit, une certaine technique du raccourci, du
rythme' (Beineix 1985: 59).[5]

Beineix had read and liked Djian's first novel, *Bleu comme l'enfer*
(which Yves Boisset adapted for the screen in 1986). He was sent *37°2
le matin* in 1984 when it was still in manuscript form, and was
immediately attracted to what he called its 'romantisme sceptique'
(Savigneau 1985),[6] its mixture of love and despair (Beineix 1985: 58).
He was particularly attracted to the way Djian 'rend le quotidien
spectaculaire. Il sait la beauté d'un instant banal' (Tranchant 1986).[7]
The title, frequently misspelt, means 37 degrees centigrade at two in
the morning, and refers, according to Beineix, to the 'body temperature in the morning, but with a slight fever which may become a real
fever by the end of the day. It could be the beginning of a serious
disease or the first hint of passion. It is also, in the feminine cycle, the
temperature of ovulation' (Beineix 1986b: 300).

Beineix worked on the adaptation, this time alone, over a period of
two months in Saint Cyprien, near Gruissan, on the Languedoc coast,
Gruissan being the site of the 1930s beach houses on stilts which are
one of the more startling images of the film. Disenchanted with his

---

3 'I made the mistake of working up the image at the expense of the narrative.'
4 'It is not necessary to extend a shot to reach emotion, and a never-ending camera
movement can generate monotony, whereas I though it could generate eternity.'
5 'I learned the discipline of the story, the technique of the short-cut, rhythm.'
6 'Sceptical romanticism.'
7 'Makes the everyday spectacular. He knows how to find the beauty of an
ordinary moment.'

experience of the producers of his two previous films, he had created his own company, Cargo Films, in November 1984, and tried to associate with some Swiss producers for *37°2 le matin*. He was unhappy with their insistence on using established stars, however. He therefore bought the producers out for 2 m. francs, replacing them with Claudie Ossard, who had produced his two advertisements, and chose a relative unknown for his hero, and a complete unknown for the role of Betty.

Béatrice Dalle (Betty) was discovered by Dominique Besnehard. She had appeared on the cover of the magazine *Photo Revue* (the cover photograph, by Rémi Loca, was in fact used for the credit sequence and poster of the film), and had never worked in film, nor was she a trained actress. Beineix was attracted precisely by her 'naturalness', which, as we shall see, played a significant part in critical reaction to the film. She made the film's director of photography, Jean-François Robin, think of one of the great stars of the classical French cinema of the 1930s and 1940s, Arletty, because of her 'gouaille bien française' (Robin 1987: 13).[8] She made Beineix, as well as the UK and US press when the film was released in those countries, think of Bardot (Beineix 1985: 58). Like Bardot, in his view, 'elle est le naturel d'une génération ... . Elle représente un certain compromis entre la sensualité et l'époque' (Beineix 1986a: 95).[9] What Beineix may have meant by 'époque' is the aura of rebellion which Dalle carries, as is suggested by another of his comments: 'Betty ... est une fille comme il en existe. Les jeunes aujourd'hui sont révoltés et je les comprends, ils ne savent pas pourquoi tout va si mal' (Pantel 1986).[10] That rebellion made itself felt on set, in that Dalle frequently complained about the costumes she had to wear, the lines she had to speak, and, especially, the amount of nudity which Beineix wanted, as she recounted in interview: 'Il y a eu des clashs. Des jours où sur le plateau, on se serait tués. A propos des scènes de nu justement. A la fin, j'avais l'impression d'être tout le temps à poil' (d'Yvoire 1986: 97; see Robin 1987: 48–49, 67–68 for an account of these upsets).[11]

8 'very French cheek.'
9 'She is the natural of a generation. She represents a compromise between sensuality and her time.'
10 'Betty is a girl like those around us. Youngsters today are rebelling and I understand them, they don't know why everything is going so badly.'
11 'There were clashes. Some days on set we could have killed each other. Over nude scenes as it happens. In the end I had the impression that I was always naked.'

Beineix had written the script with Gérard Lanvin in mind, an actor he had already wanted as the lead for *La Lune dans le caniveau* (Beineix 2001: 55). Jean-Hugues Anglade (Zorg) had started a career as theatre producer after the Paris Conservatoire, and had won the admiration of Patrice Chéreau. He was later awarded a prize as best newcomer for his role in Chéreau's *L'Homme blessé* (1983), a film about AIDS, which he had followed by the role of the roller-skater in Besson's *Subway* (1985). He was seen as one of a new type of male lead, exhibiting a certain fragility and emotion, like his contemporaries Lambert Wilson and Christophe Lambert (the latter had been the male lead for *Subway*), all, according to one reviewer, 'comédiens "à cœur"' – [actors with sincerity] – (Pascaud 1986: 25).

There were more familiar faces, such as Gérard Darmon, who was Spic in *Diva*. Dominique Pinon, who was Le Curé in the same film, as well as playing Frank in *La Lune dans le caniveau*, had a cameo part as the cocaine seller, a sequence dropped for the 1986 version of the film.

Shooting lasted from early September to mid-December 1985 and took place first in Marjevols, a village in the Lozère at the eastern tip of the Monts d'Aubrac (where some of the hilly exteriors were shot), for the piano-shop section of the film. The crew then moved to Gruissan for the opening section of the film, and finished in the Paris area for the pizzeria section and the final sequences (hold-up and hospital). Robin explains how particular attention was given to lighting effects. Early on, he and Beineix agreed that the major light source should always come from the window (Robin 1987: 15). Beineix insisted on what at might first seem like a contradiction: 'Du contraste. Pas de demi-teinte et un rendu de couleurs un peu pastel' (Robin 1987: 22).[12] That apart, Robin took care to reproduce a 1970s feel for the light in the film: 'En voyant ce soleil, je sens que le film est là, la magie du cinéma est là, dans cette lumière sèche et chaude à la fois, comme celle des photos Kodachrome d'il y a dix ans. Ce Kodachrome, j'essaierai de la retrouver tout au long des décors extérieurs à Marjevols, et plus tard à Gruissan' (Robin 1987: 29).[13] Like Beineix's paradoxical wish for a sharp contrast of pastel shades, Robin's search

---

12 'Contrasts. No half-tones and a pastel palette.'
13 'Seeing the sun, I can feel that the film is there, the magic of the cinema is there, in that light which is both searing and warm, like Kodachrome photos ten years ago. I tried to find that Kodachrome for all the exteriors in Marjevols, and later in Gruissan.'

for a light which was both searing, while also giving a sense of warmth, suggests one of the key issues in the film, the contrast between the tragic (or melodramatic) and the comic, mapped onto a different contrast, that between, as Beineix's comment on the title of the novel above suggests, disease and passion. Heat is the image that manages to combine these polar opposites, and, as Robin points out, 'il faut qu'on la sente cette chaleur, qu'on la sente comme dans le scénario et comme dans le roman, qu'elle suinte de partout' (Robin 1987: 63).[14]

Adaptation

Beineix found the adaptation difficult because Djian's style, 'qui se veut "écriture parlée", ne convient pas tellement au cinéma' (Wagner 1985: 29).[15] Nevertheless, although Djian professed dismay at Boisset's adaptation of *Bleu comme l'enfer*, he was more than happy with Beineix's adaptation, proclaiming that the novel's emotion had been retained and that 'c'est mieux que le livre' (Leclercq (1986: 44).[16] Indeed, Beineix's main objective was to convey that emotion: 'Le film est rempli d'émotions très simples, qui passent de la joie à la douleur. Emotions qui naissaient à la lecture du livre. Qu'il fallait garder sur le tournage ... Mon travail était donc de transcrire des émotions ... Il suffit de trouver l'image qui correspond' (Ferenczi 1986).[17] Beineix insisted on the fact that neither the novel nor the film were interested in psychologising: 'Cette histoire est construite à l'américaine, il n'y pas de psychologie, seulement des situations' (Robin 1987: 54).[18]

His adaptation is remarkably faithful to the novel. As he had done for *La Lune dans le caniveau*, he used much of the novel's dialogue, and some of the first-person narrator's musings are conveyed in voice-over. The longer 1991 version of the film follows the narrative

14 'That light must be felt, felt like it is felt in the script and in the novel, it must seep through everything.'
15 'Which wants to be in a spoken style, doesn't work for cinema.'
16 'Better than the book.'
17 'The film is full of very simple emotions, going from joy to suffering. Emotions aroused by the novel. That we had to keep when making the film. My job therefore was to transcribe emotions. You just have to find the image which corresponds to it.'
18 'This story is American, there's no psychology, only situations.'

events of the novel, merely omitting a few events: the narrator crashes the Volkswagen belonging to Betty's friend (ch. 2); Eddie takes his new friends to the races when he moves in (ch. 8); Betty daubs grafitti on the door of the publisher who first rejects the narrator's manuscript and subsequently goes on a shoplifting spree (ch. 10); she ransacks a supermarket during her quarrel with the narrator (ch. 16); a storm more or less destroys the hut which the narrator gives to Betty (ch. 18); the narrator discovers he has an aversion to hospitals when visiting the accident-prone Archie, Bob's son (ch. 19); he later tries boxing for fun (ch. 21); he and Betty go on holiday as the narrator tries to get her to forget her false pregnancy (ch. 22); and, finally, at the end of the novel, the security men, of whom the narrator made fools, find him so as to exact revenge, but the younger one kills the pathological older one who wants to kill the narrator (ch. 27).

Beineix added very little material. He made more of the yellow Mercedes by having Zorg pretend he was stealing the car (not in the short version of the film) and driving Betty out into the countryside. He insisted somewhat more on the importance of children for Betty by having, in the long version, a youngster practise his piano in the shop. The only other additions were minor visual details, such as Georges playing his saxophone on a merry-go-round, or the gag of Eddie's tie for the funeral, which is black, but has an unsuitably erotic image on it which causes the other three to giggle uncontrollably, thus puncturing the solemnity of the occasion. Similarly, in the novel, the narrator's first rejection letter is read by Betty, who then spraypaints the publisher's door. Beineix omits this incident, and the letter is stuffed by Eddie into his mouth to prevent Betty from reading it, in straight slapstick style. In the same slapstick vein, a mention in the novel of Eddie and the narrator's search for olives is amplified by Beineix in the long version into a comic routine where Zorg gradually gets a sales representative drunk by serving him a series of tequila rapidos.

In the introduction, I pointed out how comedy is a key component of Beineix's style. Excessive humour is one of the hallmarks of this film, and one of the major ways in which Beineix changes the novel is by pushing the novel's irony into frankly absurdist humour. As Beineix explained during an interview while shooting the film, what he was looking for was an exaggeration of implicitly comic situations into explicit comedy veering into absurdity and derision: 'Je cherche à ce que l'acteur ne joue pas en voulant faire rire. Cela se passe dans une convention de comédie parfois, puis dérape complètement et on se retrouve en pleine dérision, dans l'absurdité totale ... . J'aime les choses plutôt grinçantes et un peu ironiques' (Beineix 1985: 59).[19] Beineix's own most frequently quoted examples of the comical in the film are the two sequences that involve the policemen; indeed, in his view, the singing policeman sequence 'est une de mes trophées' (Beineix 1986a: 97).[20] As we shall see, several reviewers agreed, and it is an issue I shall return to in the analysis.

The fact that there are two versions of the film complicates the issue of adaptation. In a nutshell, the longer film, as one reviewer put it, is 'plus drôle et plus douleureux' (Pascal 1991).[21] In Beineix's view, the additional hour of footage for the 1991 version stresses the emotion which he was trying to transcribe: '(Le film) est plus beau avec ces longs moments pour l'amitié, l'amour et les mots d'amour, les chagrins et les sourires. Avec ces scènes qui n'ont l'air de rien mais qui disent tout' (Beineix 1991: 29).[22] The sense of everydayness (Zorg shopping with Betty, then later with Lisa; the foursome driving to the funeral; Betty and Zorg going out for a meal) which is implied here gives a more coherent feeling to one of the things most disliked by some reviewers of the shorter version, the constant partying, which seemed to them no more than pandering to a youth audience. As one reviewer put it in 1991, the longer version brings out the defining contrast between a life devoid of grandeur and the almost desperate urge to compensate for it by partying: 'Leur désarroi ludique, politesse d'un désespoir tour à tour feutré et paroxystique, apparaît pour ce qu'il a toujours été: le reflet d'un quotidien maussade dont toute la grandeur serait absente' (Alion 1991: 44).[23]

19 'I try to get the actor not to act while trying to arouse laughter. This sometimes corresponds to the conventions of comedy, then slips completely and you find yourself in complete derision, in total absurdity. I like things to be caustic and somewhat ironic.'
20 'one of my successes.'
21 'funnier and more painful.'
22 'The film is finer with more time spent on friendship, love and the words of love, sorrow and laughter. With those scenes which don't look like much but which say everything.'
23 'Their playful confusion, which is the polite expression of a despair alternately muffled and convulsive, appears for what it always was: the reflection of a bleak everyday reality devoid of any grandeur.'

On the other hand, the longer version also includes set pieces with secondary characters, which exacerbate the comic aspect of the film considerably: the routine with the olive representative; Zorg's discussion with the police chief who is a failed writer; the psychotic binman who hates mattresses; Zorg's purchase of cocaine from the nervous pusher played by Pinon. The last example in fact helps explain what might seem like an odd incident, Betty dropping off to sleep while Zorg tries to keep her awake. The reason Zorg cannot sleep is that he is high. Similarly, another major event included in the 1991 version is the robbing of the security company, without which Zorg's cross-dressing to gain access to the hospital seems more than a little bizarre. There is only one major sequence omitted from the short version which does not have comic overtones, Zorg and Betty's visit to the seaside and her abduction of a little boy.

The comparison I have given so far, however, does not account for other shifts of emphasis, which a more rigorous statistical analysis might help us to consider. In Table 5.1, I have tried to give some sense of how the films change the overall emphasis of the novel's narrative, this time not by the omission (or indeed addition) of narrative elements, but by the amount of time spent on the major sections of the narrative. Thus, the novel can be broadly divided into the four sections listed below, and Table 5.1 gives the proportion of each of these sections (in terms of the number of pages) relative to the novel as a whole. A similar analysis, this time based on the number of minutes, is given for each of the two versions of the film.

Table 5.1 Comparison between the two film versions showing percentage spent on novel's four main sections

	Novel	*1986 film*	*1991 film*
Beach houses	Chs 1–5, 52pp. (14%)	28 (25%)	36 (20%)
Paris	Chs 6–13, 73pp. (20%)	25 (22%)	44 (25%)
Piano shop	Chs 14–20, 120pp. (33%)	40 (35%)	60 (34%)
Betty's madness	Chs 21–27, 118pp. (32%)	20 (18%)	38 (21%)

There are a number of striking features to this set of statistics. The first is that Beineix devotes considerably more time to the opening sequence than in the novel, emphasising the iconicity of the beach houses. This to some extent confirms the criticism of those reviewers such as Frodon and Toubiana who felt that he was privileging the visual over the narrative. The second point is that Beineix also devotes more time than in the novel to the community formed by Betty, Zorg, Eddie and Lisa; indeed, this seems more important to him in the 1991 version than the iconicity of the first section. The third point, which overlaps with the second, is that whereas the novel's structure emphasises Betty's descent into madness (a full third of the novel), the films emphasise much more the happy times, and, correlatively, Betty's descent into madness is all the more vertiginous. This is especially the case in the 1986 version, which is overall less comical, because there are fewer comic cameos, and more melodramatic because there are more sequences which strike the viewer as odd, such as the final cross-dressing, because they are unexplained.

A final consideration which my approach has not yet adequately explored is that of narrative order, which will confirm points I am making here. One of the more interesting features of the short version is that, unlike the long version, Beineix changed the order of the events in the central part of the film, as can be seen from the alternative synopses above. Neither Beineix nor the reviewers talked of this, even though the change in the order changes the reading of the films; and Beineix, when I asked him why he had changed the order, was unable to answer.

In both versions, the very broad outline of the central part of each film is the same: Zorg and Betty buy a Mercedes, they have an argument, Betty announces she is pregnant just as Zorg is off to deliver a piano, he starts writing again, and then she learns that she is not pregnant after all. Two narrative elements not included in the broad outline I have just given are in different positions in the two films. In the short version Zorg rescues Archie, Bob's son, from the bathroom *before* he and Betty have an argument, but *after* the argument in the long version; Zorg gives the barn to Betty for her birthday *after* she has announced that she is pregnant in the short version, and *before* in the long version. The changes highlight one of the major differences between the two versions. The long version gives more of a feeling for the everyday, whereas the short version is not only more melo-dramatic, but more stereotypical in its delineation of character. In the long version, these two events (Archie's rescue, the birthday barn) are side by side, well after the melodrama of the chase through the town, and well before the drama of the failed pregnancy test. They form part of a short series of events whose function, I would suggest, is to stress 'life in a small town': Zorg and Betty sell a piano, the neighbour's son is stuck, it's Betty's birthday, they sell another piano, they go to the restaurant. In the short version, however, Archie's rescue occurs just before Zorg and Betty's argument. Part of the Archie sequence is Annie's melodramatic seduction of Zorg. This is to some extent neutralised in the longer version by all the other, more mundane, events surrounding it. In the short version, it serves to stress Zorg's commitment to Betty, just before she breaks down, and the implication is that Zorg is long suffering and self-sacrificing. Similarly, when in the short version Zorg gives the barn to Betty, it is after her announcement that she thinks she is pregnant. The sequence functions to confirm Zorg's attentiveness, making of him a model companion. This is re-emphasised in the short version immediately afterwards by his buying of flowers and baby clothes, and by his relatively muted acceptance of Betty's sleepiness when he wants to play. In the longer version, the birthday present is not surrounded by other instances of giving or devotion; and when they go to the restaurant, Zorg indulges in cocaine, gratifying himself, and is comically annoyed when Betty sleeps. The long version, then, does not show Zorg's devotion so starkly; it is something which emerges naturally, indeed naturalistically.

The analysis of the adaptation has raised two key issues to which I shall return: the oscillation between the realist and the melodramatic, and the disruptive function of humour. Both of these issues surfaced in the film's reception, as we shall see in the next section.

Reception

As with *La Lune dans le caniveau*, there was a sharply polarised response by reviewers, in this case between those who liked the film's romanticism and were prepared (if it worried them at all) to disregard certain aspects of the style, and those who disliked its style so intensely that they could not countenance a positive appraisal of its qualities as melodrama. Interestingly, though, there were on balance far fewer negative reviews than had been the case with *La Lune dans le caniveau*. Most reviewers appreciated, and some admired what they considered to be a simple love story relatively simply told.

The familiar charges of excess, fragmentation, and superficiality, all of which, it was suggested, prevent spectatorial identification, were levelled at the film by the first category of reviewers. For Perez, the lighting 'est presque toujours hyper quelque chose';[24] the colour makes things look like they are out of a colouring book; the music is so excessively cinema-like that it seems to double up on music which might already be there; the narrative is composed of so many 'temps forts' or high points, and so many of these are so fantastic (such as Zorg dressed as a woman) that spectators, he suggests, feel so distanced, that they experience complete indifference to the story and the fate of its characters (Pérez 1986). In the same vein, Toubiana of the *Cahiers du cinéma* complains of excessively obvious stylistic features, focusing on cinematography:

> Il sacrifie au plus facile, à ce qui fait immédiatement plaisir au spectateur. Son point fort c'est la technique, il aime faire des plans, ou plutôt des *images*, bouger sa caméra, prendre quand l'envie le démange de la hauteur, ouvrir le champ de vision du spectateur sur un soleil couchant ou un beau paysage de campagne. C'est son truc, sa carte de visite, son goût pour le 'look'. Je pense à ce camion qui file sur la route de campagne, avec le gentil gendarme qui fait au loin un signe d'adieu (une séquence qui fait mousser les bons moments), ou à la maison qui brûle, avec les deux personnages, Betty et Zorg, qui quittent le coin avec armes et bagages, la caméra s'élevant dans les airs, à l'américaine. ... Ses plans ... sont sur-signés, avec cet excès qui finit par déranger. Le film devrait atteindre la grâce et n'y réussit pas: manque de simplicité, filmage trop lourd, beauté calculée. La maison sous la lune, le soleil couchant sur cet Eldorado pour écrivain en panne (recevant comme un don du ciel le corps d'une fillette plutôt sexy), ou le vieil homme au saxo, c'est beau une fois; au bout de trois plans, c'est bonjour la carte postale (Toubiana 1986: 80).[25]

24 'always hyper something or other.'
25 'He always goes for what is easiest, for what will give the spectator pleasure. His strong point is technique; he loves constructing shots, or rather *images*, moving his camera. Going for a high angle is something he finds difficult to resist, opening the spectator's visual field onto a sunset or a beautiful landscape. It's his thing, his visitor's card, his taste for the 'look'. I am thinking of the lorry travelling on a country road, with the nice policeman waving in the background (a sequence which makes you think of the good times), or the burning house, with Betty and Zorg leaving, the camera zooming upwards ... . His shots bear his signature too overtly ['sur-signés': 'over-signed' as in 'overdetermined'], their excess is in the end unsettling. ... The house in moonlight, the sunset on

The reason Beineix does this, Toubiana suggests, is to compensate for a story 'qui hésite entre plusieurs sujets' (Toubiana 1986: 80).[26] This issue of fragmentation is taken up by several reviewers, who consider the film to be, like Pérez, made up of discrete sequences, or 'morceaux de bravoure pas forcément nécessaires à la logique de l'action' (Baignères 1986).[27] Spectators, writes another, are disconnected from the apparent subject of the film, the passion of the couple, because they are constantly sidetracked by scenes unconnected to that passion (Ostria 1986, who gives as examples, among others, the house-painting and the delivery of the piano).

Toubiana also complains of verbosity, which is part of the over-arching suggestion that Beineix is too concerned to make of this film, like the others before it, a 'statement' of the new cinema. He therefore complains of:

> Cette volonté infantile de tout dire, par la bouche des personnages ou la voix off, ... de faire du film une œuvre complète de cinéma, un manifeste de la 'nouvelle image' ... . Les personnages en disent toujours trop sur eux-mêmes ... . C'est le chahut, le babil permanent. Pas une seconde de silence. A chaque séquence, ils expriment à plein régime l'essence de leur personnage. Et au cas où le spectateur n'aurait pas saisi les méandres de leurs états d'âme, la voix off du narrateur survient pour doubler la mise et mettre à chacune de leurs déclarations les majuscules qui s'imposent. (Toubiana 1986: 80)[28]

I shall return to this issue of verbosity in my analysis.

Let us move from the issues of excess and fragmentation to the issue of superficiality. These disparate scenes, for Ostria, are superficial, either because they focus on fetish objects at the expense of

---

this Eldorado for a washed-out writer who receives the body of a sexy girl like manna from heaven, or the old saxophonist, are beautiful once, but after three times, they are no more than picture postcards.'

26 'which hesitates between several subjects.'

27 'bravura passages which are not necessary for the action.'

28 'The childish desire to say everything, through the mouths of the characters, or through the voice-over, to make of the film a complete cinematic work, a manifesto for the "new image". The characters are always speaking too much about themselves. It's a racket, constant babbling away. Not a moment's silence. In every sequence, they express full throttle the essence of their character. And just in case the spectator had not understood the rambling, the voice-over comes along to echo what is being said and to give their statements the capital letters required.'

people (for example, Eddie's kimono and erotic tie), or because they are 'aseptisés',[29] such as the (in his view) pointless photograph which the couple take of each other painting the houses, or, in the same part of the film, Betty throwing pink paint over the owner's black Citroën DS. This act, which Ostria presumes is intended to convey 'la haine unanime de leur "bof/je vous emmerde" génération'. But, in his view, it is no more than 'un geste d'esthète, qui "fait" cinéma .... Cet acte ... revient à essayer d'assommer un ennemi avec un polochon. C'est une idée *soft* et trop manifeste' (Ostria 1986: 60).[30] For Ostria, then, 'malgré la noirceur nihiliste des thèmes et la violence prêtée aux personnages, tout est clair, net, matériel, quotidien et joli comme une carte postale' (Ostria 1986: 60).[31]

As we have seen, both Toubiana and Ostria use the same metaphor of the picture postcard to convey the nature of Beineix's images. The metaphor is an interesting one, because it suggests a mixture of popularity and typicality which for these reviewers at least, combine in the stereotypical, and is linked to the notion of the simulacrum, or already seen, as we saw in comments by Chévrie on Beineix's cinema in the introduction, as well as in Ostria's comments above on the fetishisation of objects. Toubiana, similarly, reprising Chévrie, talks of 'une esthétique "chromo" qui met sur le même pied le moindre objet qui passe dans le champ et des personnages censés nous émouvoir' (Toubiana 1986: 80),[32] and one of *Télérama*'s two reviews talks even more disparagingly of 'l'ambiance chromo laqué, les tons pastel, le petit côté "cracra chic"' suggesting (stupidly) that once the film is screened on TV, spectators will no longer be able to distinguish between it and the adverts which punctuate it (Genin 1986: 21).[33] As if to underline this, Robin, the director of photography, tells us that he shot the last chili con carne of the film 'comme pour un "pack shot" en publicité, le plan du produit',[34] with the exception that the 'product'

29 'sanitised.'
30 'The unanimous hatred of their "fuck-you" generation ... an aesthetic gesture, which makes a statement that this is cinema. It's like hitting the enemy with pillows. It's too soft and too obvious.'
31 'despite the gloom and doom of the themes and the violence of the characters, everything is bright, clear, material, everyday and pretty as a postcard.'
32 'a colour-laden aesthetic which puts any old object which happens to be at hand on the same level as characters who are supposed to affect us.'
33 'a squeaky-clean feel, pastel colours, chic grunge.'
34 'like an advertising pack shot which focuses on the product.'

was carefully distressed ('tout a été soigneusement sali et patiné par la décoration comme s'il s'agissait du centième chili de Zorg dans cette cuisine rarement nettoyée') (Robin 1987: 58).[35]

Let us turn now to the more positive reviewers. If Ostria compares Dalle to a foul-mouthed schoolgirl, and Pérez simply does not mention her, Toubiana, along with other more positive reviewers, underlines her performance as one of the major strengths of the film: 'une nature', a natural, says Toubiana. Another justifies Beineix's choice of an unknown actress, saying that since it is the first time she has appeared on screen, 'pour nous, elle est vraiment Betty, et on l'aime' (Esposito 1986: 13).[36] The notion of authenticity is one to which many reviewers return: Dalle 'parle comme les filles d'aujourd'hui' (Andreu 1986c);[37] 'toute une jeunesse actuelle est dans ces yeux-là' (Chalais 1986).[38] The 'authentic' is not confined to Dalle: all the characters 'bougent comme on bouge, aiment comme on aime' (Gastellier 1986).[39]

Unlike the first category of reviewers, the second category either dismiss stylistic excess as irrelevant in the face of this newfound authenticity, or simply do not see it as excess. For one, the episodic nature of the film, which for the negative reviewers fragments the film and prevents spectatorial identification, shows a sense of rhythm: 'Le ton est si intense que les temps d'arrêt que (Beineix) s'accorde devant un paysage, un décor ou des objects, interviennent comme des moments nécessaires' (Chazal 1986).[40] For another, what is for the negative reviewers stylistic excess becomes, in a move typical of analyses of melodrama, a necessary vehicle for passion and emotion: 'Chaque plan ne dure que le temps nécessaire, chaque mouvement de caméra n'existe que pour traduire les mouvements de l'âme et les images ont la couleur des passions' (Andreu 1986b).[41]

---

35 'everything was carefully soiled and distressed by the decorators to give the feeling that this was Zorg's hundreth chili in a kitchen which was rarely cleaned.'
36 'she really is Betty for us, and we love her.'
37 'speaks like girls speak today.'
38 'the youngsters of today are in those eyes.'
39 'move like we move, love like we love.'
40 'The tone is so intense that Beineix's pauses for a landscape, decor, objects, are necessary.'
41 'Each shot lasts as long as it has to, each camera movement is there to convey the emotions and the images have the colour of passion.'

We might want to argue that both views, negative and positive, are excessive in their own right, and that, with hindsight, Beineix's own sense of the balance between romanticism and passion on the one hand and derision and irony on the other, is a more appropriate analysis: 'Roman et cynisme, c'est un mélange des deux. C'est un romantisme auquel on ne croit pas vraiment' (Beineix 1987: 43).[42] The advantage of maintaining the precarious balance between the two attitudes is that it encourages the view of the film as at least partially self-reflexive, in the way that Godard's films are. This might seem like a curious analogy, but in fact it was posited by Lenne (1986) in his review of the film in *Revue du cinéma*. He points out, more specifically, how *37°2 le matin* bears more than a passing ressemblance to *Pierrot le fou* (1966). Even Parent is somewhat taken aback by this comparison ('un rapprochement qui dut faire causer dans les chaumières'; Parent 1989: 210),[43] and yet there is a grain of truth in it. As Lenne points out, both Ferdinand (Jean-Paul Belmondo) and Zorg are writers of a sort; both are 'rescued' by a woman, who will change their lives; both will travel through France; both films show a particular type of absurdist humour; and, most importantly for Lenne, both films can be seen as beacons for their generation. Although there is considerable difference between the black humour of Godard and the derision of Beineix, neverthless, it is, I would suggest, in the complex interplay between the derisive and the passionate on the one hand, and the way in which this very interplay encourages spectatorial distancing, that the two films resemble each other.

I shall finish this review of the reviewers with the most interesting, although caustic reviewer of Beineix over the years, *Libération*'s Daney, who, like Lenne, is concerned to place Beineix within a cinematic tradition. Daney's view is that the passion–derision binary I have distinguished, following Beineix, can be relabelled (what follows is my summary of his point) 'serious but uninteresting' (for passion) and 'comical, traditional and on the whole agreeably surprising' (for derision). Daney's point is that Beineix's theme of *amour fou* is hackneyed, but that what is new in this film is a very traditional French humour based on sketches (for example, the singing policeman, and the funeral), which, suggests Daney, shows that Beineix 'est plus doué

42 'Romantic and cynical, it's a mixture of both. It's a romanticism in which you don't really believe.'

43 'A comparison which must have caused tongues to wag.'

pour la comédie que pour le drame' (Daney 1986),[44] recalling the point I made in the introduction concerning Beineix's first, short film, *Le Chien de Monsieur Michel*. That apart, Daney is also aware of Beineix's role in the context of French cinema. But unlike Lenne, who compares Beineix with Godard, Daney prefers to evoke Claude Lelouch in the early 1960s, his point being that Beineix has recycled hackneyed themes with new images, old wine in new bottles as it were:

> Lelouch, témoin de la Nouvelle Vague, avait vendu ... l'idée que les nouveautés de l'époque (la caméra sur l'épaule, le cinéma en plein air, les effets de direct tremblé, les faux raccords et les musiques engluantes) n'empêchaient pas de continuer des histoires 'vieilles comme le monde', avec une armada de petits mots à majuscules (l'Amour, La Vie, La Mort ...). Vingt ans plus tard, avec *Diva*, Beineix, témoin de nouvelles images, des rhétoriques de la séduction et de l'industrie du look, travaille lui aussi à *populariser* ce qui change dans la perception de l'image. Il potasse les nouvelles images pieuses du Cinéma pour un nouveau public et, pour ce faire, il doit faire siens les thèmes les plus incoulables (le destin qui s'acharne, l'art qui transfigure, l'amour qui sauve) comme au temps du réalisme poétique. (Daney 1986; his emphasis)[45]

Although cogently argued, the point is fundamentally flawed insofar as it is based on a fallacious distinction between form and content (the content is the same, only the form has changed), which, if taken literally, would invalidate most films, good and bad, in the history of the cinema. What else is there, one might ask, apart from love, life and death (the point being that Daney's framing of the argument is so general as to be worthless)? Allowing that there may be some similarities between Lelouch and Beineix where sentimentality is concerned, we also have to recognise that Lelouch is entirely devoid of any sense

44 'better at comedy than drama.'
45 'Lelouch, a contemporary of the new wave, sold the idea that the novelties of the time (hand-held camera, open-air cinema, jump-cuts and sentimental music) did not mean that you could not continue having age-old stories, with an armada of small words with capital letters (Love, Life, Death). Twenty years later, with *Diva*, Beineix, the contemporary of new images, of advertising rhetoric and the industry of the look, is also working to popularise what is changing in the image. He is boning up on the new icons of the cinema for a new public, and to do that he has to make his own all the imperishable themes (the arrows of fortune, salvation through art, salvation through love) just like during poetic realism.'

of irony, whereas the interest of Beineix's films, and their 'contem-
porariness', relies principally upon the tension between passion and
derision, emotion and irony, and that tension is considerably more
important than the thematic and stylistic sub-structure referred to
here by Daney. This does not invalidate Daney's overarching idea,
however, that Beineix is popularising the *Zeitgeist*, as is evidenced by
the film's appeal. What Daney's review also does is to pose very starkly
the 'problem' of a popular cinema for critics wedded to the notion of
an art cinema, and this 'problem' will form the basis of my analysis in
the next section.

As Daney pointed out in his review, a populariser will only be
vindicated by attracting a large number of spectators. That was precisely what happened. The film was released in a number of European
countries in the autumn, and in the USA in November 1986 with the
title *Betty Blue*. In all of these countries, it was very successful at the
box office. In West Germany for example, the film grossed over
$100,000 dollars in its first month, and the review in the film
periodical *Filmfaust* berated French critics for misunderstanding
Beineix (reported by Dubois 1986). In the USA it grossed some $2
million, after receiving prizes at the Festival des Films du Monde de
Montréal. The film was in fact selected in November 1986 by a group
of French critics (among them Pierre Billard, who, it may be
remembered, was one of the few critics to support *Diva*) to represent
France at the 1987 Oscars, beating *L'Effrontée* (Miller, 1985), *Sans toit
ni loi* (Varda, 1985), *Thérèse* (Cavalier, 1986) and *Tenue de soirée* (Blier,
1986). Also in November, a survey of students undertaken for *Le
Monde* revealed that the film was students' favourite film of the year,
and sixth in their list of best-ever films (Parent 1989: 201).

The long version of the film, which added an additional hour of
footage, was released in June 1991 for the Fête du Cinéma. This
version has frequently appeared on British television during the
1990s, and was screened theatrically in, unusually, an extended rerun
of five performances at the National Film Theatre in London in 1997,
as mentioned in the introduction. The tenacity of the film as a popular
film is in direct contrast to the views of French-film historians,
whether French or British, who have tended to adopt the position of
what I have called the negative reviewers of 1986.

Frodon, for example, as we have seen, likes to use Beineix as an
example of everything he hates about a certain type of postmodern

cinema. In 1986, however, he reviewed the film in a reasonably balanced way. Like Pérez and Toubiana, he stressed the excessive nature of the images and the dialogue, but considered that 'cette surenchère même balaie ce qu'un plan peut avoir de fabriqué, une phrase de trop signifiant' (Frodon 1986: 109)[46] Nevertheless, he proposed that Beineix's modernism and his search for a new cinema made of him, 'forcément, un cinéaste important d'aujourd'hui' (Frodon 1986: 110).[47] Gone is any notion of admiration a decade later in Frodon's appraisal for the centenary of cinema, which picks up the point concerning excessive images, but, following the key postmodern idea of superficiality, suggests their meaninglessness and pointlessness:

> Un scénario confus et à la dramatisation très affectée, mais sans grande importance, dans la mesure où il sert de rampe de lancement à des scènes qui impressionnent profondément la rétine, scènes menées avec une énergie certaine, pimentées de clins d'œil modernes, rétro, loufoques, coquins, sanglants, etc. Les rouages s'enclenchent, on se dira après qu'il a dû être question, aussi, de la solitude de l'artiste et du mal d'aimer, mais franchement, pendant le film, ce n'était pas le problème. (Frodon 1995: 700)[48]

Prédal is, if anything, even less generous in his appraisal; the film, for him, is a perverse mixture (his term) of downmarket popular narrative and upmarket advertising clichés: 'Cette intrigue dans la plus pure tradition des romans-photos de *Nous Deux* remis à la mode "hard" est contée avec les images qui servent dans les magazines au papier glacé à vanter les produits de luxe de la société de consommation' (Prédal 1991: 467).[49]

Curiously, although the French reviews (but not the histories here mentioned) refer in passing, usually ironically, to Betty's regressive

---

46 'That very excess sweeps away the constructedness of a shot, the over-emphasis of the dialogue.'

47 'Obviously an important contemporary film-maker.'

48 'A confused script, affected adaptation, although this does not really matter because it functions as a springboard for scenes which impress themselves on the eye, energetically composed, spiced up with various allusions: retro, crazy, saucy, bloody, etc. The machine starts rolling, you tell yourself afterwards that it was probably also about the solitude of the artist and the difficulty of love, but frankly, that really wasn't the problem.'

49 'The story, which is in the tradition of old-fashioned photo-novels brought up to date with a bit of hardcore, is told using the images which you find in glossy weeklies to sell luxury consumer goods.'

function as Zorg's muse, neither the reviews nor the histories discuss the film from a feminist perspective. Susan Hayward's brief analysis in her monumental history adopts just such a perspective, seeing the film entirely negatively. The film is, for her:

> Not a film about a young woman's progressive descent into a hellish madness, although it pretends to be just such. It is not a study in madness, or for that matter a film about man-as-victim of a nympho-maniac. Rather, it is a male fantasy of the 'supreme fuck'. It is a film constructed out of a series of video clips of madness interspersed with 'fucking' or, if you you want to go with the overt diegesis, a high-tech designer clip-film about nymphomania. (Hayward 1993: 293; Martine Beugnet in her extended discussion of the film, adopts a similar view; see Beugnet 2000)

The film was very successful among women spectators, however, a fact which Hayward finds 'worrying' (Hayward 1993: 293). Guy Austin addresses this issue directly, pointing out that Hayward's view 'fails to account for its appeal as a female fantasy, and therefore can only condemn for their false consciousness those female spectators who find pleasure in the film' (Austin 1996: 63). Rather, the film explores a variety of issues which are likely to be of interest to female spec-tators, Austin suggests, such as Betty's desire for Zorg, and her desire to have a baby. 'Such episodes testify to a more melodramatic element within the narrative, existing alongside the "male sexual fantasy" which would construct Betty's body as a spectacle' (Austin 1996: 64). Emma Wilson has more recently taken up this problem, suggesting that 'within hetersosexual identification, female images of desirability can still be an object of female fascination. This may be liberating rather than masochistic' (Wilson 1999: 59).

In the analysis which follows, I shall be expanding on the issue of the film as a combination of melodrama and soap opera, genres which share similar concerns, and which are traditionally seen, rightly or wrongly, as 'women's genres'.

The female spectator, soaps and melodrama

It will be remembered that fragmentariness was one of the chief criticisms by negative reviewers of the 1986 version (even though, as I have shown, that version is much less based in the everyday than the

1991 version, and has a tendency to melodramatic intensity). This is because, I would suggest, those reviewers did not recognise how the film was functioning as soap, that is to say, by establishing a realist grounding in everyday events, into which are inserted typical points of intensity whose function is to elicit emotion, an emotion all the more intense because it is grounded in, but shown in sharp relief from, quotidian banality.

When discussing the release of the longer version of the film, Beineix said in interview that he had always released films which were shorter than he would have wanted, and that his vocation was that of a serial or soap-opera writer: 'Ma vocation est d'être feuilletoniste. J'ai toujours tourné des films trop longs que j'ai montés trop courts' (Beineix 1991: 29). The word 'feuilleton' does not only refer to television serials or soap operas, but also to literary or scientific commentaries originally appearing in newspapers or periodicals. Both senses derive from the fragmentary nature of what is produced. Whichever of two senses Beineix may have had in mind, I would suggest that the film fulfils both of the meanings: it is structured as a series of events in the life of Betty and Zorg, going from the relatively banal (odd jobs, a pregnancy) to the highly melodramatic (a sensational robbery, a murder). But, by the same token, the film is also, indirectly, a commentary on the relative hopelessness of a lost generation, and indeed, was taken as such by the youth audiences of the 1980s, who ensured its success. I shall explore both senses in this analysis. The first is the way in which the film can be seen, and indeed analysed, as a combination of melodrama and soap opera.

To suggest that the film functions like soap opera might seem surprising, and clearly there are strict limits to such an analogy. The film was not conceived for television. It is not a series, although it has an episodic construction.[50] Its 'episodes' do not end, as is usual for

50 Indeed, that episodic construction is emphasised in the recently released DVD version by the common practice of dividing the film into 'chapters. These are: 'Betty et Zorg'; '500 bungalows à repeindre!' (500 bungalows to be repainted); 'Les mémoires d'Adolf Hitler' (Adolf Hitler's memoirs); 'On se tire' (we split); 'Eddy sayoles'; 'Les éditeurs ça lit pas' (Publishers don't read); 'La plainte' (The complaint); 'Le deuil' ('Mourning'); 'La proposition d'Eddy' (Eddy's proposition); 'Les vestiges d'une civilisation' (The vestiges of a civilisation); 'La crise' (The crisis); 'Des pianos à prix coûtant' (Cost-price pianos); 'Le cadeau de Betty' (Betty's present); 'Le dernier des aventuriers' (The last of the adventurers); 'Test négatif' (Negative test); 'Le monde est trop petit pour elle' (The world is too

soap opera, on a cliffhanger which generates suspense; rather, there is a gradual build-up of tension, more obviously akin to film melodrama. And then, unlike soaps, there is no attempt to establish concurrent interlocking narratives, no matter how well developed the secondary characters may seem.

But the film nevertheless shares features with soap opera. The effect of community which interlocking narratives help establish in soaps is gestured at by Betty and Zorg's interactions with Eddie and Lisa in the first half of the film, and with Bob and Annie in the second half, and these 'secondary' characters are in many ways as 'real' for us (and for reviewers, it will be remembered) as the central couple.

A second shared feature is that their 'reality', their 'genuineness', which is one of the prerequisites for audience involvement in soap operas (Ang 1987: 33–34), is at least partly dependent on a fairly obvious point, but which spectators might forget: the 'ordinariness' of the central characters, who are, as far as their 'station in life' is concerned, an ex-secretary and a plumber. I would hasard the guess that most spectators do not think about the couple's 'station in life' or their class. They are representative of a generation which felt itself to be classless because marginalised (however fallacious that view might be in reality). As Beineix pointed out, unlike tragedy where one finds exceptional individuals in exceptional situations, in this case, 'ce sont des gens ordinaires dans des situations ordinaires qui finissent par devenir exceptionnels' (Leclercq 1986: 45).[51] Ordinariness and specialness combine in exemplarity, as is already at issue in Zorg's name and Zorg and Betty's ages.

The first-person narrator of the novel does not have a name. Beineix chose Zorg because, according to him, 'après la lettre "Z" il n'y a plus rien' (Savigneau 1985),[52] and 'pour ne pas l'appeler comme tout le monde' (Beineix 1986a: 93).[53] The comment suggests Zorg's combination of absolute ordinariness and specialness. He is so ordinary that he can be given a name which does not exist, and which,

---

small for her); 'Joséphine'; 'Le rapt de l'enfant' (Kidnapping a child); 'L'accident' (The accident); 'Etat de choc' (State of shock); 'Les deux doigts de la main' (The two fingers of the hand).

51 'they are ordinary people in ordinary situations who end up becoming exceptional.'

52 'after the letter Z there is nothing.'

53 'so as not to call him like everyone else.'

by implication, denies him the identity one might associate with being given a name; he has a 'degree zero' identity, as it were. He is nothing because he has nothing, wants nothing, and therefore has nothing left to lose; there is nothing beyond Z, as Beineix says. But then, partly because of the unusual name, he is also somehow special. Poised on the edge of having/being nothing, he is both supremely ordinary and supremely special. The appeal of such a character for a young student audience is easy to imagine, therefore, because they, like he, are part of society without being committed to it in the way that a full-time job commits you. He is a character in transition, as are the 18 to 22-year-old students who, it would seem, made (and continue to make) a cult of the film. Zorg's age, and more particularly Betty's age in the film, make them exemplary of that age group, in the same way that the combination of ordinariness and specialness does. Betty and the narrator are 30 and 35 respectively in the novel, but Beineix wanted unknown actors rather than stars, which meant choosing actors of a lower age (Beineix 1986a: 93). In the event, Dalle was 21 at the time of shooting (instead of 30), and there is a twentieth-birthday celebration in the film, and Anglade was 30 (instead of 35).

A third feature shared by the film and soaps has to do with the unimportance of the social context. The reason we may well forget the social context is that the concentration on the daily lives of these three couples ignores social reality unconnected to them; 'social problems and conflicts get short shrift or are not dealt with in an adequate, that is, structural way', as Ang says of *Dallas* (Ang 1985: 59). To return to a criticism levelled at Beineix's *Diva*, *37°2 le matin* is not a film with a 'message'; its function is to elicit raw emotion rather than to establish a view on society, a point which can be made about melodrama as well as soaps: 'Melodrama is typecast as a form interested solely in gut reaction, in emotional thrill which has no social significance. Tragic emotion, by contrast ... is linked to the correctly managed body politic ... . Melodrama ... is portrayed as degrading the connection between performance and civic society' (Shephard 1994: 25).

Indeed, the problematic fit between the concentration on character at the expense of the social context leads to a fourth shared feature. This is what Ang calls 'external unrealism' (Ang 1985: 47), a *mise en scène* which is at odds with the pessimism of the narrative. In terms which recall the censoriousness of some reviewers at Beineix's picture-postcard images, Ang points out how the luxury of the place

and the beauty of the people in *Dallas* seem 'to belong to the optimistic image world of advertising, an optimism that does not fit in
with the pessimistic world of soap opera, so that mise-en-scène in
itself produces a chronic contradiction' (Ang 1985: 78). In this light,
Ostria and Toubiana's criticism of the contradiction between pessimistic themes and optimistic *mise en scène* seems a wilful disregard of a
productive tension.

Similarly, the complaint made by Toubiana that the characters in
37°2 le matin talk too much, can be explained by soap's continual
'emotional display' (David Thornburn quoted in Ang 1985: 68). Such
display is an essential part of what Ang calls 'emotional realism' (Ang
1985: 45), which contrasts with the realism of the classical Hollywood
cinema, and for that matter the realism of French cinema. *37°2 le
matin* shares with soaps and film melodrama a particular relationship
with affect, which Ang calls, following Raymond Williams, a 'tragic
structure of feeling', 'tragic because of the idea that happiness can
never last for ever but, quite the contrary, is precarious' (Ang 1985:
45–46), a sentiment which Betty occasionally echoes when she
complains that everything is against her.

This leads to the feeling of fatalism, of inevitably being a victim,
characteristic of the melodramatic imagination, which has led to film
melodrama and soap opera being seen as women's genres: 'It is
mainly women who are susceptible to the melodramatic imagination,
a type of imagination which appears to express mainly a rather
passive, fatalistic and individualistic reaction to a vague feeling of
powerlessness and unease' (Ang 1985: 82). This fatalism, as much as
'the "male sexual fantasy" which would construct Betty's body as a
spectacle' (Austin 1996: 64), is clearly a problem in that it seems to
reinforce all the usual female stereotypes. This in turn makes it
difficult to account for the film's success, unless, as Austin points out,
one assumes false consciouness on the part of the youth audiences
who flocked to see it.

One of the more obvious ways in which we might obtain answers
to help solve this problem is the kind of ethnographic study undertaken by Ien Ang and Jackie Stacey in film studies, or Janice Radway
in literary studies (Ang 1985; Stacey 1994; Radway 1987). However,
quite apart from the fact that I have not undertaken such a study, and
therefore have no empirical data on which to base any findings, there
are two objections to this approach. The first is that to be methodical,

it would have been necessary to do the same thing for Beineix's other films. Second, and more important, there are methodological problems associated with such ethnographic studies, as Sue Thornham points out when contrasting the 'real' women of ethnographic surveys and the 'abstract' woman constructed by psychoanalytical or 'text-based' film theories: 'As the category of "real women" itself becomes less certain – crossed by differences of class, location, race, ethnicity, sexual orientation – the "female spectator" as social subject becomes as theoretically problematic as her textual counterpart' (Thornham 1997: 90). Consequently, I shall be using 'text-based' theories of melodrama in what follows, in the attempt to explain the problematic attraction of women spectators to a film which appears to reinforce all the old stereotypes: Betty is presented to us as a sexed body, a male fantasy of, as Hayward puts it, 'the supreme fuck' (Hayward 1991: 293). She sacrifices everything for her man, acting as the driving force behind him. He in turn sacrifices her, fetishising her in a literary work. She is therefore doubly his muse, what drives him, and what he writes about. How could women spectators find pleasure in this type of scenario, over and above issues, as Austin suggests, which are likely to be of interest to female spectators?

A first answer is recognition which functions as compensation. This recognition can work in a number of ways. If soap operas and film melodramas have been seen as 'women's genres', it is partly because, as Brunsdon points out, they presume 'the culturally constructed skills of femininity – sensitivity, perception, intuition and the necessary privileging of the concerns of the personal life' (Brunsdon 1981: 36). We can see an example of this in the sequence when Betty watches Zorg knock down the partition wall in the flat above the piano shop. Zorg plays the fool and, in dialogue lifted straight from the novel, likens himself to Stallone in *Rocky 3* (Stallone, 1982), to which Betty answers that he reminds her of him trying to write his book. Zorg answers that he doesn't see the connection, and she says that it does not surprise her (Djian 1986: 170/Djian 1989: 156–57). The novel subsequently makes it clear that Zorg understands perfectly well what she means, despite his answer, whereas the film, which does not have a voice-over corresponding to the novel's text at this moment, leaves a sense of mutual incomprehension. The sequence, depending on your gendered point of view, would suggest Betty's impractical idealism at seeing a great writer in Zorg (from Zorg's point of view), or her high hopes constantly thwarted by Zorg (from Betty's point of view). Betty reads the breaking down of a wall as a metaphor for connecting with his creativity, something which he cannot understand, precisely because he is not sensitive enough. This confirms, as Modleski puts it, that women in melodrama 'carry the burden of feeling for everyone' (Modleski 1987: 331). Women spectators, then, like Radway's readers of romance fiction, might recognise in such a scenario 'the failure of patriarchal culture to satisfy its female members' (Radway 1987: 151). Radway sees this leading to 'utopian wish-fulfilment fantasy through which women try to imagine themselves as they often are not in day-to-day existence, that is, as happy and content' (Radway 1987: 151), hardly an apt description of *37°2 le matin*. Mulvey sees a more critical recognition operating for women spectators of melodrama, a recognition which is more in tune with the pessimism and violence of *37°2 le matin*: 'There is a dizzy satisfaction in witnessing the way that sexual difference under patriarchy is fraught, explosive and erupts dramatically into violence' (Mulvey 1987: 75).

A second type of compensation is role reversal. The violence in *37°2 le matin* is mostly instigated by Betty herself, and motivated by frustration at being constantly thwarted in her desires, whereas Zorg is considerably more compliant and accepting. Betty's violence is frequently associated with breaking out of constraining spaces (throwing objects out of the beach house, punching her fist through a glass door), and this is associated with movement: emptying the beach house is a prelude to leaving; breaking the glass is a prelude to running through the streets. Stereotypically, movement outside domestic space is associated with men rather than with women. Zorg, on the other hand, is content to stay put and to accept misfortune. He spends much of his time cooking, and literally and figuratively repairing, either objects (repainting houses, fixing defective plumbing), or situations, whether with Betty, with people she has provoked (the beach house owner, the pizzeria customer, the publisher), or with people he himself has unwittingly provoked (Richard the policeman, Annie who tries to seduce him). This confirms a point made by Modleski in her discussion of *Letter from an Unknown Woman* (Max Ophuls, 1948), which I shall return to, that 'one of the appeals of such a film for women is precisely its tendency to feminise the man, to complicate and destabilise his identity' (Modleski 1987: 332).

These two forms of compensation – giving shape to disappointment, and role reversal (showing that men can be feminised and women can be as aggressive as men) – because they are compensation, merely confirm women within potentially oppressive roles. Betty, like Pearl in *Duel in the Sun* (King Vidor, 1946), must die, it could be argued, because she has transgressed patriarchal codes, she has not kept a woman's 'place'. The female spectator who identifies with these characters has only momentarily enjoyed a certain degree of 'masculinisation'. As Mulvey so memorably puts it, 'the female spectator's fantasy of masculinisation (is) at cross-purposes with itself, restless in its transvestite clothes' (Mulvey 1989: 37).

Moreover, Betty's violence is contained by two features familiar in certain types of melodrama. The first is the fact that the story is told in flashback from Zorg's point of view, and this is emphasised by Zorg's voice-over. Betty as a character is therefore doubly put into (his) perspective, her desires framed as attractive turbulence in the quiet life to which he aspires, her story 'interpreted' by him.

The turbulence she brings is also contained by what Doane calls a 'medical discourse' (Doane 1987: 38–69). This refers partly to the narrative fact of mental illness, which turns Betty's desires into 'hysteria'. In *37°2 le matin* Betty's gradual deterioration has an inexorable logic to it. There is a series of hysterical fits, all of which have to do with liquids, usually blood, and each one becoming more serious, as well as getting closer and closer to involving her own body. Betty first throws paint over the beach house owner's car in a fit of anger. She then draws blood when she attacks the pizzeria customer, and has a nervous fit. Then she draws her own blood when she punches her fist through a glass door. Later Zorg finds her with her hair roughly cut and make-up daubed grotesquely over her face. Like Rosa (Bette Davis) in *Beyond the Forest* (1949), 'the signs of her excessive desire are inscribed on her body in a hyperbolic manner' (Doane 1987: 42). Betty begins to hear voices inside her head, and, finally, after this series of events which inscribe symptoms of her malaise on or in her body, she attempts to evacuate part of that body by tearing out her eye. As Doane points out, it is 'the symptoms of the female body which "speak" while the woman as subject of discourse is inevitably absent' (Doane 1987: 66).

Doane also means by 'medical discourse' films in which a doctor figure functions as 'reader or interpreter, ... the site of knowledge which dominates and controls female subjectivity' (Doane 1987: 43).

In *37°2 le matin* the doctor figure only occurs towards the end of the film as a minor character, and is necessary because Zorg has committed himself to Betty, as is suggested by the mimicry of the tomato sauce over his face to imitate Betty's excessive make-up. Nevertheless, elements of a medical discourse surface in a 'natural' way during the course of the film, as characters comment on Betty's behaviour. This is done implicitly by Eddie after the pizzeria scene, and explicitly by Bob, who comments ruefully that his wife 'a le feu au cul' and that Betty 'est à moitié dingue';[54] bracketing the two women together in this way makes clear the link established by Doane between excessive desire and 'madness'.

What of the female spectator in this theoretical structure? Melodrama encourages qualities already associated more with women than with men, 'excess of emotion, sentiment, affect, empathy', leading to 'a proximity to the image which is the mark of overidentification and hence a heighened sympathy' (Doane 1987: 67). As a result, Doane suggests, the female spectator maps onto the hysterical character: 'Unable to negotiate the distance which is a prerequisite to desire and its displacements, the female spectator is always, in some sense, constituted as a hysteric' (Doane 1987: 67). The purpose of the medical discourse is to re-establish distance. The female spectator adopts the male–medical perspective, and she is thus de-hystericised. Another way of looking at the process is discussed by Doane in her chapter on the melodramatic love story, where the feminisation of the man (which we have already noted in *37°2 le matin*) allows the female spectator to identify with both the man and the woman, subject as well as object. As Doane points out, it is often difficult to tell who is the protagonist of the story in such films. It is Zorg's narrative, but the focus, as the English title makes clear, is Betty (Doane 1987: 117). The two become one at the end of the film: Zorg dresses as Joséphine, repeats things she might have said if she were still with him, and says to Betty before he kills her, 'Toi et moi on est comme les deux doigts de la main. Personne nous séparera.'[55] An omission in the adaptation is significant in this respect. In both versions of the film, even in the longer one which includes the robbery of the security company, what is omitted at the end of the film is Henri's visit to Zorg to exact

54 'mine has hot pants, and yours is half crazy' (Djian 1989: 263).
55 'You and me, we're like two fingers of the same hand. Nobody will ever separate us.'

revenge. The function of this scene in the novel is to demystify Zorg's feminine identity, since Henri is accompanied by the younger security man who thought that Zorg really was a woman, and much of the dialogue centres on this (self-)deception. Both novel and film re-establish Zorg's masculinity by having him write, and exchange a few words with the white cat who speaks with Betty's voice. Zorg may have come close to being (like) Betty, but Betty and her unknowability[56] are re-established, serving as the motivation for Zorg's creativity. By omitting a scene which demystifies Zorg's feminisation, therefore, the film allows the female spectator to 'be' both Zorg/Joséphine as well as the cat/Betty.

Whichever of these two views one adopts – the de-hystericisation of the female spectator by identification with the doctor figure, or the double identification with both female and male protagonists – the result is broadly the same as Mulvey's masculinisation of the female spectator who must don transvestite clothes.

One way out of this theoretical impasse, to return to the question under discussion – how could women spectators find pleasure in this type of scenario – is what Doane calls the masquerade, which allows distance to be created between the spectator and the screen image: 'Rather than overidentifying with it, she can *play* with the identifications offered by the film, manipulating them for her own pleasure and purposes. Whereas Mulvey's "transvestite" spectator must imagine herself a man in order to obtain cinematic pleasure, Doane's "feminine" spectator ... plays at being a woman' (Thornham 1997: 56; her emphasis). There are scenes which might encourage such play: examples are Betty moving in, when the camera slowly pans up her body in close-up, followed by her asking Zorg whether he finds her attractive; and, in the long version, her provocative pose dressed in a violent red dress on the bonnet of the yellow Mercedes. Such scenes overemphasise a certain type of feminine display, whose very excessiveness (in camera work emphasised by dialogue in the first example, and *mise en scène* in the second) allows female spectators to see that display as play.

56 As Doane says, commenting, in her discussion of *Cat People* (Tourneur, 1942), Freud's' article on narcissism, 'The cat is the signifier of a female sexuality which is self-enclosed, self-sufficient, and, above all, object-less. This sexuality, in its inaccessibility, forecloses the possibility of knowledge, thus generating a string of metaphors – cat, criminal, child, humorist' (Doane 1987: 51).

Then there is the excessive nudity in the film, of which Dalle complained, which, it could be argued, is another form of display, rather than, as one reviewer put it, 'ce voyeurisme qui étouffe le film sous un érotisme plat et vulgaire'[57] (Macia 1986). Betty is seen naked throughout the film, and some of it is evidently provocative, as in the scene where Betty pushes the owner off the verandah onto a heap of sand below. The spectators during this scene are forced to adopt the point of view of the owner/voyeur as Betty aggressively displays her pudenda, struggling with Zorg who is trying to contain her and shouting, direct to camera: 'Vas-y, maintenant, va, mate, espèce d'enculé, va. Eh bien, tiens, vas-y maintenant, regarde, mate. Allez, t'es bien placé là maintenant'.[58] Although the scene is in the novel, in it the owner does not fall from a great height, he is merely pushed down some steps by Betty, without falling over; and the dialogue I have just transcribed is not in the novel either. The changes emphasise three things: the distance between male spectator and female object of that spectator's gaze; the female body as display; and the female object's resistance to being made an object precisely by overemphasising her body as erotic attraction.

Generally, though, nakedness in the film connotes less display than intimacy with Zorg. Zorg is seen naked as much as Betty, whether in the opening love-making sequence, or during the middle part of the film when the two of them wander about the house without any clothes on. As one (female) reviewer pointed out in relation to the opening sequence, although it applies with even more force to the later sequences, there is an equality in that nakedness: 'pour la première fois au cinéma, nudité masculine et nudité féminine sont traitées également' (Jamet 1986). This is certainly very different to Bardot's more obviously provocative nudity in *Et Dieu créa la femme* (Vadim, 1956), or her displays of 'animal' passion as she dances, watched in both cases by immobile and fully-dressed men.

The high degree of intimacy which the two of them have, coupled with their frequent nudity, suggests a final issue, that of fantasy, which does not necessarily attempt to impose a moral judgement on the content of the fantasy. Female, as well as male spectators can

---

57 'Voyeurism which stifles the film with its flat and vulgar eroticism'.
58 'Go one then, ogle, asshole. Well, look, go on, look, ogle. Go on, you're just in the right place now.'

adopt the various positions suggested by the film – oppressed woman, rebelling woman, masquerading woman (but also fatalistic man, rebelling man, feminised man) – without this necessarily impinging on their reality as social (and political) subjects:

> In the play of fantasy we can adopt positions and 'try out' those positions, without having to worry about their 'reality value' ... . We can occupy those positions without having to experience their actual consequences. It may well be, then, that these identifications can be pleasurable, not because they imagine the Utopia to be present, but precisely because they create the possibility of being pessimistic, sentimental or despairing with impunity ... . Fantasy ... is a dimension of subjectivity which is a source of pleasure *because* it puts 'reality' in parentheses, because it constructs imaginary solutions for real contradictions which in their fictional simplicity and their simple fictionality step outside the tedious complexity of the existing social relations of dominance and subordination. (Ang 1985: 134–35; her emphasis)

The couple's nudity, in this optic, functions not just as erotic display for its own sake (which is what it might first be taken to be), but as the affirmation of a possible lack to which some spectators might wish to aspire.

Ultimately, then, the film constructs a set of overlapping possibilities for the female spectator. True, as Austin points out, one of its fundamental pleasures might well be that it evokes issues which are likely to be of interest to female spectators, such as Betty's desire for Zorg, and her desire to have a baby. But there is much more to it than mere evocation. Pleasure can be derived from compensatory mechanisms, such as giving shape to disappointment, and role reversal (male feminisation, female masculinisation). In practice this would mean that female spectators derive pleasure from this film because they are able to say something like 'she is too good for him, she at least fights for what she wants, she is more of a man than he is.' Role reversal can be complicated by double identification, allowing the female spectator to be both the feminised Zorg and the masculinised Betty: the film makes 'it possible both to be what patriarchal cultures demand without sacrifice and to transform men into beings with whom sexual rapport is possible' (Lapsley and Westlake 1992: 47). Further, Betty's violence, which from one perspective is hysteria, is, from another, a metaphor for rebellion, and part of an aggressive masquerade which allows the female spectator considerable latitude in fantasy: 'The hysteric is a woman asking what it is to be a woman; or, more precisely, and given the determination of female roles by male-dominated society, what it is to be a woman for a man. Hysteria then may be seen as a questioning of and protest against the positions assigned to the female subject' (Lapsley and Westlake 1992: 37).

Betty's ultimate hysterical act is to tear out her eye. It is very literally a hysterical act in that the eye can be seen as the baby she wanted to 'give' to Zorg ('je ne suis même pas foutue de te faire un enfant', she says),[59] and which would have equated to what he gave her, his book. It is also the ultimate rebellion against erotic object-ification, as well as the ultimate rebellion against what Lacan would term the impossibility of love (Lapsley and Westlake 1992: 28–30). Adopting Lapsley and Westlake's Lacanian perspective, the eye repre-sents the *objet a*, the unrepresentable of the subject: 'To be a subject is to be looked at from somewhere other than the position from which one sees. What is desired in love is to be seen by the Other as one wishes to be seen, to overcome the split between the eye of the subject and the gaze of the Other' (Lapsley and Westlake 1992: 30). Betty cannot overcome this split and therefore removes one side of the equation, the eye of the subject, leaving Zorg's gaze. To paraphrase Dorothy Parker, the couple run the gamut of the emotions from B(etty) to Z(org), but they can never incorporate the (*objet petit*) *a* within that circuit, because it is the condition of their relation in the first place;[60] there is some logic that the eye should be ex-corporated.

Deriding the law

It would not be unreasonable to assume that the film was successful as much because it attracted male spectators as female spectators. Quite apart from the probable pleasure to be gained from Zorg's feminisation for male spectators, and which I do not have the space to discuss here,[61] one of the film's features with which both men and

59 'I can't even fucking well make a baby for you.'
60 This could be represented by the following, where 'a' is the *objet petit a*, 'b' Zorg's book, 'B' is Betty, and 'Z' is Zorg: $a(B + Z > b)$.
61 See Silverman 1988 and Creed 1993 in particular, and, for a summary of their work, Thornham 1997: 93–116.

women can identify is the derision of the law. Both male and female spectators are positioned, by identification with Betty and Zorg, outside the law, just as the film positions itself outside the law of 'consistent' narrative by its sudden bursts of absurdist humour. The singing-policeman sequence is not only a good example of such absurdist humour, but the one preferred by Beineix himself, as mentioned above, for whom it is clearly an element not just of disruption, but of subversiveness: 'La base du rire ... c'est ... un moment où les choses se dérèglent. Ce sont les rapports du pouvoir, quand ce dernier devient excessif: il devient ridicule. Mais c'est aussi quand on confronte les grand sentiments, les choses éternelles avec l'éphémère. De là naît le comique' (Beineix 1987: 42).[62] Beineix's project is as much to deflate pomposity, whether in terms of morals or in terms of film narrative, by derision. Like irony, derision functions as a kind of protection, both for the disempowered youth audiences of the 1980s, as, one may assume, for Beineix himself, in constant disagreement with the film 'establishment'.

It is worth looking at the singing-policemen sequence a little more closely to complete this analysis. In what follows, I shall bring together aspects of Beineix's adaptation strategies, his visual strategies, and link them to his moral position. Table 5.2 represents the singing-policeman sequence, with numbered shots, a description of what is in the shot, and a transcription of the dialogue. In the far right-hand column, there is the extract of the novel which corresponds to this sequence. Betty, it will be remembered, has just announced to Zorg that she is pregnant, as he is rushing off to deliver a piano to a client on a borrowed lorry with his neighbour Bob. He is stopped for speeding by Richard, the zealous policeman, who, once Zorg has told him that he is about to be a father, becomes sentimental, and eventually lets him go.

The sequence in the film compresses two consecutive sequences in the novel, a visit in the Mercedes to a prospective client, and the follow-up delivery in a lorry (Djian 1986: 244–48, 254–56/Djian 1989: 224–25, 233–34). Most of the material in the film is, as can be

---

62 'The basis of laughter is the moment when things go wrong. Take power; when power becomes excessive, it becomes ridiculous. But it's also when one you place grand feeling, eternal truths next to the ephemeral. This gives rise to the comical.'

Table 5.2 The singing policeman sequence in *37° 2 le matin*

Shot] Content	Dialogue [sound]	[Corresponding extract from novel]
1] Bob	Bob: Ben dis donc, qu'est-ce t'as là, t'a pas l'air dans ton assiette, t'es tout palo.	J'ai donc sauté dans la voiture et je suis sorti de la ville. Sur les trottoirs, j'ai
2] Zorg (reverse shot)	Zorg: Oh la la, Bob, on est vachement ...	compté vingt-cinq bonnes femmes avec des landaus.
3] Foot on brake	[Brakes screech]	J'avais le gosier sec et je
4] Pram crosses	Bob: Putain.	réalisais pas bien ce qui
	Zorg: T'as remarqué le nombre de bonnes femmes qui se promènent avec des landaus, Bobbie?	arrivait, c'était quelque chose que j'avais jamais envisagé sérieusement. Les images traversaient
	Bob: Ah, mais non, celle-là elle est passée après.	mon crâne comme des fusées.
	Zorg: Mais non.	Pour me calmer, je me
5] Piano on lorry	Bob: Oh là là, dis donc, ça monte là, pousse pas les vitesses, ce camion est en rodage.	suis concentré sur la conduite de la Mercedes. La route était belle. Je suis passé à 160 devant la
	Zorg: Ah, écoute je pousse rien là, c'est un turbo, quand même, merde.	voiture de flics sans m'être rendu compte de rien. Un peu plus loin, il me forçait
	Bob: Ah c'est un turbo, c'est un turbo, oui tu diras ça à Momo.	à m'arrêter. C'était encore Richard. Il avait de belles dents, saines et régulières,
6] Lorry	[Bird song; lorry in distance]	il a retiré un calepin et un
7] Zorg and Bob in cab	Zorg: Ecoute, merde, je suis à 40 là.	stylo de sa poche.
	Bob: T'es à 40, t'es à 40, t'es pas à 40, t'es à 80.	
8] Lorry passes police	Zorg: Bon, ben je suis à 80, qu'est-ce que c'est sérieux.	
9] Richard stops them	Zorg: Oh merde.	
10] Bob	Bob: Hé, t'es sûr que tu l'as ton permis?	
11] Zorg (reverse shot)	Zorg: Hein? Non, pas vraiment.	
12] Richard stops them	[Engine stops]	

Shot] Content	Dialogue [sound]	[Corresponding extract from novel]
13] Same as 11	[Bird song and goat bells until 21]	
14] Richard and Zorg	Zorg: Comment ça va? Vous me reconnaissez?	
15] Richard and Zorg (reverse shot)	Richard: Vous roulez à 100kh avec un véhicule dont la vitesse est limitée à 60kh. Sur un tronçon de voie départementale, classée vicinale, lui-même limitée à 50 kh. Bon début, bon début. Allez hop. Contrôle des papiers, contrôle du véhicule, le grand jeu quoi. Zorg: Excusez-moi, j'étais un peu dans les nuages. Richard: Ne vous faites pas de bile, si je vous trouve un ou deux grammes d'alcool dans le sang, je vais vous ramener les pieds sur terre, moi. Zorg: Si c'était que ça, monsieur l'agent, mais je viens d'apprendre que je suis papa.	– Maintenant, chaque fois que je vois cette bagnole, je sais qu'il y a du boulot pour moi, il a grincé. Je savais pas du tout ce qu'il me voulait, je savais même pas ce que je faisais sur cette route. Dans le doute, je lui ai souri. Peut-être qu' il était comme ça, planté en plein soleil, depuis le lever du jour ... ? – Si je comprends bien, il a ajouté, vous vous êtes dit que de changer un pneu, ça vous donnait le droit de rouler comme un dingue ... Je me suis enfoncé le pouce et l'index dans le coin des yeux. J'ai secoué un peu la tête. – Bon sang, j'étais complètement ailleurs ...
16] Bob (reaction shot)	Richard: Pardon? Zorg: Oui ...	j'ai soupiré. – Vous faites pas de
17] Richard (reverse shot)	Zorg: Papa. Richard: Vous n'auriez pas une cigarette ? Zorg: Ah, si, bien sûr.	bile. Si je vous trouve deux ou trois grammes d'alcool dans le sang, je
18] Zorg and Bob in cab	Zorg: Tenez.	vais vous ramener les pieds sur terre.
19] Same as 16 (camera further back)	Richard: Les pères de famille sont les derniers aventuriers des temps modernes.	– Si c'était que ça, j'ai dit. Mais je viens d'apprendre que je suis papa ... ! Il a paru hésiter un
20] Bob		instant puis il a refermé
21] Same as 20	Richard: Eh alors, vous verrez	son carnet avec le stylo au

Shot] Content	Dialogue [sound]	[Corresponding extract from novel]
	les joies, les peines aussi, les peines. [He sings Yves Duteuil song] *Prends un enfant par la main/Pour l' emmener vers demain/Pour lui donner de la confiance en son pas/Prendre un enfant pour un roi/*	milieu et l'a reglissé dans sa poche de chemise. Il s'est penché vers moi. – Vous auriez pas une cigarette ? il a demandé. Je lui en ai donné une et il est resté tranquillement appuyé sur ma portière
22] Bob (same as 21)		pour la fumer et me parler de son fils de huit mois qui
23] Same as 20	*Prendre un enfant dans ses bras/Pour la première fois* [Music starts]	traversait le salon à quatre pattes et des différentes marques de lait en poudre
24] Lorry leaves		et des mille et une petites
25] Lorry in sunset		joies de la paternité et tout et tout. Je voyais le coup que j'allais m'endormir pendant qu'il me faisait un cour sur les tétines. Quand au bout d'un moment il m'a fait un clin d'œil en me disant qu il fermait les yeux et que je pouvais partir, ben je suis parti. (Djian 1986: 245–46)
1] Bob	Bob: Look, what's the matter, you don't look at all right, you're all pale.	I hopped in the car and drove out of town. On the street I counted twenty-five women with strollers. My
2] Zorg (reverse shot)	Zorg: Oh là là, Bob, we're really ...	throat was dry. I had trouble getting my mind
3] Foot on brake	[Brakes screech]	around what was
4] Pram crosses	Bob: Shit. Zorg: Have you noticed the number of women walking around with prams, Bobbie? Bob: Ah, no, that one almost copped it. Zorg: No she didn't.	happening – it was an eventuality I'd never seriously considered. Images raced through my mind like rockets. To calm myself down, I
5] Piano on lorry	Bob: Oh, là là, look here, we're going uphill, don't force the gears, this lorry	concentrated on the drive. It was beautiful. I passed the cop car, I was going

Shot] Content	Dialogue [sound]	[Corresponding extract from novel]
	is running in.	eighty. A minute later he
	Zorg: Look, I'm not forcing	stopped me. Richard again.
	anything, it's a turbo	He had nice, straight teeth.
	after all, shit.	He took out a pad and a
	Bob: Ah it's a turbo, it's a	pen.
	turbo, you tell that to	
	Momo.	
6] Lorry	[Bird song; lorry in distance]	
7] Zorg and Bob in cab	Zorg: Listen, shit, I'm only doing 40.	
	Bob: You're doing 40, you're doing 40, you're not doing 40, you're doing 80.	
8] Lorry passes police	Zorg: Well, alright I'm doing 80, it's not that serious.	
9] Richard stops them	Zorg: Oh shit.	
10] Bob	Bob: Oi, are you sure you've got your licence?	
11] Zorg (reverse shot)	Zorg: What? No, not really.	
12] Richard stops them	[Engine stops]	
13] Same as 11	[Bird song & goat bells until 21]	
14] Richard and Zorg	Zorg: How are you doing? Do you remember me?	
15] Richard and Zorg (reverse shot)	Richard: You're doing 100kh in a vehicle with a speed limit of 60kh. On a section of a Bob-road classed as a local road, which has a limit of 50 kh. It's a good start, a good start. All right. Your papers, vehicle check, the whole thing.	'Every time I see this car I know it means I have a job to do,' he whined. I had no idea what he wanted me for – no idea of what I was even doing on this road. I smiled at him dubiously. Perhaps he had been standing there in the sun all day, ever since dawn
	Zorg: Look, I'm sorry, I was dreaming.	'Maybe you think that changing your tyre gives
	Richard: Don't you worry about it, if I find that you've got one or two	you the right to drive like a maniac ... ?' I shoved my index finger and thumb into

Shot] Content	Dialogue [sound]	[Corresponding extract from novel]
	grammes of alcohol, I'll bring you down to earth	the corners of my eyes. I shook my head.
	Zorg: If that was all, officer, but I've just learned I'm going to be a father.	'Jesus, I was somewhere else,' I sighed. 'Don't worry. If I find two
16] Bob (reaction shot)	Richard: Sorry? Zorg: Yes ...	or three grams of alcohol in your blood, I'll bring you
17] Richard (reverse shot)	Zorg: A dad. Richard: You wouldn't have a cigarette would you? Zorg: Yes, of course.	right back down to earth.' 'If it was only that,' I said. 'I just found out I'm going to be a daddy!'
18] Zorg and Bob in cab	Zorg: Here you are.	He seemed to hesitate for a moment, then he
19] Same as 16 (camera further back)	Richard: Fathers are the last adventurers of modern times.	closed his pad, with his pen stuck inside, and put it back in his shirt pocket. He
20] Bob		leaned over to me.
21] Same as 20	Richard: And so you'll see the joy, the sorrows too, the sorrows. [He sings Yves Duteuil song] *Take a child by the hand/To take him to tomorrow/To give him confidence in his steps/Take a*	'You wouldn't have a cigarette, would you?' he asked. I gave him one. Then he leaned against my door, puffing peacefully, and told me all about his 8-month-old son, who had just
22] Bob (same as 21)	*child for a king/*	started crawling across the living room on all fours,
23] Same as 20	*Take a child in your arms/ For the first time* [Music starts]	and all the various brands of formula, and the thousand-and-one joys of
24] Lorry leaves		fatherhood. I almost dozed
25] Lorry in sunset		off during his lecture on nipples. Finally he winked at me and said he'd look the other way this time, that I could go. I went. (Djian 1989: 225)

seen, derived from the first visit in the Mercedes; indeed, a considerable section of the dialogue comes straight from the novel. Replacing the car by a lorry, however, allows a series of emphases. The first is the emphasis on speed, underlined by Bob's comment about the strain on the engine. The second is the emphasis on motherhood, underlined by quantity in the novel (25 prams), but by visual effect in the film, as an extreme low-angle shot shows the lorry braking abruptly in front of a single pram. Both of these emphases serve to underline Zorg's confusion at potentially being a father. A third emphasis is structured like the second: Richard is dominated by the lorry in a series of low-angle shots (Richard standing in front of the lorry as he calls for Zorg to stop; Richard looked down on by Zorg in the shot-reverse-shot conversation section), just as, interestingly, the mother was dominated by the lorry as she pushed the pram over the road.

The visual side of the sequence thus uses *mise en scène* literally to diminish the stature of the policeman, an effect which is emphasised even more by the dialogue. Whereas in the novel, Richard's talk of the joys of paternity is in reported speech, which conveys Zorg's feeling of not quite being able to focus on what Richard is saying, in the film Richard begins, absurdly, to sing a well-known sentimental song. The absurdity is underlined by Bob's reaction shot (a blankly uncomprehending face); and both the absurdity and the sentimentality are amplified in the various shots at the end of the sequence: a long-distance shot of Richard slowly and deliberately waving goodbye, framed by the lorry's ramps, followed by an extreme long shot of the lorry in the sunset, distorted by a wide lens, being waved at by people on the roadside. The singing avoids the need to replicate Richard's details about his son's feeding habits and other joys of paternity, thus serving a compressive function. That compressive function is largely outweighed, however, by the sequence's comic function, centring principally on the disruption of Richard's role as a policeman.

The immense leap from Richard as law dispenser to Richard as sentimental father is derisory in ways that the novel is not. It maintains the diffidence of the novel's narrator to the law, but introduces, as Beineix points out, caustic irony, a distancing for the spectator, which echoes the novel narrator's marginality from everything around him. (Marginality in the novel is also conveyed by irony, although this irony is less caustic, less absurdist; its function is mainly to distance the narrator from events and people.) Spectators laugh (and my experience of spectators watching this film is that this is the sequence where they laugh most), but laugh *knowingly*, by which I mean that they watch themselves laughing. The spectator feels something like this, I would venture: 'This is absurdly funny, so absurd that it does not square with what I was expecting, which only makes it funnier, but in so doing calls into question what I really was expecting, and thus calls my responses into question, which is absurd because this is a simple story, and the comedy which disrupts this simple story is itself simple, but that does not square with what I was expecting ... .' And so on.

It is no coincidence that Beineix should emphasise the comical with sequences involving policemen. There is a 'doubling' effect. Spectators are implicated in the film's narrative through identification with Zorg, being made to feel his panic at the thought of being a father through the various techniques outlined above. But at the same time they are forced out of that identification by a complex derision, which works at the level of both character and narrative. At the level of character, the 'law' represented by Richard is absurd (in the sense of absurdly comical); fatherhood is absurd for Zorg (in the sense that it is unreal); Richard, like Zorg, is a father; so fatherhood-as-law is absurd (in the combined sense of unreal and comical). At the level of narrative, Beineix calls on spectators to stand back from the law of the narrative, to put into question the notion of consistent tone upon which a simpler narrative might have depended, and to position themselves sideways in the elsewhere of mockery and by implication, I would suggest, self-mockery.

As Beineix said, 'J'ai toujours aimé le burlesque et rêvé de faire une comédie (Beineix 1986a: 97). What is perhaps most surprising is that the burlesque is *also* directed at the main protagonists. It is not a little disconcerting to read that one of the scenes which we might have felt was touching, Zorg's birthday cake in the boot of the Mercedes, was directed by Beineix with total derision in mind: 'Zorg est un désabusé, un dérisoire. Quand il offre la cabane à Betty, ce gâteau d'anniversaire allumé dans le coffre de la voiture est la preuve de ce dérisoire!' (Beineix quoted in Robin 1987: 34).[63] The problem, surely,

---

63 'Zorg is a cynic, who turns everything into derision. When he offers the cottage to Betty, the birthday-cake lit up in the boot of the car is proof of that derision!'

is that the cynicism here attributed to Zorg is not manifest in Anglade's performance. On the contrary, Anglade is touching as Zorg *because he is so sincere*, and that sincerity matches Betty's desire, giving it the (imaginary) complementarity, which is arguably essential to romance. There is, then, a mismatch between Beineix's wish to introduce into his melodrama the same kind of critical distancing one finds in Sirk, and the powerful emotions elicited by the narrative and by the performance of the two central protagonists. It is as if Beineix is saying 'get close', at the same time as he is saying, 'stand back, don't let yourself get hooked', or to recall Beineix's own formulation of this mismatch: 'Roman et cynisme, c'est un mélange des deux. C'est un romantisme auquel on ne croit pas vraiment' (Beineix 1987: 43).[64]

One way of looking at this mismatch is to see it as double-coding, a way of helping the spectator indulge in what can no longer be believed in, as in Umberto Eco's example of the lover saying 'As Barbara Cartland would put it, I love you madly'.[65] Another way of looking at it is to see it as the exact opposite, a moral streak which would *not* want us to indulge in 'unearned emotion' (Plantinga 1997: 385). That would be to become too much like Joséphine who steals hearts (the young security guard's) and who kills the person s/he loves, leaving nothing but the unstable gap of desire, and not enough like Zorg, the artist, after whom, to recall Beineix's comment on his name, there is nothing.

64 'Romantic and cynical, it's a mixture of both. It's a romanticism in which you don't really believe.'
65 Quoted by Lapsley and Westlake 1992: 28, who make a similar point about *Pretty Woman*.

References

Alion, Yves (1991), '*37°2 le matin*, l'intégrale', *Revue du cinéma* 474: 44.

Andreu, Anne (1986a), 'Jean-Jacques Beineix: "Djian et moi, on est frères de sang"', *L'Evénement du jeudi*, 3–9 April: 84.

Andreu, Anne (1986b), '37°2 d'émotion', *L'Evénement du jeudi*, 10 April.

Andreu, Anne (1986c), 'Hors champs: Béatrice Dalle', *L'Evénement du jeudi*, 10 April.

Ang, Ien (1985), *Watching Dallas: Soap Opera and the Melodrmataic Imagination*, translated by Della Couling. London and New York, Methuen. Originally published in 1982.

Austin, Guy (1996), *Contemporary French Cinema*. Manchester and New York, Manchester University Press.

Baignères, Claude (1986), 'Dérives', *Le Figaro*, 14 April.

Beineix, Jean-Jacques (1985), 'Jean-Jacques Beineix: le virage', *Starfix*, 30 November, 58–59.

Beineix, Jean-Jacques (1986a), 'Le choix de Beineix', *Première* 109: 90–99.

Beineix, Jean-Jacques (1986b), 'Universal mariner', *Monthly Film Bulletin* 53/633: 300.

Beineix, Jean-Jacques (1987), 'Interview', *Séquences* 129: 40–47.

Beineix, Jean-Jacques (1991), 'Poussée de fièvre', *Télérama* 2163 (26 June): 29–31.

Beineix, Jean-Jacques (2001), 'Autant en emporte le divan: Jean-Jacques Beineix et Jean-Hugues Anglade', *Ciné-Livre* 4: 54–59.

Beugnet, Martine (2000), *Marginalité, sexualité, contrôle: cinéma français contemporaines*, Paris, L'Harmattan.

Brunsdon, Charlotte (1981), '*Crossroads*: Notes on soap opera', *Screen* 22/4: 32–37.

Chalais, François (1986), 'Fiévreux: *37°2 le matin*', *Le Figaro Magazine*, 12 April.

Chazal, Robert (1986), '*37°2 le matin*: L'eau et le feu', *France-Soir*, 12 April.

Creed, Barbara (1993), *The Monstrous Feminine: Film, Feminism, Psychoanalysis*. London, Routledge.

Daney, Serge (1986), ''Petite fièvre', *Libération*, 14 April.

Dazat, Olivier (1986), 'Coups et blessures', *Cinématographe* 120: 71.

Djian, Philippe (1986), *37°2 le matin*. Paris, J'ai Lu, no.1951. First published Paris, Bernard Barrault, 1985.

Djian, Philippe (1989), *Betty Blue: The Story of a Passion*, translated by Howard Buten. London, Abacus, 1989; translation first published in Great Britain by London, Weidenfeld and Nicolson, 1988.

Doaner, Mary Ann (1987), *The Desire to Desire: the Woman's Film of the 1940s*, Basingstoke, Macmillan.

Dubois, Nathalie (1986), 'Beineixportation', *Cinématographe* 125: 8–9.

D'Yvoire, Christian (1986), 'Bétrice Dalle: "J'aime ce qui est trop"', *Première* 109: 96–97.

Esposito, Marc (1986), '*37°2 le matin*, *Première* 109: 13.

Ferenczi, Aurélien (1986), '*37°2 le matin*: tout Paris a la fièvre', *Le Quotidien de Paris*, 9 April.

Frodon, Jean-Michel (1986), 'Beineix: la chasse au trésor', *Le Point* 707: 109–10.

Frodon, Jean-Michel (1995), *L'Age moderne du cinéma français: De la Nouvelle Vague à nos jours*. Paris, Flammarion.

Gastellier, Fabian (1986), '*37°2 le matin*', *Les Echos* 14609, 9 April.

Genin, Bernard (1986), 'Peuplée de fantômes', *Télérama* 1891: 21.

Hayward, Susan (1993), *French National Cinema*. London and New York, Routledge.

Jamet, Dominique (1986), 'Chaud les passions chaud', *Quotidien de Paris* 1985, 9 April.

Lapsley, Robert and Michael Westlake (1992), 'From *Casablanca* to *Pretty Woman*: The politics of romance', *Screen* 33/1: 27–39.

Leclerq, Jérôme (1986), 'L'adaptation sans douleur', *Cinématographe* 118: 42–45.

Lenne, Gérard (1986), '*37°2 le matin*', *Revue du cinéma* 416: 52–53.

Macia, Jean-Luc (1986), 'Beineix en état de surchauffe', *La Croix*, 10 April.

Modleski, Tania (1987), 'Time and desire in the woman's film', in *Home is Where the Heart is: Studies in Melodrama and the Women's Film*, edited by Christine Gledhill, London, BFI: 326–38. First published in *Cinema Journal* 23/3 (1984): 19–30.

Mulvey, Laura (1987), 'Notes on Sirk and Melodrama', in *Home is Where the Heart is: Studies in Melodrama and the Women's Film*, edited by Christine Gledhill, London, BFI: 75–79. First published in *Movie* 25: 53–56 (1977–78).

Mulvey, Laura (1989), 'Afterthoughts on "Visual pleasure and narrative cinema" inspired by King Vidor's *Duel in the Sun* (1946)', in *Visual and Other Pleasures*, Basingstoke and London, Macmillan, 29–28. Originally published in *Framework* 15–17 (1981), 12–15.

Ostria, Vincent (1986), '*37°2 le matin*', *Cinématographe* 118: 60.

Pantel, Monique (1986), 'Beineix a filmé, avec folie, une histoire folle d'un amour fou', *France-Soir*, 4 April.

Parent, Denis (1989), *Jean-Jacques Beineix: Version originale*, Paris, Barrault Studio.

Pascal, Michel (1991), 'En vedette: *37°2 l'intégrale*', *Le Point*, 29 June.

Pascaud, Fabienne (1986), 'Jean-Hugues Anglade: acteur "à coeur"', *Télérama* 1891: 25.

Pérez, Michel (1986), 'Un petit train de fièvre', *Le Matin*, 10 April.

Plantinga, Carl (1997), 'Notes on spectator emotion and ideological film criticism', in *Film Theory and Philosophy*, edited by Richard Allen and Murray Smith, Oxford, Clarendon Press, 372–93.

Prédal, René (1991), *Le Cinéma des Français depuis 1945*, Paris, Nathan.

Radway, Janice (1987), *Reading the Romance*, London, Verso. First published in 1984 by the University of North Carolina Press.

Robin, Jean-François (1987), *La Fièvre d'un tournage: 37°2 le matin*. Paris, Séguier.

Savigneau, Josyane (1985), 'Jean-Jacques Beineix: amoureux d'un récit', *Le Monde*, 2 May.

Shephard, Simon (1994), 'Pauses of mutual agitation', in *Melodrama: Stage, Picture, Screen*, edited by Jacky Bratton, Jim Cook, Christine Gledhill, London, BFI, 25–37.

Silverman, Kaja (1988), 'Masochism and male subjectivity', *Camera Obscura* 17: 31–67.

Stacey, Jackie (1994), *Star Gazing: Hollywood Cinema and Female Spectatorship*, London and New York, Routledge.

Thornham, Sue (1997), *Passionate Detachments: An Introduction to Feminist Film Theory*, London, New York, Sydney, Auckland, Arnold.

Toubiana, Serge (1986), 'Les oripeaux du look', *Cahiers du cinéma* 383–4: 79–80.

Tranchant, Marie-Noëlle (1986), '*37°2 le matin*', *Le Figaro*, 9 April.

Wagner, Jean (1985), 'Le cœur sur pilotis', *Télérama* 1874: 28–29.

Wilson, Emma (1999), *French Cinema since 1950: Personal Histories*, London, Duckworth.

10 Betty cleans up (*37°2 le matin*)

11 The publisher who should not have refused Zorg's book
(*37°2 le matin*)

12 Zorg pursues Betty (*37°2 le matin*)

13 Betty as Ophelia (*37°2 le matin*)

14 Zorg as Joséphine (*37°2 le matin*)

15 Zorg as *femme fatale* (*37°2 le matin*)

16 Zorg finds inspiration (*37°2 le matin*)

17 Roselyne about to seek solace in church (*Roselyne et les lions*)

18 Thierry does the beam (*Roselyne et les lions*)

19 Roselyne and Thierry's final number (*Roselyne et les lions*)

20 Roselyne's lonely gaze of triumph (*Roselyne et les lions*)

6

Roselyne et les lions (1989)

Synopsis

Thierry, who daydreams at school, offers his services to Frazier, the lion tamer, in return for lessons in a local zoo, where Roselyne is also learning. Taking the stage name D'Alembert, he learns how to tame the lionesses, impressing his schoolteacher, Bracquard. But he is resented by Frazier, especially when he suggests manoeuvres to Frazier and succeeds, despite Frazier's scorn. Frazier realises that Thierry and Roselyne are in love, and takes the opportunity of Thierry's foolhardiness in the cage to throw him out. Thierry and Roselyne leave the town on Thierry's motorbike in search of lion-taming work.

They ask for work at the Cirque Zorglo but are told that they would have to start with other animals. They are unsure what to do. Roselyne lights a candle in the local church, and sees a votive plaque with the same name as Thierry's schoolteacher. Bracquard comes to meet them, and bolsters their confidence by telling them that they are on a journey of initiation, and, more practically, by giving them money. They return to the Cirque Zorglo and wait for an opportunity, while suffering the constant taunts of Markovitch, the lion tamer. Their opportunity arises when Thierry sees Markovitch trying to sell dangerous lions to a colleague, who, grateful, tips Thierry off that a circus agent is looking for a new lion-taming act on behalf of the Munich-based Koenig Circus. Thierry and Roselyne strike a deal with him, only to find that the lions he wants them to use are Markovitch's. Nevertheless, Roselyne puts on a perfect performance and they are hired, with Roselyne as the tamer and Thierry as her trainer.

Thierry and Roselyne are introduced to Klint, the tiger tamer, who takes a dislike to them. They are dispirited when they botch their first training session with Markovitch's three lions, the lions being on heat. Koenig tells them that he has bought them four more lions, and he makes Roselyne a star by using her photo for the circus's poster and having her interviewed by a newspaper over a champagne dinner. Thierry, jealous, drives her hard in the next day's training session. Told by Koenig that they should do the beam, Thierry, rather than endanger Roselyne, reluctantly spreadeagles himself on it; the lights go off at the key moment and he is wounded as the lion slips. Koenig asks Klint to take over the training with the lions, but Klint is not up to it, almost fainting in the cage. He subsequently commits suicide. Koenig asks Thierry to take over the tiger act, but Thierry refuses, saying that he has an act in mind.

Bracquard visits them, and shows them how he has trained his cat. Thierry and Roselyne put on their show, with Roselyne dressed in a small bikini and Thierry masked and caped to represent Death. The show is a triumph.

Background

As he had done after *La Lune dans le caniveau*, Beineix had gone on a three-month cruise in his yacht after the release of *37°2 le matin*, visiting Stromboli before going on to the Peleponnese islands. He met the film-maker Maroun Bagdadi in Athens, with whom he had been discussing the possibility of starring in the main role of Bagdadi's new film, *L'Homme voilé* (1987), the story of a doctor turned terrorist in Lebanon. After some hesitation, Beineix turned the offer down; Bernard Giraudeau eventually took on the role. On his return, Beineix went to the Montreal Festival, where *37°2 le matin* was representing France, and took advantage of his visit to pursue his pet project, the vampire film based on Behm's novel. David Puttnam, recently arrived at Columbia Pictures, took considerable interest in the project, as did Madonna briefly, looking for a role that might give her the success of *Desperately Seeking Susan* (Susan Seidelman, 1985), after the failure of *Shanghai Surprise* (Jim Goddard, 1986). Beineix was offered a variety of scripts to work on by many studios, including films which were later made by others (among them *The Princess Bride*, Rob Reiner, 1987), but failed to secure the funding for the vampire film. On his return from the USA, he made more advertisements for Valentine paints, as he had done in 1985 and 1986, and once more collaborated with the lion tamer Thierry Le Portier whose big cats were used in the ads. Seduced by Le Portier's life story, Beineix decided to adapt it to the screen. He co-wrote the script with Jacques Forgeas (a schoolteacher friend of Richard Bohringer whom he had met while preparing *Diva*) over a period of seven months (November 1987 to May 1988).

During 1987 Beineix had directed two public-utility advertisements, one on road safety, and the other as part of the government's AIDS campaign. The latter had starred Gérard Sandoz, a television actor with many series and advertisements behind him, but with only a couple of brief appearances in feature films (*La Nuit, tous les chats sont gris*, Gérard Zingg, 1977; *La Boum*, Claude Pinoteau, 1981). Beineix was interested in him for the role of Thierry partly because he bore an uncanny resemblance to the lion tamer.

In 1987, Beineix had also directed ads for the Italian clothes company Stefanel, one of which starred Isabelle Pasco. The two of them became lovers. Pasco had started her career as a model at the age of 17, and by the time she met Beineix in 1987 had starred in five films, always playing the role of the innocent but slightly perverse child-woman (*Ave Maria*, Jacques Richard, 1984; *Hors-la-loi*, Robin Davis, 1985; *Le Mal d'aimer*, Giorgio Treves, 1986; *Sauve-toi Lola*, Michel Drach, 1986; and an Italian film, *Qualcuno in ascolto*, Faliero Rosati, 1988).

Beineix used several of the same people as for *37°2 le matin* in the new film, such as Pierre Befve for sound, Jean-François Robin for the photography, Jacques Mathou, who was Bob the grocer in *37°2 le matin*, in the role of Monsieur Armani, the director of the Cirque Zorglo. There were other familiar faces: Catherine Mazières, manager on Beineix's previous films, was now promoted to producer; Gabriel Monnet, who was Gérard's father in *La Lune dans le caniveau*, played the role of Frazier the lion tamer.

As with Beineix's previous films, considerable attention was paid to lighting and music. The film's lighting scheme shows a slow modulation from the bright summer light dominated by the yellows and reds of the beginning of the film, to colder greenish colours for the Koenig Circus, intended to translate the development from innocence to loss of innocence, from the Edenic garden to the devilish city.

Where music was concerned, Beineix wanted particular emphasis on harsh metallic sounds. These were remixed with a musical score by Reinhardt Wagner (who had collaborated with Beineix on several adverts), based on a combination of circus music and nostalgia: 'Il compte retravailler en studio toute une palette de timbres dérivés à partir de heurts métalliques (barreaux de cage, portes, barre, grille, fourche, etc.), dont les échos éveilleront la musicalité toute particulière des arènes de métal où travaillent les grand félins' (Parent 1989: 75).[1]

Initially intended to start in the spring of 1988, shooting was delayed until the summer while Beineix and Forgeas reworked the script. Shooting lasted sixteen weeks, 18 July to 3 November 1988, in four main locations: a zoo in Marseilles for the first part of the film; Donnemarie-Dontilly, a village in the Marne, for the Cirque Zorglo; the disused Valexis factory in Noisy-le-Sec, near Paris for the Koenig Circus training hall, and Amiens Circus for the Koenig Circus's spectacle. The final lesser location was Thierry and Roselyne's hotel room in Munich, actually L'Auberge Autrichienne in Brussels (rebaptised Bosphore Hotel-Bar) with its back onto the platforms of the city's Gare du Midi.

Sandoz and Pasco trained with Le Portier for nine months so as to be able to work with the lions. Some of the more dramatic shots were, however, achieved without the presence of humans in the cage, by using the Louma camera, controlled remotely with the use of a video screen. Normally on a crane, the head of the Louma was fixed onto a small trolley which had to be manoeuvred manually for the dramatic shots of the lions running into the cage. A similarly complex, and considerably more dramatic shot in the final sequence is what looks like a crane shot as Roselyne is lowered into the cage from high up in the big top. In fact, two sets of rails were built onto the terraced seats of the auditorium, one for the camera on a trolley, and the other for the counterweight.[2]

---

1 'He wanted to work on a whole palette derived from the shock of metal on metal (the cage walls, doors, bars, railings, pitchfork, etc.), whose echos would evoke the very special musicality of the iron arenas where the big cats work.'

2 These details can be seen on the film of the film, Le Grand Cirque (1989) directed by Bruno Delbonnel, and produced by Cargo Films. See also Parent 1989: 145–46.

Reception

Given the polemics to which Beineix's previous films had given rise, reviewers' reactions to *Roselyne et les lions* were in the main surprisingly positive, if somewhat muted. The general feeling was that the film was slow and simple, and the finale excessive. As was the case with Beineix's previous films, reviewers split on these issues. Some reviewers considered the film's slowness to be positive, and others negative. Similarly, the simple narrative was seen by some as overly simplistic. The finale was seen by most to be excessive, particularly in relation to what precedes it, although one or two appreciated its baroque splendour.

The film was seen as slow because of the repeated training sessions in the lead-up to the finale. For some, this translated as laboriousness (Le Morvan 1989) or self-indulgence (Gasperi 1989), not least because of what they saw as the stereotypical simplicity of the characters, both principal and secondary. So for one, the shock of the confrontation between Roselyne and the lions is dissipated by 'des personnages artificiels dans leur comportement et superficiels dans leur pensée' (Baignères 1989),[3] and for another, once the spectator realises, as is the case early on, that the story is one of initiation and that the two youngsters will inevitably succeed, 'il n'y a plus d'attente, plus de surprise venant d'eux' (C. 1989: 24).[4]

For others, including the two most important cinema journals, *Cahiers du cinéma* and *Positif*, the training sessions are what redeem the film. For *Cahiers du cinéma*, these translate 'une émotion brute' where the youngsters convey 'une sexualité sauvage', and the film is successful largely because it is 'un joli documentaire sur le domptage de lions' (Katsahnias 1989: 78).[5] For *Positif*, apart from the finale, the film is realist and well paced, and Beineix's best film:

> Beineix, se tenant à son sujet, sobrement, est en train de réaliser son meilleur film. Avec juste ce qu'il faut de réalisme, voilà une narration précise, contenue, sans temps mort. Le tempo est professionnel: aux

---

3 'characters who are artificial in their behaviour and superficial in their thinking.'
4 'you don't expect anything, any surprises from them.'
5 'raw emotion ... untamed sexuality ... a pretty documentary on lion-taming.'

relâchements succèdent les moments forts, et l'humour sait à point équilibrer les séquences les plus tendues. (Amiel 1989: 60)[6]

Similarly, if we now turn to the issue of simplicity, Pérez, who had been less than generous about *Diva*, underlines what he calls Beineix's modesty in adhering to a simple story-line which conveys emotion without an excess of talk (Toubiana's criticism of the characters in *37°2 le matin*, it will be recalled) or of 'images modernes que (la jeunesse) est censée réclamer' (Pérez 1989: 158).[7] The principal characters are fascinating for several reviewers, partly no doubt because they knew that Sandoz and Pasco had undergone a long period of training, and that they faced real dangers in the ring. This creates not just emotion, as *Cahiers du cinéma* had suggested, but 'une tension électrique, qui brise la lenteur du récit' (Macia 1989: 24),[8] and the characters become attractive through a mixture of heroism and fragility:

> Ces deux adolescents blonds, frère et sœur, cousin et cousine, en lutte contre les médiocres et les méchants, dans leur quête d'une vie plus forte, plus intense, ont quelque chose d'héroïque et de fragile, une pureté sans mièvrerie .... Ils s'aiment et se heurtent, ne transigent avec rien ni personne, se soutiennent toujours l'un l'autre, plus loin, plus haut. Ils sont justes et émouvants, on ne peut que les aimer. (Braudeau 1989)[9]

The reviewers of *Libération*, however, were not convinced by Beineix's apparent simplicity, which they preferred to see as simplistic in the worst possible sense. Thus, both Lefort and Daney underline what they see as spurious idealisation. Their principal criticism is what they see as 'un monde moralisé et extrêmement simplifié, destiné à tenir la complexité du monde à l'écart' (Daney 1989).[10] Thus, they remind

6 'Beineix, keeping to his subject, soberly, makes his best film. With just the right amount of realism, here we have a clear, restrained story-line without lulls in the action. The rhythm is professional: slackening of the pace is followed by moments of intensity, and humour counter-balances tenser sequences.'

7 'Modern images which youth is supposed to want.'

8 'An electric tension, which breaks the slow pace of the narration.'

9 'These two blond adolescents, brother and sister, cousins, who struggle against second-raters and villains, in their quest for a life less ordinary, more intense, have something of the heroic and the fragile about them, an unsoppy purity . They love each other, they argue, they refuse compromise over everything and everybody, they always support each other, as they go further and higher. They ring true and they are moving, you cannot but help like them.'

10 'a world which has been moralised and extremely simplified, whose function is to put to one side the complexity of the world.'

us that Beineix's films always suggest a simple binary between bad adults and good youngsters. Daney cattily points out that such stereo-types and the hankering for a lost purity which accompanies them corresponds both to the cinema of the *tradition de qualité* which preceded the *nouvelle vague* (and which Beineix professes to detest) and Beineix's own childhood. He links this to pre-Americanisation, pointing out, as had Jameson for Jules, that Beineix's young boys represent a very traditional France, and that in all of Beineix's films there is 'un petit Français affublé d'une belle Femme, qui la possède sans vraiment la mériter',[11] a match which he derisively labels 'noces de Tintin et de Miss France' (Daney 1989).[12] The tone is, as usual with Daney, gratuitously spiteful, but the substance is of some interest, and I shall return to it.

If reviewers were split over the pace and simplicity of the film, most agreed that the finale was kitsch, a term found in several reviews (Macia 1989; Pérez 1989), even if it was palpably sincere in its emotion (Bernard 1989: 30), accurate in its rendering of the wonder of the circus (Macia 1989), or beautiful in its imagery (Coppermann 1989). Some went further, particularly if they had appreciated the 'realism' of the first part of the film. So, for the reviewer of *Positif*, the finale is nothing short of catastrophic (Amiel 1989: 60). Only Bassan, writing a review in the same issue of *Revue du cinéma* in which he proposed the term neo-baroque for the films of Beineix, Besson and Carax, saw it as the highlight of the film, which turns the visual into the visionary (his terms; Bassan 1989: 13).

Curiously, if some reviewers suggested at least implicitly that the film was an allegory by referring to the legend of Saint Blandine, a Christian slave fed to the lions in the reign of Marcus Aurelius (see for example Dagouat 1989: 127; in fact, the allusion to Blandine is made by Frazier early on in the film, and then again by Thierry before the fateful rehearsal with the beam), few were prepared to follow Beineix's often-repeated suggestion in interview that the film could be read as an allegory about cinema itself, 'une dénonciation farouche du monde du spectacle' as one put it (C. 1989: 24).[13]

---

11 'a canny little Frenchman saddled with a beautiful woman, and who has her without having really deserved her.'
12 'the marriage of Tintin and Miss France.'
13 'a fierce denunciation of show business.'

If we turn now to histories of French cinema, we can see that Siclier is not entirely right when, in the very few lines he accords the film, he says that it was favourably received and that 'le consensus critique est total' (Siclier 1991: 259).[14] Both Frodon and Prédal point to the same tension as the film's reviewers, that between a relatively simple story-line, which they both see as the film's strength, and the grandiloquent and excessive lyricism of the finale (Prédal 1991: 468; Frodon 1995: 701), which they both see as its weakness. Similarly, Austin, who has less to say about this film than any of the others, emphasises this tension, and the fact that the film is an allegory, but considers that the defence of style becomes an end in itself and that style 'finally wins out in the overblown spectacular ending' (Austin 1996: 124).

In the following analysis, I shall return to the issue of allegory, but first will consider briefly the context of the *film animalier*, as it was labelled by reviewers in the mid-1980s.

The *film animalier*, Beineix and Besson

Reviewers, indeed, and even more so interviewers, made much of the apparent parallels between *Roselyne et les lions* and Besson's *Le Grand Bleu* (1986), seeing these films, along with Annaud's *L'Ours* (1988), as part of a trend: films which focused on animals as much, if not more, in the case of Annaud's film, than humans. The appellation *film animalier* is a misnomer, however, since there already existed, as Siclier points out, a tradition of films focusing on animals, but with a considerably more documentary slant (Siclier 1991: 274–75). Clearly, none of the three films is remotely documentary, even if *Roselyne et les lions* was said by several reviewers to have a documentary feel to its first section, due to the relatively sober photography. Beineix made it very clear that in his mind, *Roselyne et les lions* was not 'un film animalier de plus mais une métaphore poétique' (Beineix 1989b).[15]

That is not to say, however, that there are not similarities between Besson and Beineix's films, as Bassan's article in *Revue du cinéma* that year points out. One of the major points he makes, that the heroes of

---

14 'There is a complete consensus.'
15 '(not) just one more *film animalier* but a poetic metaphor.'

the *cinéma du look*, lost in a fatherless world, find difficulty in communicating, and tend to retreat into themselves, despite the best efforts of women to draw them out, is a point which Beineix was fond of making in interviews in the run-up to *Roselyne et les lions'* release. Besson's film is about regression (Beineix 1989a: 129; Beineix 1989c: 106), about the disappearance of the father, with the adult becoming like a child 'marqué à jamais par la disparition du père' (Beineix 1989d).[16] Beineix seems to agree that this leads to similarities between the films, namely 'une nostalgie de l'innocence', the search for a paradise lost incarnated in animals which are pure and unchangeable (Beineix 1989b).

Beineix is also keen, however, to differentiate *Roselyne et les lions* from *Le Grand Bleu*. His film is enclosed in a cage whereas Besson's opens out onto the limitless sea; Besson's film is concerned with competition, whereas in *Roselyne et les lions* 'c'est l'habileté qui compte, pas le score' (C. 1989: 25);[17] Beineix's film is about showmanship, whereas the hero is solitary in Besson's; there is constant eroticism through fear because of the almost permanent presence of the lions in Beineix's film, whereas, Beineix suggests, because the dolphins are rarely seen in Besson's film, the film 'joue sur l'imaginaire' (C. 1989: 25).[18] In fact, Beineix on a number of occasions signals that in his view *Roselyne et les lions* has much more in common with one of the films he went to see while making his own, Adjani and Nuttyens's *Camille Claudel* (1988), since both of them can be seen as metaphors 'de la mise en scène et du spectacle' (C. 1989: 24).[19] I shall therefore now turn to an analysis of the allegorical gesture of the film.

Allegory

Northrop Frye points out that 'we have actual allegory when a poet explicitly indicates the relationship of his images to examples and precepts, and so tries to indicate how a commentary on him should

16 'marked forever by the father's disappearance.'
17 'it is skill which counts, not the score.'
18 'Plays on the imagination.'
19 'For directing a film and for show business.' See also Beineix 1989e: IV for a similar comment; see Parent 1989: 115 for the list of seven contemporary films Beineix watched while shooting.

proceed' (Frye 1957: 90). Beineix did exactly this in interviews in the week of the film's release, his point being that the taming of the lions represented the artist's shaping of matter into poetic ideas. I shall quote two passages from different interviews, so as to be able to comment on them subsequently:

> Les animaux représentent la matière. La cage, le lieu scénique. C'est dans la cage que le dompteur trouve l'inspiration. Sur la page que l'écrivain trouve les mots. Le spectacle est fait des peines, des douleurs, des renoncements de l'artiste. Le fauve est couleur, lumière, force brute. Il faut faire passer le lion dans le cerceau, avec grâce. Dans cette histoire, ce n'est pas le cirque qui m'a intéressé, mais cet effort, cette tension qui a lieu dans un cercle, qui est le lieu de tous les regards. (Beineix 1989a: 129)[20]

> Un film sur l'artiste qui met en forme la matière brute, représentée par les fauves. La répétition figure cette lente progression du désir, de l'idée. (Beineix 1989d)[21]

The problem with allegory is that what is signified is not always clear to anyone else, particularly if the allegory is a personal vision, hence the need for directorial commentary. Indeed, the longer first quotation is Beineix's correction to his interviewer's statement that the film is obviously a metaphor for the director and his star, in which, he suggests, the big cats might be the films. It is tempting to think that it is perhaps the overly directorial aspect of the allegory which attracted previously critical reviewers, in particular those of the *Cahiers du cinéma*, because they could see the film as a very personal statement by an auteur. By the same token, it might well have been the overly directorial aspect which alienated the youth audience that had previously supported Beineix, because that audience might well have felt excluded from this personal vision.

Beineix's allegorical vision corresponds to what Honig calls apocalyptic allegory, which 'casts a cold eye on man's social and moral

---

20 'The animals represent matter. The cage, the stage. It is in the cage that the tamer finds inspiration. On the page that the writer finds the words. The show is composed of the efforts, the pain, the renunciations of the artist. The big cats are colour, light, brute force. You have to make the lion go through the hoop, gracefully. In all this, it is not the circus which interested me, but the effort, the tension which occurs in a circle, which is the focus for all eyes.'

21 'A film on the artist who shapes raw matter, represented by the big cats. Rehearsing signifies the slow progress of desire, of the idea.'

nature, and criticizes the failures and imperfections of man and his laws. Apocalyptic [allegory] frequently becomes the refuge of heretical imagination defying the contingencies of legalism and the status quo' (Honig 1960: 107). We need to note just how close this description is to Beineix's position in relation to the critical establishment, as the youth- and image-oriented director of the *cinéma du look* who rejects the modernist cinema of the new wave. Even more important are the religious connotations in Honig's description.

Allegory is closely related to religion, frequently referring to religious ritual (*A Pilgrim's Progress*, for example). The connotations of Saint Blandine add an obvious religious flavour to the allegory, as was pointed out by several reviewers. It is hardly surprising, then, that Beineix, in the first quotation referring to allegory above, uses language which his interviewer points out has religious overtones (the issue of 'grace'). Nor is it surprising that there is a church sequence in which Roselyne realises what she and Thierry should do, a sequence which, with its excessive camera angles and movements, and its portentous music, seems out of place in the first, more realist part of the film, as was pointed out by several reviewers.[22] Allegory tends to impose structure and order on the more diffuse intuition or revelation of myth. Indeed, Fletcher suggests that allegory is akin to scientific order, opposed to the dream time of myth: 'Allegory makes an appeal to an almost scientific curiosity about the order of things' (Fletcher 1964: 69). It is significant in this respect that Thierry's stage name is that of one of the major Enlightenment thinkers, D'Alembert, and that he imposes the order of a particular performance on the 'wild' Roselyne, insisting on perfecting the act. If Thierry represents rationality and order, Roselyne represents its opposite, since it is she who goes to the church, and it is no accident that the finale of the film parallels the cinematography and music of the church sequence earlier, since, arguably, it represents the triumph of Roselyne and the dream at the expense of Thierry and allegorical order. As Bracquard says to the couple when he visits them in Munich, quoting Eluard, the surrealist poet, 'le plus court chemin d'un point à l'autre n'est pas la

---

22 Beineix has pointed out that his films often have churches in them (quoted in Parent 1989: 171 in the context of his Catholic upbringing). One thinks of Betty and Zorg's chase through the town to a church on a hilltop (rather than the industrial estate of the novel), and the dreamlike cathedral in which Gérard and Loretta are married (again, a change from the novel).

ligne droite mais le rêve'.[23] The quotation is not an unintegrated contingency signalling an ad-like punch-line, as Lefort suggests (who thinks that it looks like 'un slogan pour le Crédit Agricole'; Lefort 1989),[24] but a clear indication of a tension within the structure of the film between Roselyne's dream and Thierry's order, both of which are contained in the ritual of allegory.

Beineix's response to the interviewer who suggested that he was using religious language to explain his allegory was, in appearance at least, eccentric: 'Je pourrais employer un langage de *torero*' (Beineix 1989a: 129).[25] There are obviously, however, parallels between lion taming and the bullfight; indeed, the film itself arguably signals as much in the finale, when Roselyne takes off her red cape with the flourish of a *torero*. There is also implicitly here an allusion to the work of Michel Leiris, who explains in a well-known essay, 'De la littérature considérée comme une tauromachie',[26] written in 1945–46, how he decided to make himself the subject of his work. Such 'confessional' writing, where the writer reveals everything about himself, including his fantasies, is similar to bullfighting, Leiris suggests, in that it means taking considerable risks (upsetting close family, going against good taste, and so on). Even more apposite is Leiris's comment that he intended to combine dreams and a classical structure, which, in his view, are also combined in the bullfight: 'Si j'ouvrais bien ma porte aux rêves (élément psychologique justifié mais coloré de romantisme, de même que les jeux de cape du torero, utiles psychologiquement, sont aussi des envolées lyriques), je m'imposais ... une règle aussi sévère que si j'avais voulu faire une œuvre classique' (Leiris 1968: 19).[27] Both of these points can be applied to Beineix's project in this film. First, the film is 'classical' in structure in its simple narrative of initiation, as praised by the reviewers of the *Cahiers du cinéma* and *Positif*. At the same time it incorporates the dream, as intimated by

23 'the shortest path from one point to another is not the straight line but the dream.'
24 'a slogan for the Crédit Agricole [one of the large banks].'
25 'I could use the language of the bullfight.'
26 'Literature considered as bullfighting.'
27 'If I was opening my door to dreams (a psychological element which was justified although coloured with romanticism, in the same way that the torero's play with the cape, psychologically useful, is also a lyrical flight of fancy), I was imposing on myself a rule as severe as if I had wanted to write a work in the classical vein.'

Bracquard's comment quoted above, particularly in those sequences which these periodicals did not like for their 'excess', namely the church sequence and the final gothic sequence. Second, it is clear that the film, and the final sequence in particular, is a very personal statement by Beineix, showing a fascination with Pasco reminiscent of Carax's fascination for Juliette Binoche in *Mauvais Sang* (see Vincendeau 1993).

The parallel with Leiris's bull-fighting metaphor is nevertheless less instructive than the more general issue of allegorisation. The film might well be considered an allegory of itself, as was suggested by Beineix to Parent, echoing what he said in interview above about the cage acting as a focus for the gaze:

> La première partie du film sera celle de la fascination. Comme Roselyne et Thierry, le spectateur restera en dehors du cercle magique. Puis progressivement, lors de la phase d'initiation, il pénétrera dans la cage ... au contact des bêtes; enfin lors de la phase de domination, il sera à la fois dedans et dehors, lion et dompteur, public d'un cirque et spectateur d'un film. Ainsi la forme est-elle en accord parfait avec le fond. (Parent 1989: 86)[28]

But the film could well be considered an allegory of Beineix's own trajectory, as hinted by Coppermann, who sees Roselyne and Thierry as representing 'un défi au monde qui, peut-être, est un peu le sien' (Coppermann 1989). This is borne out by a comment made by Thierry to Koenig as he negotiates for the gothic spectacle of the finale: 'C'est pas une question de contrats, c'est une question de style. Je veux faire ce que je veux, comme j'ai envie, à ma manière, ou ça ne m'intéresse pas'.[29] What both of these versions of allegory – the film as allegory of itself, and the film as allegory of Beineix's trajectory – have at their centre, quite literally, is the gaze on Roselyne. The film, although ostensibly about a rite of passage involving both a boy and a girl, is, as its title suggests, more concerned with Roselyne than Thierry.

28 'The first part of the film will focus on fascination. Like Roselyne and Thierry, the spectator will stay outside the magic circle. Then gradually, during the initiation phase, the spectator will go into the cage and make contact with the animals; finally, during the domination phase, the spectator will be both inside and outside, lion and trainer, a member of the audience in a circus and spectator of a film. In this way the form corresponds perfectly to the content.'

29 'It isn't a question of contracts, it's a question of style. I want to do what I like, as I like, in my own way, or else I'm not interested.'

The gaze on Roselyne reaches a climax in the finale. Evidently, we are supposed to be stunned by the visual splendour of the finale, and, as reported above, many reviewers saw it as excessive. The finale, far from being an unnecessarily excessive theatricalisation of the more 'documentary' training, is the key to an understanding of the film and its allegorical imperative.

Baroque allegory and the triumph of woman's gaze

The work by theorists of allegory to which I have referred has so far explained how we can view allegory as an example of Beineix's defiantly visual 'heretical imagination'. It has also allowed us to conceptualise the relationship between Thierry and Roselyne as one of order and rationality versus wildness and dream. It has not yet been able to help us explain the impact of the uncanny (in the strong Freudian sense of *unheimlich*) gothic images in the finale, nor the impact of the finale in theoretical terms. To do this, I shall turn to the work on baroque allegory by Walter Benjamin,[30] who, in the same way that the other commentators mentioned in the introduction to this book felt that the baroque sensibility was a feature of postmodernism, saw baroque allegory as a way of explaining particular features of modernism.

Like many other analysts of allegory, Benjamin suggests that allegory arises when symbols fade away, or, to put it another way, the notion of the singular divine collapses into a plurality of allegorical gods and goddesses who function as ciphers. Benjamin thus contrasts transcendent meaning, or the 'image of organic totality', and plural, fragmented meanings, 'amorphous fragment(s)' with an emphasis on the visual (Benjamin 1977: 176–77). This collapse leads to melancholia and is figured most obviously in the all-pervasive dreamlike images of Death's head and the ruin. The baroque image is, Benjamin suggests in a famous phrase 'a fragment, a rune' (Benjamin 1977: 176), by which he means something which excites the imagination to decipher its obscure meaning. As Buci-Glucksmann explains, allegory's fragmenting effect is similar to modernism's distancing

---

30 Benjamin's major work on allegory is contained in his doctoral thesis on German baroque drama, *Ursprung des deutches Trauerspiels*, written in 1924–25, published in 1928.

techniques: 'L'allégorie anticip(e) sur le rôle du choc, du montage et de la distanciation dans l'avant-garde du XXᵉ siècle, brise son object, et fixe le réel par une sorte d'effet d'étrangeté, semblable à la logique de l'inconscient' (Buci-Glucksmann 1984: 69).[31] The style appropriate to allegory, Benjamin writes, is 'une écriture émotionnelle' (Buci-Glucksmann 1984: 69).[32] As Buci-Glucksmann points out, 'une telle écriture émotionnelle excède de part en part l'ordre linguistique, car elle exprime précisément *le deuil comme sentiment* (Buci-Glucksmann 1984: 69; her emphasis).[33] We find this particular complex of notions in the finale of *Roselyne et les lions*.

Most obviously, there is Thierry dressed up as Death, in a decor of gothic ruins, these two images being inexplicable, 'runes' demanding interpretation. These images are powerful first and foremost because they convey emotion, or 'mourning as feeling', precisely because they are so excessive in relation to what precedes them. We are not sure what the images are telling us, but we are 'stunned' by them, in the strong sense of having our rationality anaesthetised by images seemingly extracted from a dream. The finale is like a dream in relation to the everydayness of what precedes it. It is a dream which has its roots in what precedes it, but is an excessive version of it, an overflow, figuratively like the dry ice that billows and curls across the set.

Thierry and Roselyne are, during most of the film, more like twins than lovers. The finale apparently changes this. Thierry is transformed into Death, wearing his inside, the skeleton, outside. He is the opposite of life, and the representation of a terminal baroque melancholy, gazing on the ruins around him, and on Roselyne. Roselyne is transformed into the opposite, a statue, not life decayed, but life petrified, all outside without an inside, the ultimate spectacle within this spectacle of a spectacle; unlike Thierry, who gazes on her, she gazes out at the audience. She appears to be statuesque because the light bounces off her body, making it seem 'hard', an impression all the stronger when she places herself on the stone slab for Wotan to

---

31 'Allegory ... shatters its object and fixes reality by a kind of alienation effect similar to the logic of the unconscious' (Buci-Glucksmann 1994: 70).

32 'that stirs the emotions' (Buci-Glucksmann 1994: 70). I am using her translation of 'erregende Schrift' rather than 'stirring writing' as in Benjamin 1977: 176.

33 'such writing "that stirs the emotions" completely overflows the linguistic order, for it expresses *mourning as feeling*' (Buci-Glucksmann 1994: 70).

pick the rose off her naked body. (It is an impression grounded in reality, since her 'body' does not breathe; it was a silicone replica.)

Arguably, the connotations are more complex than this. We need to bear in mind the explicit references to Saint Blandine, the slave torn apart by lions in Christian mythology. When Roselyne places herself on the stone slab, waiting for the lion to approach, it recalls the scene in the butchery where Klint and Thierry prepare the meat for the lions and tigers. In this analogy, Roselyne is like the dead meat, waiting to be sliced up; an early scene where Thierry and Roselyne unload raw meat from the back of Frazier's van, and where they are insistently framed against the meat, suggests this. But whether we see her as 'dead meat', the dead centre of the performance, or as a statue, she is nevertheless, like Thierry, but differently, a representation of death. As Buci-Glucksmann points out, 'la *pétrification* (le corps-pierre, le corps-marbre, le corps figé et gelé) est une métaphore baroque par excellence' (Buci-Glucksmann 1984: 183; her emphasis).[34] Death's head (Thierry) and the petrified body (Roselyne) among the ruins: the three key images of the baroque, as identified by Benjamin, signifying, broadly speaking, a collapse in values.

The message suggested by the finale's iconography may seem very bleak. Clearly, however, the finale is intended to suggest something more akin to triumph. The possibility of redemption emerging from ruin is, as it happens, also vital to Benjamin's view of baroque allegory. The vision of death in baroque allegory 'is not just a symbol of the desolation of human existence. In it transitoriness is not signified or allegorically represented, so much as, in its own significance, displayed as allegory. As the allegory of resurrection. Ultimately in the death-signs of the baroque the direction of allegorical reflection is reversed; on the second part of its wide arc it returns, to redeem' (Benjamin 1977: 232). We may recall in this respect Beineix's view that the film is about the struggle of the artist to shape his material, the film therefore being an allegory of itself, a statement by Beineix about the redeeming power of art (a position also outlined in the dialogues of *Diva*, it may be remembered).

The finale of the film, then, is an *apotheosis*, in both the figurative sense of the finale, and in the more original sense of the admission of

---

34 '*Petrification* (the stone body, marble body, fixed and frozen body) is a baroque metaphor *par excellence*' (Buci-Glucksmann 1994: 138).

ordinary mortals to the home of the Gods. The finale functions as the spectacular amplification of what precedes it, and we read it as precisely this: the spectacular accomplishment of what was already a spectacular training, the spectacle which contains and magnifies the preceding spectacle, as if a grand overmantel mirror had been placed on the wall opposite a smaller, more mundane mirror.

Thierry, however, 'dies', remaining the one-dimensional character he has been throughout the film. If he is dressed in black in the finale, it is because the light reflected in the metaphorical mirrors I have just evoked must be absorbed by him, so that we cannot see him, for it is Roselyne who must be seen and be the scene of fantasy, she must be the centre of the narrative and the centre of the gaze. This is made clear to us by the sequences where Koenig turns her into a 'star' much to Thierry's jealous dismay. She is dressed to be a star, interviewed, photographed, and, finally, used as an image on the Circus poster. This is just a preparation for what happens in the finale, where she is fixed in the limelight, extensively visible, and multiple: she is both the wild beast ('elle va le bouffer',[35] says a character of her as he watches Thierry train her in Koenig's Circus) and the slave who might get eaten; she is very much alive and fragile for us in the face of the lions, while at the same time being 'dead meat' through the iconography of the film; she is very active during most of the film, while during the finale, the non-diegetic rock music which drowns out ambient sound, and the slow motion as well as the play of light, turn her more into the statue I referred to above. In this hall of mirrors, then, Roselyne, is at the dead centre, and multiply double.

Do these multiple doublings point us in the direction of the classic dichotomy virgin–whore? Is Roselyne at one and the same time virginal in her statuesque inaccessibility, and whore in her fetishisation as spectacular body, around and over which Beineix's camera lingers in the finale? I would rather suggest that this simplistic dichotomy is transcended. As Buci-Glucksmann says of Benjamin, it is 'une logique de l'excès qui se pétrifie, se cristallise en idée fixe, en point de rencontre "mystique" de tous les sens, de tous les contraires' (Buci-Glucksmann 1984: 222).[36] The characteristic of such a sensibility, she continues, is that the body is taken out of circulation, taken out of the

35 'she'll have him for dinner.'
36 'A logic of excess which petrifies or crystallizes in the *idée fixe*, in the mystical meeting-place of all meanings and all opposites' (Buci-Glucksmann 1994: 159).

arena of the gaze which would normally transform it into a visual commodity. What remains is the 'fascination pour une matière corporelle exclue de toute circulation marchande, une matière ultime et morte' (Buci-Glucksmann 1984: 222).[37] Making Roselyne metaphorically part-dead matter, in the ways I have suggested above, is therefore a way of *preventing* the gaze from turning her into a fetishised commodity. It is consonant with Beineix's view of art, as we saw in *Diva*, as somehow spiritual, a redemptive activity in both secular and religious senses, and which woman actualises (in this the diva and Roselyne are different from Loretta and Betty, who are not connected to art, even though they may 'perform' in other ways).

Roselyne's triumph is conveyed in the close-up on her face; 'mon film est dans le regard final de Roselyne ... . Un regard de triomphe, mais aussi de solitude totale', said Beineix (Frodon 1989: 16).[38] Roselyne's triumph is followed almost immediately by Thierry literally tearing off his 'face', Death's head. He tosses it up into the air, and we see it rise in three brief slow-motion shots. The image is uncanny in the same way that Buci-Glucksmann suggests that the baroque image of the severed head is uncanny. It is a trope which conveys 'la peur panique du sexe et de la castration, l'obsession d'une virilité frappée d'impuissance, l'impossible jouissance du féminin' (Buci-Glucksmann 1984: 211).[39] The image of the severed head and its connotations is hardly surprising in a narrative which elevates woman to a realm combining fetishisation and hysteria.

We should not forget that Roselyne is never injured by the lions, unlike Saint Blandine; whereas Thierry, in the same sequence where he mentions the Saint, spreadeagles himself like Christ on the beam, and his leg is sliced open in a clear image of castration. The severed head of the final sequence merely repeats what has been happening throughout, as Roselyne takes over the narrative and triumphs over the fetishising gaze by returning a gaze of immense solitude.

37 'Fascination for corporeal matter excluded from all commodity circulation, a final, dead matter' (Buci-Glucksmann 1994: 159).
38 'My film is in Roselyne's final gaze. A gaze of triumph, but also of total solitude.'
39 'Panic fear of sex and castration, obsession with virility smitten with impotence, the impossible *jouissance* of the feminine' (Buci-Glucksmann 1994: 154).

Unlocking the father

Thierry is not the only male to fade away. All the significant males in the film are undermined in one way or another. Markovitch, the stereotypically macho lion tamer of the Cirque Zorglo, is made fun of by Petit Prince, and is humiliated by Roselyne when she manages to tame lions which we have been told are untameable. Klint, the tiger tamer, loses his nerve when asked to tame the lions, and commits suicide. Koenig is forced to accept Thierry's conditions for remaining. His humiliation is emphasised by the camerawork, as Thierry looms over him in a low-angle shot, and during the finale, Koenig, who likes to control, gasps that what he is seeing 'n'est pas dans le programme'.[40] Of all the significant males, it is perhaps the schoolteacher Bracquard who is the most interesting. He is introduced in the very first sequence in a position of authority, but as the film progresses, that authority is diminished. First, after criticising Thierry at school, he is filled with admiration as he watches Thierry tame the lions. Later in the film, while his protégés train big cats, he struggles comically to train his pet cat. This undermining even extends to a minor detail. When Roselyne has her bright idea in the church, that she and Thierry should ask Bracquard for a loan, it is after looking at a votive plaque next to the statue of the Virgin Mary. That plaque has the name of Bracquard on it, but the Christian name, Raymonde, is that of a woman. Bracquard, then, is not only undermined, but feminised. The reason for this, I would suggest, is that whereas the other significant males are stereotypes, and therefore easily dismissed, Bracquard is the most developed character after Thierry and Roselyne, and acts as the missing good father (which is why I cannot agree with Tom Milne's view that he 'seems imposed on the film rather than an integral part of it'; Milne 1989: 374). In his role as father, he is much more of a threat.

The threat is different for the two main protagonists. We never see Thierry's family, and early on he assumes a stage name. His frequent clashes with other significant males in the course of the film suggests an obvious Œdipal structure as the son struggles against the shadow of the father. This is all the more obvious to us since Roselyne does not seem to reject her family or her family name; she does not have a stage name, and we do see her mother, if only briefly. For Thierry,

40 'isn't on the programme.'

then, Bracquard threatens to replace the father he has rejected and left behind. The narrative must therefore undermine him as much as, if not more than Thierry himself, so that Thierry may survive the Œdipus. In the event, this is precisely what happens. It is far from ironic that Bracquard should be such a pale imitation of Thierry when it comes to training cats.

The father is also important for Roselyne. Pressed by the journalist for a good story, she tearfully tells of how she was abandoned by her father when young. He worked as a mechanic for the Pinder Circus, where she had her first encounter with a lion. The tamer, who called her 'le petit ange blond',[41] asked her to choose a lion, and took her into the cage. Lion taming for Roselyne has thus become a means both of rejecting her real father who abandoned her, as well as a means of finding a substitute father. Bracquard, then, is for her even closer to the missing father than he might be for Thierry, because the lion taming goes back into her earliest memories. Bracquard is an echo, through his cat, of that elusive liontamer of her memories. She is the one who makes Bracquard's cat dance when he visits them in Munich, reminding us of the kinds of anthropomorphic games children tend to play with such animals.

Despite her closeness to Bracquard as good father, Roselyne floats free. For her to do so, the father must fade away; indeed, all the males, including Thierry, who is the last male in the series, must fade away. In this respect, Roselyne may be the centre of the story, its focus; but Thierry is the key, as the paternal name he has rejected, Serrurier, meaning locksmith, suggests. The film is about the gradual humiliation and disappearance of the male. Roselyne is twice referred to as Saint Blandine, suggesting that it is she who will suffer from the jaws of the lion. But it is Thierry, not Roselyne, who is almost literally crucified by Wotan as he stretches out on the beam.

41 'little blonde angel.'

References

Amiel, Vincent (1989), 'Jean-Jacques et les anges (*Rosleyne et les lions*)', *Positif* 339: 60–61.
Austin, Guy (1996), *Contemporary French Cinema: an Introduction*, Manchester and New York, Manchester University Press.

Baignères, Claude (1989), 'Le contenant et le contenu', *Le Figaro* 12 April.

Bassan, Raphaël (1989), '*Roselyne et les lions*: L'étoile et le troubadour', *Revue du cinéma* 449: 13–14.

Beineix, Jean-Jacques (1989a), 'Beineix: tourner, ça fait mal', *L'Express*, 7 April, 128–29.

Beineix, Jean-Jacques (1989b), 'Les cris et les rugissements de Beineix le révolté', *Le Journal du dimanche*, 9 April.

Beineix, Jean-Jacques (1989c), 'Le dompteur d'images', *Le Nouvel Observateur*, 6 April, 106–07.

Beineix, Jean-Jacques (1989d), 'Jean-Jacques Beineix: "Une réflexion sur l'artiste qui, comme un dresseur ..."', *Le Quotidien de Paris* 2921, 10 April 1989: 27–28.

Beineix, Jean-Jacques (1989e), 'Beineix critique Beineix', *Le Monde*, 13 April 1989, IV.

Benjamin, Walter (1977), *The Origin of German Tragic Drama*, translated by John Osborne, London, NLB. This edition originally published as *Ursprung des deutches Trauerspiels*. Frankfurt am Main, Suhrkamp Verlag, 1963.

Bernard, Jean-Jacques (1989), '*Roselyne et les lions*', *Première* 146: 30.

Braudeau, Michel (1989), 'Cœur de lion', *Le Monde*, 13 April.

Buci-Glucksmann, Christine (1984), *La Raison baroque: De Baudelaire à Benjamin*, Paris, Galilée.

Buci-Glucksmann, Christine (1994), *Baroque Reason: The Aesthetics of Modernity*, translated by Patrick Camiller, London, Sage.

C., S. (1989), 'Fauve qui peut ... la vie', *7 à Paris*, 12–19 April, 22–25.

Coppermann, Annie (1989), 'Les fous dans la cage', *Les Echos* 15366, 12 April.

Dagouat, Marylène (1989), 'Dans la gueule du lion', *L'Express* 1970, 7 April, 127.

Daney, Serge (1989), 'Les petits Français de Beineix', *Libération*, 3 May.

Fletcher, Angus (1964), *Allegory: The Theory of a Symbolic Mode*, New York, Cornell University Press.

Frodon, Jean-Michel (1989), 'Jean-Jacques Beineix: Le cinéma de l'émotion', *Le Point* 864, 10 April, 14–16.

Frodon, Jean-Michel (1995), *L'Age moderne du cinéma français: De la Nouvelle Vague à nos jours*, Paris, Flammarion.

Frye, Northrop (1957), *Anatomy of Criticism. Four Essays*, Princeton, New Jersey, Princeton University Press.

Gasperi, Anne de (1989), 'Le bond dans l'absolu', *Le Quotidien de Paris*, 12 April.

Honig, E. (1960), *Dark Conceit. The Making of Allegory*, London, Faber & Faber.

Katsahnias, Iannis (1989), '*Roselyne et les lions*', *Cahiers du cinéma* 419–20: 78.

Lefort, Gérard (1989), 'L'avis public numéro un', *Libération* 13 April.

Leiris, Michel (1968), *L'Âge d'homme*, Paris, Livre de Poche. Originally published by Paris, Gallimard, 1946.

Le Morvan, Gille (1989), 'La vie des bêtes (suite)', *L'Humanité*, 12 April.

Macia, Jean-Luc (1989), 'Beineix en sa période fauves', *La Croix*, 13 April, 24.

Milne, Tom (1989), '*Roselyne et les lions*', *Monthly Film Bulletin* 56/671: 373–75.

Parent, Denis (1989), *Jean-Jacques Beineix: Version originale*, Paris, Barrault Studio.

Pérez, Michel (1989), 'L'amour et les fauves', *Le Nouvel observateur* 1276, 20 April, 158.

Prédal, René (1991), *Le Cinéma des français depuis 1945*, Paris, Nathan.

Siclier, Jacques (1991), *Le Cinéma français, 2: de Baisers volés à Cyrano de Bergerac 1968–1990*, Paris, Ramsay Cinéma.

Vincendeau, Ginette (1993), 'Juliette Binoche: from gamine to femme fatale', *Sight and Sound* 3: 22–24.

7

IP5 (1992)

Synopsis

Tony sprays graffiti on a wall as Jockey sings. Tony collects the photo Jockey has taken of his art at a photo booth, and is beaten up by Lulu and his skinhead gang, who take his collection of photos. He agrees to take a delivery-van full of garden gnomes to Grenoble in return for his collection. Jockey returns home to find his father drunk once again. His father collapses in the shower. Gloria, the night nurse from the hospital, gives him medication. Tony is visibly taken by Gloria. He tries to pick her up the next day, but she spurns him, calling him 'an empty shell'. He spends part of the night spraying the wall opposite her flat. She spurns him again. Tony and Jockey leave for Grenoble with the delivery. Tony phones Gloria on the way, but she turns him down a third time, saying she is moving to Toulouse. Tony and Jockey stop in a motorway café. The man on the neighbouring table tells Jockey off for stealing the batteries out of someone's walkman. Tony nuts him in the toilets and takes his car keys, heading off for Toulouse, much to Jockey's dismay, because Tony had promised to take him to see the snow in the mountains.

Tony crashes the car in a forest, but takes the car of a man who has stopped to relieve himself after killing a couple of rabbits with his car. They discover Léon Marcel in the back, and throw him out. Tony lets Jockey drive, but Jockey crashes the car, and Tony is stuck behind his jammed seatbelt. Léon arrives and gives Jockey a knife to cut the belt. The car blows up as they walk into the forest. Léon heals Tony by placing his hands upon him, calling him, like Gloria, 'an empty shell'. He pulls the supposedly dead rabbit from under his cape, which runs off. He walks into a lake; Tony and Jockey search his bag, discovering a revolver, and stealing his money. Tony and Jockey leave him, and try to steal a car in a motorway café. They are caught by two policemen. Léon, who is in the back, saves them by confirming their story about a lost key. The three of them go into the café. While Léon is in the toilet, Tony and Jockey search his bag once more, discovering that he belongs to an asylum. Léon collapses in the toilet, but heads off for the forest once more as soon as a doctor has treated him. Tony follows him, but Jockey refuses. Tony finds Léon 'purifying' himself in the rain. They head off for the main road to Toulouse; Jockey follows them, and eventually catches them up. Léon tells them he is looking for an island surrounded by large trees (the 'pachyderms' of the title; the '5' refers to Beineix's fifth film); he tries to get them to communicate with the trees. Tony, irritated by their wanderings, nuts Léon just as Jockey discovers another lake. He swims into the lake, and is rescued by Tony when they realise he cannot swim. Over a campfire, Léon tells them how he was trying to find the place where, as a young man on vacation, he fell in love with Clarence, one of two twins, swimming in the lake; he had left at the end of the holidays after a quarrel with Clarence and had never seen her again.

The following morning, Léon announces that he is giving up his quest, but Tony and Jockey persuade him to go to the village where his love lived. Tony and Jockey find the surviving twin, Monique, who is a butcher's wife, and persuade her to pretend she is Clarence. Léon and Monique talk about old times. Léon pulls his gun on her, but tells her he knows she is not Clarence. Monique tells him that Clarence had committed suicide by drowning after the quarrel. Tony and Jockey find Léon in a deserted railway station waiting for a train. They take him with them. Tony stops in the countryside to spray a large hoarding. Jockey plays with Léon's gun, and lets it off. Léon collapses as he runs towards Jockey. They take him to a hospital in Toulouse, and wait along with Léon's family outside the intensive care unit. Léon dies in the night with Jockey at his bedside. Gloria, who works in the hospital, has overheard Jockey tell Léon how much Tony loves her. She goes to Tony who is sitting morosely in a nearby café. He rejects her advances at first, but they make up. They are almost run over by Jockey who has taken the dead Léon in a car to see the snow. Jockey looks out onto the snow at the top of a hill, sobbing as he shouts Léon's forest cry. Tony, who has followed him with Gloria, stops his car and shouts back.

Background

In 1991, Jacques Forgeas, who had collaborated with Beineix for *Roselyne et les lions*, gave the script of *IP5* to Beineix, who worked on it for a couple of months. There were familiar names on the team: Robin for the photography, Yared for the music, Monnet, who played Frazier in *Roselyne et les lions*, as the village butcher. Yves Montand had let it be known that he wanted to work with Beineix. Since his acclaimed Papet in *Jean de Florette/Manon des Sources* (Claude Berri, 1986), the 70-year-old Montand had acted in two disappointing films, *Trois places pour le 26* (Jacques Demy, 1988), a musical in which he played himself, and *Netchaïev est de retour* (Jacques Deray, 1991), a thriller based on a novel by Semprún. The 25-year-old Olivier Martinez, a graduate from the Paris Conservatoire, had had a bit part in *Plein fer* (Josée Dayan, 1990), but was otherwise unknown. The 11-year-old Sekkou Sall was selected from a group of hopefuls. Shooting lasted eleven weeks from September to November 1991. Montand died of a heart attack on 9 November 1991, three weeks before the end of shooting, and much was made at the time of the possibility that his death could have been caused by Beineix demanding that he go into the cold water of the lake. When the film was eventually released, in June 1992, the debates were revived, and the film became the 'last Montand' rather than the 'fifth Beineix'.

This was in spite of an extensive marketing campaign with a 3.9 m. franc budget: Beineix's location photographs were shown ten days before the film's release in one of Paris's large bookstores (FNAC-Etoile), and subsequently went on tour for a month in the FNAC stores of nineteen major cities and towns. The film's release coincided with the release of Yared's score and a novelisation of the film by Forgeas and Beineix, as well as a large format, lavishly illustrated storyboard. Much was also made of the fact that the film's soundtrack was digitalised (by a French firm, LC Concept). Several large cinemas in Lyons, Marseilles and Paris chose to exhibit it in this format. Indeed, the film was the first to be screened in Gaumont's new giant 650-seat screen cinema on the Place d'Italie. Just prior to the film's release, Martinez was awarded a prize for his role as Tony (a prize which, coincidentally, had been awarded the previous year to his partner in this film, Géraldine Pailhas).

Reception

In interviews preceding the film's release, Beineix suggested that the film was a moral allegory ('une allégorie, le récit d'une initiation (qui) tient plutôt de la morale que de la métaphysique'; Beineix 1992b).[1] He likened the film to Cocteau's *La Belle et la Bête* (1946), claiming that both films were a 'cinéma naïf' (Beineix 1992c: 33). Reviewers, on the other hand, saw not a simple cinema, but a simplistic cinema. Beineix was 'trop intellectuel pour se laisser aller au lyrisme qui aurait pu hausser son film au-dessus de la simple parabole écologique et de la fable sentimentale' (Martin 1992).[2] The charge can be decomposed into three main areas of criticism.

First, reviewers took exception to the superficiality of the themes and of the imagery. The themes 'se superposent sans vraiment se mêler' (Amiel 1992: 68).[3] What might be considered the principal theme of myth is imposed on the film: 'La mythologie reste à l'état de croûte ... , au sens pictural du terme, qui dit à la fois la couche superficielle mais aussi l'espèce de noir qui a recouvert le tableau où les figures sont prises dans une pâte de peinture ou de cinéma – du son, de la lumière, des idées, du sens' (Giavarini 1992).[4] Amiel criticises the stereotypically ad-like images of nature: 'la cathédrale des arbres, la brume mystérieuse du matin, le silence infini des sommets neigeux' (Amiel 1992: 68).[5]

Second, reviewers complained that Beineix undermined the sense of mystery which he claimed to want to generate; 'mystère des lieux, des lumières et surtout des personnages', Beineix writes in the storyboard (Beineix 1992a: 232).[6] Reviewers felt that Léon was stripped of his mystery when it is revealed that he was the one who left his lover, and that his lover had committed suicide; 'et voilà détruit le mythe de

---

1 'an allegory, the story of an initiation which is more moral than metaphysical.'
2 'too intellectual to let himself go in the lyricism that could have lifted his film above a simple ecological parable and sentimental fable.'
3 'are superimposed without really mixing.'
4 'The mythology is no more than a layer in the painterly sense, which means both the paint at the surface and the sort of black patina which has covered the painting where the figures are caught in an impasto of paint or cinema – of sound, light, ideas, meaning.'
5 'the cathedral of the trees, the mysterious morning mists, the infinite silence of the snowy mountaintops.'
6 'mystery of the locations, of the lighting, and especially of the characters.'

cette immense passion plus forte que la mort' (Baignères 1992).[7] As Macia says, 'Beineix nous lance sur la piste d'un film fantastique puis nous déçoit cruellement en nous en donnant les clés, fort banales' (Macia 1992).[8]

Third, the sense of mystery is even more undermined by an unequal struggle between the real (or hyper-real) and the fantastic, the magical realist on the one hand and the 'reportage social' (Heymann 1992)[9] on the other. As Macia less charitably puts it, 'on passe du clip au docurama pour les Eaux et Forêts' (Macia 1992).[10] Even *Studio*, a keen supporter of Beineix's work, complained about the lack of imagination which, in their view, hampers the fantastic: 'Au lieu d'ouvrir tout grand la porte de l'imaginaire, ils ont multiplié les parades, les personnages périphériques et les situations anecdotiques. Comme s'il avaient eu peur de perdre pied, comme s'ils avaient tenu à fair *aussi* un film réaliste' (Lavoignat 1992: 17; his emphasis).[11]

Télérama ran its usual for/against column. Murat, writing 'for', was one of only a small handful of reviewers who unreservedly praised the film for its rhythm and its colour, the appealing sincerity of its characters, and what this let one suppose might be Beineix's sensitivity (Murat 1992: 35). Writing against, Trémois, who claimed to be a supporter of Beineix because she admired the way the characters in his previous films had been swept up in 'une spirale vertigineuse',[12] underlined what she felt was the superficiality and banality of the film: 'Ici, ni spirale ni vertige' (Trémois 1992: 35).[13]

One might imagine that the film did not do very well. It is true that it fared worse than *Diva* and *37°2 le matin*, and worse than films by other directors working in the *cinéma du look*, such as Besson (whose *Nikita*, 1990, had 3,786,613 spectators), or those working in the derision genre, such as Chatiliez (whose *Tatie Danielle*, 1990, had 2,151,463).

---

7 'and so the myth of that huge passion stronger than death is destroyed.'
8 'Beineix sends us on the trail of a fantasy film only to disappoint us cruelly by the very banal keys that he gives us.'
9 'social report.'
10 'You go from the advertising clip to the docudrama for a national forestry authority.'
11 'Instead of opening wide the doors of the imagination, there are endless displays, peripheral characters and anecdotal situations. As if they had been afraid to lose their footing, as if they wanted to make a realist film as well.'
12 'vertiginous spiral.'
13 'Here, there is neither upward spiral nor intoxication.'

But, to put this in perspective, the film had about the same number of spectators as Carax' s *Les Amants du Pont-Neuf* (1991; 867,197), and more spectators than Rochant's youth film *Aux yeux du monde* (1991; 149,198).

Frodon's 1995 film history follows the generally negative appraisal covered above. For him, the film is a confused and naïve fable. Unlike the reviewers of the film, however, Frodon pays particular attention to the iconic function of Montand, who began in the music hall, and eventually became one of cinema's leading politically engaged actors. He suggests implicitly that the initiation of the narrative is paralleled by the transmission of a continuity at the level of film history, 'comme si ce dépositaire d'un pan de l'histoire du cinéma fait de spectacle à l'ancienne (le music-hall) et d'idées (l'engagement) devait transmettre à la génération nouvelle un secret dont, manifestement, Beineix n'a pas idée – pas plus que sur des jeunes qu'il ne représente qu'au travers de clichés' (Frodon 1995: 701).[14]

Austin, in the only English-language history to have covered this film, also addresses the idea of Montand as icon. Unlike Frodon, however, who implies that Beineix's use of Montand is unthinking, Austin sees it as a critical move on Beineix's part:

> Montand represents at once the ostensible wisdom of age and the iconic power of French cinema in the three decades preceding the *cinéma du look*. Moreover, he constantly chastises Tony in terms which recall the usual critiques of Beineix's work, calling him an 'empty shell' and informing him that the woods surrounding them are no film set. A more conventional narrative would simply settle for a rite-of-passage movie in which Léon would educate his young charges. Beineix, however, after initially portraying Léon as a mystical figure at one with nature, slyly explores the deceit and despair beneath the old man's façade, thereby both eschewing sentimentalism and calling into question the mythical status of past French cinema. (Austin 1996: 125)

The key to the film is Montand. He functions as the father figure who, as Austin rightly suggests, is slowly undermined, just as Depardieu, I have argued, is undermined in *La Lune dans le caniveau*. The undermining is paradoxical, however, because sentiment, if not sentiment-

---

14 'As if this guardian of part of the history of the cinema made of old-time spectacle (the music-hall) and ideas (political commitment) was to transmit to the new generation a secret of which, manifestly, Beineix has no idea, no more than he has of the youth whom he represents only through clichés.'

ality, as well as derision, is never far from the scenes involving Montand. It is this paradox which will form the focus of the following analysis.

Undermining the shaman father

The film is on the surface a confrontation between simple binaries. The principal binary is that of inexperienced youth–wise old age. As Beineix says in the storyboard, 'entre Léon Marcel et les deux adolescents il y a confrontation probable de deux univers' (Beineix 1992a: 234).[15] Mapped onto this binary are several others. City is contrasted with forest, again stressed by Beineix: 'La forêt est un monde étrange, différent. Habitué que je suis à la ville, je perds mes références. Notre monde de citadin est un monde rectangulaire, parallélépipède. L'absence de marques, de signes, d'angles, rendent la forêt troublante' (Beineix 1992a: 222).[16] Tony's bright paint is contrasted with the luminous greens of the forest. Fire is associated with the city (the car which explodes at the edge of the forest; the papers which Léon burns to eradicate his traces in the system), whereas water is associated with the forest, particularly the 'pluie lustrale' or purifying/cleansing rain. Finally, stealing (of books, batteries, cars, suits) is contrasted with giving; Léon 'heals' Tony, and, as Tony points out to Jockey, he 'saves' them more than once.

The binary structure is set up for us to understand that what Léon represents is good, and what Tony and Jockey represent is bad. Tony does not have a soul, he is an empty shell, says Léon, echoing Gloria. Tony and Jockey are, Léon says, thieves and liars, who cannot connect with nature, whereas we see Léon 'connecting' on a number of occasions, the most impressive of these being first his walking on the water of the first lake – 'C'est Jésus, ou quoi?',[17] says Tony, astonished – the second being Léon standing, arms outstretched like Jesus, in a shaft of light as the 'pluie lustrale' 'cleanses' him.

---

15 'between Léon Marcel and the two adolescents there is the probable confrontation of two universes.'

16 'The forest is a strange, different world. Accustomed to the city, I lose my bearings. Our urban world is a rectangular, parallelepipedal world. The absence of marks, of signs, of angles, make the forest a disturbing place.'

17 'Is he Jesus, or what?'

Léon's role then is that of the shaman who initiates the novice, leading him out of childhood and ignorance into adulthood. All the hallmarks of ritual in tribal societies, as described by Mircea Eliade, the historian of religions, for example, are there. The initiation takes place in a secluded location away from 'society', although it must still be part of it. (One of the more disconcerting aspects of the film is the way in which the forest is not the magical labyrinth which reviewers apparently wished it to be. Roads and cafés are never far.) Léon is from an asylum, echoing the well-known link between madness and insight: 'Certaines maladies graves, surtout les maladies psycho-mentales, sont considérées comme un signe que le malade a été choisi par les êtres sur-humains pour être initié, c'est-à-dire torturé, mis en pièces et "tué", afin d'être ressuscité à une existence supérieure' (Eliade 1976: 163).[18] His walk on the water is a version of the bridge between heaven and earth which has become difficult to cross because of mortality (see Eliade 1974: 375–8). Trees are another form of communication in primitive religions between heaven and earth (Eliade 1975: 229ff.): 'Ce sont des dieux',[19] says Léon, telling Jockey that birds are a means of connecting with the tree god. 'Les oiseaux sont les gardiens du temple. Si je pose ma main sur la branche d'où vient de s'envoler cet oiseau, je me sens relié à lui'.[20] Animals, but especially birds, as Eliade points out, are crucial in shamanic ritual (Eliade 1974: 136–37).

The initiation involves 'losing one's way' (Beineix's suggestion that in the forest one loses one's reference points), trials by fire (the car in which Tony almost burns) and water (he swims to save Léon, and cleanses himself with Léon in the 'pluie lustrale'; see Eliade 1975: 165ff.). It involves violence; as Beineix says, commenting on Tony's attack on Léon, 'si Tony en vient à la brutalité on a l'impression que c'est le Vieux qui l'y a poussé presque dans un rituel d'initiation, de mise à l'épreuve' (Beineix 1992a: 242).[21] It involves becoming a child

18 'Certain serious illnesses, especially mental illnesses, are thought to be the sign that the sufferer has been chosen by superhuman beings to be initiated, that is to say tortured, wrent into pieces and "killed" so as to be born again into a superior existence.'

19 'They are gods.'

20 'Birds are the guardians of the temple. If I put my hand on the branch from where a bird has just flown, I feel that I am connected to the bird.'

21 'when Tony becomes aggressive, we get the impression that the old man has pushed him to it, almost in a ritual of initiation, a putting to the test.'

again, eating acorn porridge, and purifying the system; when Tony vomits the mixture, Léon explains to him that it is the thymus gland which is being purified. Reality and fiction intermingle in this instance, as Beineix explains that the substance used to simulate the porridge was baby food, 'une bouillie à base d'aliment pour enfant. La scène veut que les acteurs aient l'air dégoûté. Nul besoin d'en rajouter, ils le sont vraiment' (Beineix 1992a: 288).[22] Becoming a child once more, in a return to Mother Earth which leads to a death and rebirth, is a ritual structure common to nearly all systems. When Beineix suggested in interview that the forest was the womb (Beineix 1992f: 59), he was echoing primitive myths of the earth as source of life: 'La terre est Mère, c'est-à-dire qu'elle engendre des formes vivantes en les tirant de sa propre substance ... . Tout ce qui sort de la terre est doué de vie et tout ce qui retourne à la terre est à nouveau pourvu de vie' (Eliade 1975: 219).[23]

Some reviewers suggested that *IP5* was a film riding on the back of the ecological movement ('sentencieusement écologiste', Heymann 1992;[24] 'mystique vaguement écologiste',[25] Lenne 1992: 35). As I hope to have shown, the discourse is more focused and coherent than this might suggest, as Beineix himself was at pains to point out:

Je parle de la forêt dans sa dimension mythologique et spirituelle. L'arbre, c'est l'arbre de la Genèse, l'arbre généalogique, l'arbre de la connaissance et de la mémoire ... Et la forêt, c'est le lieu de l'initiation et du passé profond de l'humanité. Le lieu où l'on perd ses références et où l'on éprouve ses limites. Un lieu d'éveil pour le regard et l'esprit. Quand on va dans la forêt, on rend visite à des 'pachydermes', à des dieux. On retrouve des valeurs spirituelles que la civilisation des villes a perdues. (Beineix 1992d)[26]

22 'a gruel using baby cereal. The scene required the actors to be disgusted by it. They didn't have to try very hard, they really were.'
23 'The earth is Mother, that is to say it gives birth to living forms by pulling them from its own substance. Everything which comes from the earth is endowed with life and everything which returns to the earth is once again given life.'
24 'Sententiously ecological.'
25 'Vaguely ecological mysticism.'
26 'I am speaking of the forest in its mythological and spiritual dimension. The tree is the tree of genesis, the genealogical tree, the tree of knowledge and memory. And the forest is the place of initiation and of humanity's deepest past. The place where you lose your bearings and where you test your limits. A place of awakening for the eyes and the mind. When you go into the forest, you visit the "pachyderms", the gods. You rediscover spiritual values which the cities have lost.'

Beineix links this renewal of values to the search for the missing father: 'Cette société n'a pas confiance en elle. Elle se sent coupable de tout. De la pollution, de la nature violentée, alors, elle se cherche un père' (Stouvenot 1992).[27] He insists that although the film is apparently about three males searching for a woman (Jockey looking for his mother, Léon and Tony looking for a lost love), in fact what the two youngsters find is the father, by which he means Léon (Beineix 1992c: 34). Clearly, the combination of the father figure who is very much in contact with Mother Earth forms the ideal figure of value opposed to the failing fathers. The latter are absent: 'notre société a tué le père puisque ce n'est plus lui qui donne la nourriture' (Beineix 1992c: 34); 'le père n'existe plus. C'est l'immense sujet de société nord-européen, nord-américain: la famille orpheline' (Beineix 1992e: 52).[28] Or the father is negatively connoted, as the parallelism between Jockey's real father and Léon demonstrates. Both have cardiac arrests, both try to purify themselves with water; indeed, it is in so doing that Jockey's father precipitates his heart problem, whereas Léon pointedly stresses the healing properties of the 'pluie lustrale' which Tony thinks might cause even more problems. But Jockey's father drinks and gambles and is looked after by his son, whereas Léon turns into a surrogate father for Jockey by the end of the film, as the emotional bedside conversation between them and the final apotheosis of the father on the hilltop suggest.

However close Léon is to the birds he has so much respect for in the final scene, he is of course dead, and metaphorically blind with his dark glasses, doubly castrated. As Austin points out, the binary which I have explored is complicated by a critical distancing, effected principally through derision and comedy. This is typical of Beineix's previous work. There is a difference here, however. Although derision and comedy is located mainly in secondary characters, as in the previous films, in *IP5* derision is also located in the character of Léon.

Where secondary characters are concerned, comedy is generated by the skinhead Lulu, who, like Pinon's Le Curé in *Diva*, speaks in a curiously emphatic voice. Just as Le Curé was derided when the music

---

27 'This society no longer has any confidence in itself. It feels guilty about everything. Pollution, the rape of nature, so, it is searching for a father.'

28 'our society has killed the father because it is no longer he who provides food.' 'The father doesn't exist any more. It is the burning social topic in North European and North American societies: the family without a father.'

he listens to on his walkman turns out to be traditional French accordion music, so too Lulu is derided when we find out that the delivery he forces on Tony is a vanload of large garden gnomes. The BMW driver (played by Fabien Behar, the olive seller of the long version of *37°2 le matin*) who tells Jockey off for stealing batteries from someone's walkman is humiliated by Tony in one of the film's more frankly comic scenes, which, as Beineix admits, is unrelated to the plot (Beineix 1992a: 88). The military man whose car they steal in the forest is derided not just by the stereotypically bombastic brass band music he plays in his car, but also by his extremely noisy farting; this scene is perhaps more obviously linked to the themes of the film, since Beineix points out how for him this character represents a society out of touch with nature: 'Mon personnage est un tueur de lapins. C'est un carnivore, donc il pète. Et tout ça sur une musique militaire. Il y a l'idée de la chair, l'idée du carnassier, et du carnage. C'est pour moi l'arrogance d'une civilisation sûre d'elle et déjà décadente' (Beineix 1992f: 60).[29] Finally, the two policemen who think that they have caught car thieves are ridiculed when Léon 'saves' Jockey and Tony, much to the surprise of all concerned, as the car window opens and he dangles the keys in front of them.

The military man, and even more the policemen are figures of authority, whom, as we have seen in the previous films, Beineix takes great delight in mocking. In this film, Léon is also a figure of authority, of moral authority, and he does not escape debunking. This begins with the last example I have given of the two policemen. Up to that point, Léon has been a mysterious, almost magical figure. Indeed, his sudden reappearance in the back of the car, echoing his first appearance in the back of the military man's car, combined with more apparently magical feats, in this case the possession of the car keys at exactly the right moment, might seem to confirm his status. But the sequence takes away as much as it accords him. First, the two policemen, who both have the same moustache, address each other as 'Marcel', Léon's surname. The gag undermines both the policemen and Léon by its absurd multiplication of Marcels. Second, any apparent magic is dispelled when Léon returns the car keys to their

29 'My character is a rabbit-killer. Therefore he is a meat-eater, and so he farts. And all of this happens with a military music accompaniment. It is for me the arrogance of a civilisation sure of itself and already decadent.'

English owners, leaving us to assume that he had hitched a lift and had agreed with them that he would sleep for a while in their car.

The comical effect of near-twin policemen is echoed later in the village when Tony and Jockey visit the butcher's shop. Just as the butcher is saying that the two sisters were identical twins, there is a cut to two large pig's heads on a tray, ridiculing both the policemen called Marcel of the earlier sequence, and the two sisters who changed Léon Marcel's life, thereby ridiculing him indirectly. The remaining sister, Monique, has none of the charisma we might have associated with the water-nymph fantasy evoked by Léon in the forest. She is turned into a figure of fun by her prosaic appearance and poor dress sense; she has to be told by Jockey to remove her ridiculous hat and earrings before meeting Léon. Léon himself, a figure of moral authority in the forest, has that authority gradually dismantled in the village. He produces a whole string of credit cards, his 'magic' veering wildly away from the ecological to the materialistic, as is stressed by Jockey: 'Putain! Il a la Gold. Et une pour voyager en First. Moi qui le prenais pour un naze'.[30] He steals the wedding suit of the father of the bride, just like Jockey steals a suit for him, showing that he is no better than they are, even if he insists that courtesy dictates a letter of apology. He has stage fright before meeting Monique, and has to be morally supported by Tony and Jockey. Even the *mise en scène* stresses the falling away from initiatory mystery into social banality by paralleling forest and village: the village church is shot in a wide lens low-angle shot, as were the trees in the forest, and, as in the forest, there is a bird, but it is a mechanical bird (given to Jockey by Léon) which drops out of the sky clumsily, whereas the birds in the forest flew upwards.

The most interesting element of Léon's diminishing stature is the Lüger he carries with him, since it is used to undermine both Léon the character and Montand the star. In the forest the Lüger is a dramatic prop, a source of fascination for the two youths. It remains so until the village, when we eventually realise why Léon carries it with him: to shoot his erstwhile lover. But this element of high drama is undermined when, having played along with the deception, Léon reveals that he knew all along that 'Clarence' was in fact Monique. The

30 'Fuck me! He's got the Gold. And a card for first-class travel. There was me thinking he was a bit of a wanker.'

revolver also functions as an essential support for Montand's star image, as Beineix points out in the storyboard when commenting on the fact that it is the first time in the film that Léon is seen holding the revolver: 'A le regarder, le pistolet à la main, je me remémore toutes les armes avec lesquelles je l'ai vu dans les films. *Police Python [357]* [Alain Corneau, 1976]. *Le Cercle rouge* [Jean-Pierre Melville, 1970] ... Ici, aucun culte pour l'arme à feu. Pas de mystification, juste un peu de dérision' (Beineix 1992a: 300).[31] The derision in question is the uselessness of the weapon; as Léon says to Tony who asks him where the Lüger is, knowing full well that Léon has not as he claims thrown it in the lake, 'tu crois qu'on tue le passé?'.[32] The weapon's uselessness indirectly parallels Léon's 'fall', and Montand's degradation. I claimed above that this begins in the village, but this is not entirely the case, if we consider not just the narrative, but Montand's body.

Beineix makes frequent reference in the storyboard and in interviews to the way in which the normally dandyish Montand had to show his old age and frailty in the film: 'Il ne se trouvait pas assez à son avantage, avec sa barbe pas rasée de tout le film, ses cheveux emmêlés, son visage sans maquillage. Je lui disais: "Attention, tu fais le coquet." Mais en même temps il acceptait sans tricher cette dégradation apparente. Et de ce courage, je lui suis reconnaissant pour toujours' (Pantel 1992; see also Beineix 1992a: 156).[33] Indeed, one of the more startling aspects of the film is the exposure of Montand's ageing body, in all senses of the word. There is the constant allusion to heart trouble in the dialogue, his two cardiac arrests, made all the more troubling by Montand's death in similar circumstances, as well as the unkemptness alluded to by Beineix here. But more startling still is the real physical exposure of his body at a key moment of the film, when he strips down to his underpants at the first lake. There is something shockingly paradoxical about the combination of eco-

---

31 'Looking at him with the gun in his hand, reminds me of all those guns he held in his films. *Police Python [357]*. *Le Cercle rouge*. Here, there is no cult for the firearm. No mystification, just a little bit of derision.'

32 'do you think you can kill the past?'

33 'He was worried that he didn't look at his best, with his stubble through the whole film, his tangled hair, his face without make-up. I said to him: "Careful, you're getting too worried about your appearance." But at the same time, he accepted without trying to get round it this apparent degradation. I am forever grateful to him for this courage.'

logical fantasy (this is the lake of the nymphs) and Montand's frail white body with its sagging skin. It is a paradox made all the more acute by two things. First, by Montand's very obvious attempt to hold himself erect, the paradox here being that between erectness and the 'fall' of age and of the skin; and second, Léon/Montand's apparent walk on the water like Jesus, the paradox here being between the defiance of the elements and gravity on the one hand, and, again, the 'fall' into old age and mortality. As the reviewer of the *Cahiers du cinéma* pointed out, the sense of the sacred which defines and differentiates the sacred from the profane depends on terror. Léon's 'magical' feats do not engender the sense of the sacred, but there is a sense of terror located in Léon's body: 'De vraies apparitions ne peuvent venir que d'une vraie peur. Ce n'est pas tant lorsqu'il marche sur l'eau ou surgit à l'arrière d'une banquette, que Montand figure le mieux une apparition, mais quand il ôte ses vêtements et montre son torse nu, ce corps d'homme vieux, fripé comme celui d'un bébé' (Giavarini 1992: 86).[34]

That terror, Giavarini suggests, is the passing of time, which turns the son into a father. The film, for her, shows 'Beineix s'arrêtant devant une figure crainte, sans doute haïe (et toutes ses dénégations ne pourront que mieux nous en convaincre): un vieux. Et moins parce qu'il craint en lui la mort que parce que le temps se voit en lui' (Giavarini 1992: 86).[35] Far from denying the Œdipus, Beineix stresses the conflictual aspect of his relationship with his father, whom he describes as 'une espèce de mélange de père sévère et de père très fier de son fils' (Beineix 1992f: 59).[36] He also freely admits to the childlike pleasures he takes in his films, whether it is in fetishised objects such as the car ('Les autos, il y en a toujours dans mes films. C'est un reste de mon enfance. Je continue à jouer aux petites voitures'; Beineix 1992a: 196),[37] or in the undermining of father figures. For him, it is

34 'Real apparitions can only come from a real fear. It is not so much when he walks on the water or when he appears in the back of a car that Montand best approximates an apparition, but when he undresses to bare his torso, the body of an old man, wrinkled like that of a child.'
35 'Beineix stopping in front of a figure of fear, a figure he no doubt hates (and all of his denials can only convince us all the more): an old man. And less because he fears death in him than because time can be seen in him.'
36 'a sort of mixture of the strict father and the father who is very proud of his son.'
37 There are always cars in my films. It's a hangover from my childhood. I still play with toy cars.'

clear that these are linked to a desire for Œdipal transgression: 'Une volonté de transgression. Ça vient des rapports avec mon père' (Beineix 1992f: 60).[38] The film, I am suggesting, points to a Beineix caught on the cusp between the rule-breaking son and the moralising father, the son who takes delight in the father farting, and the father who is seeking to instil moral values in the son: 'je veux surtout parler d'éthique; il faut rester droit, droit comme une lame' (Beineix 1992b),[39] he said, quoting one of Léon's lines to Jockey.

The reader will no doubt have noticed that I have moved away from a universalising psychoanalytical perspective to a very particularising auteurist perspective. *IP5* is in many ways Beineix's most personal film. Although it is like all of his films, about obsession, and particularly about obsessive love, it is less about the ostensible object of the quest (Gloria is no Betty, and Monique is undermined) than it is about the quest itself. That quest, I am suggesting, is less about the other/lover who helps define the self, than about the self in a more direct sense: the *auteur*. I am using the word here in the double sense of a self-identity, the origin which answers the question 'who am I?', and in the sense of film director, what we as spectators might understand as the origin of the discourse of which we are the onlookers, and who answers the question 'who is speaking?'

IP5 is the first film where Beineix had free rein with the narrative. As he has frequently pointed out, with his first three films he was in a sense merely illustrating a story, and even in the fourth he was using someone else's story, Le Portier's biography. In *IP5*, he was using Forgeas's original script, but the film is framed by two very personal statements penned by Beineix himself. Beineix has stated that he reworked the conclusion of the film, which did not exist in Forgeas's version (Beineix 1992e: 50). I have already pointed out how intensely emotional the final sequence is, and the way its effect depends to a large extent on the death of the father. The opening sequence of the film is just as personal, and it seems appropriate to end by considering the beginning, the 'rap du tagueur'. I shall quote the last three stanzas:

38 'A need to break rules. It comes from my relationship with my father.'
39 'I especially want to talk about ethical issues. One must stay straight, as straight as a knife blade.'

> Dans ce monde qui réprime
> Par mes zébrures je m'exprime
> Et à grands jets de peinture
> Je fais l'amour avec les murs
> Je fais l'amour avec les murs
>
> Vous lancez à mes trousses
> Vos brigades de voieries
> Mais j'ai pris le maquis
> Oui j'ai pris le maquis
> Jamais j'aurai la frousse
> La ville pour moi c'est la brousse
> De l'époque sombre des cavernes
>
> Aux lueurs néons des temps modernes
> Je ne suis qu'une signature
> Une immense rature. Ra Ra Ra. Ture-Ture-Ture
> Rature.[40]

Given that the signature in question is the title of the film, the rap can be read self-reflexively as Beineix the director who made his hallmark by reinstating colour, and hounded by the critics. There is even the touch of masochism in the pun of the final word, which means both a crossing out (of a word, for example) and, in the figurative and colloquial sense, a failure. The death of the father brings about the death of the son. Perhaps it is no accident that the phrase 'coquille vide', or empty shell, is repeated so frequently in the film. For that very reason, Beineix thought he might use it as the film's title at one point, rejecting that option because it could be too easily used by ill-intentioned reviewers to describe the film (Beineix 1992a: 80). But it is not the film which is an empty shell. The son is empty, and an empty distorted signature at that, since 'coquille' is as frequently used to mean a typographical error as it is a shell. The son is no more than an error, the wandering mistake of the father. As has been the case with all of Beineix's films, this film is about the struggle between the rule-breaking son and rule-making father. It is in this film, however,

---

40 'In this world, left on the shelf/I use the spray to express myself/With the coloured painted scrawls/I make love to city walls/I make love to city walls/The top men send after me/Their city cops by duty bound/But I've gone underground/Yes, I've gone underground/I'll never let fear in, I'm free/Life is one big jungle see/From the gloomy caveman days/To the latest neon craze/I'm nothing but a signature/One big failure Fail-Fail-Fail Lure-Lure-Lure/Failure'

that the struggle is resolved in favour of the death of the father, and the ultimate guilt of the son.

This may explain why, from one perspective at least, Beineix did not make any more feature films during the 1990s after *IP5*, retreating into documentaries whose subject is either foresaken children, foresaken buildings or people who have retreated into themselves, whether by choice, such as the *otaku*, or by force, such as Bauby.

References

Amiel, Vincent (1992), '*IP5: L'Île aux pachydermes*', *Positif* 378: 68.

Austin, Guy (1996), *Contemporary French Cinema*, Manchester and New York, Manchester University Press.

Baignères, Claude (1992), 'Chronique d'une mort annoncée', *Le Figaro*, 14 June.

Beineix, Jean-Jacques (1992a), '*IP5: L'Île aux pachydermes*, Paris, Dargaud.

Beineix, Jean-Jacques (1992b), '*IP5*: Montand au pays des tagueurs', *Le Point* 1029, 6 June.

Beineix, Jean-Jacques (1992c), 'Le mal aimé', *Télérama* 2213, 10 June, 32–34.

Beineix, Jean-Jacques (1992d), 'Jean-Jacques Beineix: un cinéaste en quête de sagesse', *Le Figaro*, 12 June.

Beineix, Jean-Jacques (1992e), '*IP5* Le nouveau Beineix: Montand l'émotion', *Première* 184: 46–52.

Beineix, Jean-Jacques (1992f), 'Jean-Jacques Beineix: les racines du ciel', *Studio* 64: 59–61.

Eliade, Mircea (1974), *Le Chamanisme et les techniques archaïques de l'extase*, Paris, Payot; originally published in 1968.

Eliade, Mircea (1975), *Traité d'histoire des religions*, Paris, Payot. Originally published in 1964.

Eliade, Mircea (1976), *Initiations, rites, sociétés secrètes. Naissances mystiques: essai sur quelque types d'initiation*, Paris, Gallimard. Originally published in 1959.

Frodon, Jean-Michel (1995), *L'Age moderne du cinéma français: De la Nouvelle Vague à nos jours*, Paris, Flammarion.

Giavarini, Laurence (1992), 'Opus morbidum', *Cahiers du cinéma* 458:86.

Heymann, Danièle (1992), '*IP5*', *Le Monde*, 13 June.

Lavoignat, Jean-Pierre (1992), '*IP5*', *Studio* 64: 17.

Lenne, Gérard (1992), '*IP5: L'Île aux pachydermes*', *Revue du cinéma* 484: 35.

Macia, Jean-Luc (1992), 'Montand, dernière', *La Croix*, 13 June.

Martin, Marcel (1992), 'Chercher la femme', *Révolution*, 11 June.

Murat, Pierre (1992), 'Pour: rêve en couleurs', *Télérama* 2212: 35.

Pantel, Monique (1992), 'Beineix raconte la rencontre d'un homme et d'un personnage', *France-Soir*, 12 June.

Stouvenot, Michèle (1992), 'Un Beineix qui va vous étonner', *Le Journal du dimanche*, 7 June.

Trémois, Claude-Marie (1992), 'Contre: vide existentiel', *Télérama* 2212: 35.

21 Tony the *tagueur* (*IP5*)

22 Léon absorbs the energy of the *pluie lustrale* (*IP5*)

23 Léon/Montand and old age (*IP5*)

24 An old man walks on water (*IP5*)

25 The pigs' heads (*IP5*)

26 Michel wonders what to do with the body (*Mortel Transfert*)

27 Michel's dream (*Mortel Transfert*)

8

Mortel Transfert (2001)

Synopsis[1]

Michel Durand est psychanalyste. Ses journées s'écoulent dans la torpeur feutrée de son cabinet entre les petites plaintes d'une professeur de mathématiques chahutée, les fureurs d'un éjaculateur précoce et les récits sado-masochistes d'Olga Kubler, une perverse kleptomane. Une vie somme toute banale pour un thérapeute, si l'étrange et séduisante Mme Kubler, profitant de l'assoupissement de son médecin, n'avait eu la fâcheuse idée de se faire étrangler sur le divan. La neige tombe sur Paris, les doux flocons tourbillonnent dans les rêves du docteur ... 19 heures. Carillon. Fin de la séance. Olga ne bouge plus. Cette fois, Michel Durand est complètement réveillé.

Que s'est-il passé? Qui a tué l'épouse du promoteur escroc, Max Kubler ? Pourquoi Michel Durand a-t-il si mal aux avant-bras? Peut-on commettre un assassinat en dormant? Trêve de questionnement ... Il faut agir. Se débarrasser du corps. Et vite. Car le commissaire Chapireau lui aussi mène l'enquête et Max Kubler cherche sa femme comme un fou ...

Cette course délirante, dans laquelle Durand est entraîné bien malgré lui, le mènera dans un univers où rêve et réalité se confondent, et où meurtres et fantasmes le disputent à toutes les perversions.

---

1 The synopsis which follows is the official synopsis published at the time of the film's release. Given that at the time of writing the film has not been released in the UK or USA, I have respected Beineix's wish not to reveal the detail of the story in an extended synopsis.

Avec, au bout du chemin, et comme un message d'espoir, la douceur sensuelle d'Hélène, l'amante, la complice, la femme aimée.²

Background

Bereavement after *IP5* turned Beineix away from feature film-making, despite several propositions from American producers, *Alien Resurrection* (Jeunet, 1997) and *The Avengers* (Chechik, 1998) among them. During 1999 Beineix worked to raise money for his long-standing project, the comic vampire film based on Behm's novel. The film was to cost something like 250–300 m. francs (£2.5–3 m). The project fell through with only 170 m. francs raised (from TF1, the French TV company, UGC, UGC International, and the German company Odeon), despite being promoted with Jean Reno in the lead role. Subsequently, however, a new feature film was planned, as alluded to by Beineix in the foreword to this volume, *Mortel Transfert*, based on a novel of the same name by Jean-Pierre Gattégno (1997). This was a co-production between Cargo Films and Odeon, one of the contributors to the funding of the vampire film. Gattégno's earlier novel, *Neutralité malveillante* (1992) had been adapted for the screen by Francis Girod with the title *Passage à l'acte* (1996, starring Daniel Auteuil as a psychiatrist).

2 'Michel Durand is a psychoanalyst. His days drift by in the muffled torpor of his consulting room between the complaints of a maths teacher played up by her pupils, the rantings of a premature ejaculator, and the sado-masochistic stories of Olga Kubler, a perverted kleptomaniac. It would have been the very picture of a typical therapist's life if the strange and seductive Madame Kubler, taking advantage of her doctor's drowsiness, had not had the unpleasant idea of allowing herself to be strangled on his couch. The snow is falling in Paris, and the soft snowflakes swirl around in the doctor's dreams ... . 7 p.m. The clock strikes. End of session. Olga doesn't move. This time Michel Durand is wide awake.

What happened? Who killed the wife of Max Kubler, the crooked property developer? Why are Michel Durand's arms hurting so much? Can you murder someone while asleep? Enough questions, he needs to do something. Get rid of the body, quickly. Because Police Commissioner Chapireau is investigating and Max Kubler is going crazy looking for his wife.

Durand, caught up against his will in a mad chase, will enter a universe where dream and reality get confused, and where murders and fantasies fight it out with perversions. And at the end of the road, a glimmer of hope, in Hélène's soft embrace, his lover, his partner, the woman he loves.'

As with so many of his other feature films, Beineix chose to work with familiar faces for this new adaptation. Jean-Hugues Anglade plays the role of a psychoanalyst, Michel Durand, who is in the habit of dropping off to sleep while listening to his patients. The music was provided by the composer of *Roselyne et les lions*, Reinhardt Wagner, who also plays a bit part, that of a blind man, as does Gérard Sandoz, the young hero of *Roselyne et les lions*, in the role of a police inspector. Some of the paintings in the film were produced by Pierre Peyrolle, who had designed the 'Try another world' poster in *La Lune dans le caniveau*.

There were a number of newcomers. Hélène de Fougerolles had acted opposite Anglade in Alexandre Jardin's *Prof* (2000), and had impressed Beineix in Arthur Joffé's *Que la lumière soit!* (1997). Here she plays the role of the sexually perverse kleptomaniac Olga, whom Durand wakes up to find strangled on his couch. The veteran Théâtre Français actor Robert Hirsch (who had appeared most recently in Blier's *Mon Homme*, 1996) appears in the role of Zlibovic, Durand's own psychoanalyst. Faithful to his commitment to multi-ethnic casts, Beineix has the Yugoslav Miki Manojlovic in the role of Erostrate, the drunk. He had acted in several films by Emir Kusturica, but had most recently appeared in Ozon's *Les Amants criminels* (1999). There was Yves Rénier, a well-known TV actor (particularly for the title role in the series 'Le Commissaire Moulin'), in the role of Max Kubler. Finally, there was Catherine Mouchet, whom Beineix had seen as the psychologist in Philippe Harel's *Extension du domaine de la lutte* (1999).

Mortel Transfert went into production in April 2000. It was made over 14 weeks, released in France on 10 January 2001, and in Switzerland on 24 January. It was subsequently shown at various festivals: the *polar* festival at Saint-Quentin-en-Yvelines (January 2001), and the Berlin festival (February 2001).

One of the more interesting features of the release of the film, particularly when compared to the earlier features, is the mounting of an extensive interactive website, with a trailer and lists of events. Although not unusal in itself for the period, the site, more unusually, included e-mails from spectators and electronic versions of a number of reviews, both good and bad.

A further point of interest is the very extensive marketing campaign mounted by Cargo Films, with a number of TV and radio appearances by Beineix and the two leads, and interviews by Beineix in a wide variety of outlets (see the bibliography). As well as the general press, such as *L'Express*, and standard trade magazines such as *Première*, Beineix gave interviews to medically oriented magazines, such as *Psychologies*, and, with Ovidie, the hard-porn actress who plays in the SM video on Kubler's television, to *Hot Vidéo*, a magazine devoted to the pornographic video industry.

Reception

The general reaction to the film was that its mixture of genres, thriller and comedy, had not gelled in quite the way Beineix had intended. Beineix pointed to the oscillation between the sacred and the profane, the grotesque and the morbid (Beineix 2000a: 22), suggesting that this mixture of genres would appeal to a younger audience brought up on Almodóvar (Beineix 2001b). Some reviewers found the mixture to their liking. One called the film 'un petit bijou'[3] (Anon. 2001a: 7). Another pointed to its 'savant dosage entre un onirisme et un réalisme teinté d'humour noir et un esthétisme très léché' (Menguy 2001).[4] The thriller/comedy mix for many created a strong atmosphere, a word appearing frequently in reviews (Anon. 2001b; Anon. 2001c; Coppermann 2001), along with the words 'malaise' (Attali 2001, Quéméré 2001), and 'macabre' (Maupin 2001; Heymann 2001; Sotinel 2001). Several reviewers, following Beineix's lead (Beineix 2001b: 108), pointed to a similarity of atmosphere with Scorsese's yuppie comedy thriller of 1985, *After Hours* (for example Royer 2001),[5]

---

3 'a little gem.'
4 'a clever mix of dream and reality tinged with black humour and a very polished aestheticism.'
5 The hero, Paul, goes to SoHo to spend the night with Marcy, whom he has just met in a coffee-house. Marcy turns out to be unstable, but he cannot return home as he has lost his money. In his attempt to escape Marcy (who commits suicide after he has left her) and to return home, he encounters a series of bizarre characters. Events and characters appear to be connected as his night turns into a nightmare: the bartender who offers to lend him money turns out to be Marcy's boyfriend; Paul is mistaken for a burglar and pursued by a mob; he ends up being hidden in a sculpture which breaks open on the street the following morning when it falls out of the van belonging to the burglars who have taken it.

and parallels with some of Hitchcock's thrillers (Gaillac-Morgue 2001; Lalanne 2001; Malterre 2001).

The majority of reviewers, however, found the mixture simply disconcerting, without any redeeming features: 'un méli-mélo d'idées ... (un) bizarre bricolage' (Loiseau 2001);[6] 'd'incessants décalages comiques et de maladroites envolées romantiques' (Quéméré 2001).[7] Others took against the erotic aspect of the film. *Première*'s critic, for example, in the issue following an extended interview with Beineix, talked of 'intermèdes éroticoconvenus, façon porte-jarretelles sur fond bleuté un peu passés de mode' (Katelan 2001).[8] A word frequently used was 'vulgar' (Anon. 2001d; Larcher 2001).

The film disconcerted reviewers in the etymological sense of the word, with some suggesting that Beineix had given too much rein to his fantasies, and that the film would have been better served by being more focused (Katelan 2001), whereas others suggested the opposite. *Libération*'s critic, for example, applauded the black humour which reminded him of Hitchcock's *The Trouble with Harry*, suggesting that Beineix could have exploited the comedy more fully: 'moins produit, plus lâché, il pourrait ... s'abandonner à cette pente caustique et délirante' (Lalanne 2001).[9]

A further criticism, reminiscent of the criticisms of *Roselyne et les lions*, was that the film was too impersonal, too cold, too cerebral. Indeed, *Studio*'s reviewer, a journal which had supported Beineix during the 1980s, pointed out what for him seemed a paradox: 'un film impersonnel où il ne s'implique jamais, et un film où il ne cesse de semer des indices d'ordre privé' (Lavoignat 2001).[10] *L'Humanité*'s reviewer suggested that Michel Durand is the alter ego of Beineix himself, and that the film is a self-reflexive exercise 'd'autodérision chez un cinéaste cérébral' (Guilloux 2001).[11] Pushing this idea further, Pascal Mérigeau suggested that the film showed a profound self-disgust (Mérigeau 2001).

6 'a hotch-potch of ideas ... knocked together any old how.'
7 'constant comic interludes and clumsy romantic flights of fancy.'
8 'stereotypical erotic interludes, of the old-hat type with suspenders on blue background.'
9 'less produced, more relaxed, he could let himself go in this caustic and surreal vein.'
10 'an impersonal film where he never gets involved, and a film where he never stops dropping clues of a private nature.'
11 'Self-derision in a cerebral film-maker.'

As usual, then, Beineix's new film, like his others, caused contradictory reactions, with the same kind of criticisms levelled against his previous films: a pompous style too close to the advertising aesthetic, heavy humour, improbable and confusing plots, stereotypical and underdeveloped characters, distance, irony, derision, verging on masochistic self-derision. And, as before, some reviewers were unreasonably virulent in their criticisms. It is worth quoting in full a short review from *Les Inrockuptibles*, transcribed on the *Mortel Transfert* website:

> Si on écrit ce qu'on en pense vraiment, on va encore dire que les critiques s'acharnent sur Beineix, qu'ils préjugent les films avant de les voir, qu'ils font les malins, etc. Pourtant, on ne connaît pas personnellement JJB, on n'a rien contre lui, et de toute façon, on rédige nos papiers en fonction d'un film, pas d'une personne. Alors on va la faire très courte. Scénario abracadabrantesque, personnages inexistants, comédiens (intrinsèquement bons) ici exécrables, mise en scène superficielle et boursoufflée, style oscillant entre la noirceur frelatée des années trente et le glacis publicitaire des années quatre-vingt, humour à côté de la plaque tuant la crédibilité du projet, tunnels explicatifs plombant définitivement l'affaire, enjeu du film insaisissable. C'est du Z chiadé, un polar psycho-sexuel sans queue ni tête tellement au-delà de la nullité cinématographique qu il en deviendrait presqu intéressant s'il n'était aussi ringard et prétentieux. Mortel ennui. (Kaganski 2001).[12]

This kind of reaction was infrequent, however, and most reviewers, while finding the film slow, also acknowledged its debt to the kind of psycho-sexual thrillers made by Hitchcock or Buñuel, and the intriguing mystery which Beineix's film has in common with some of their films: 'il émane de *Mortel Transfert* le charme mystérieux et tenace de ces films qui oscillent d'un bout à l'autre entre l'ironie et

---

12 'If I write what I really think, people will yet again say that I'm hounding Beineix. Yet I don't know Beineix personally, I've got nothing against him, and anyway, I write my reviews according to the film, not the person. So I'll make this one very brief. A cock-and-bull story, characters who are nonentities, actors (in themselves good) here awful, direction superficial and bombastic, a style oscillating between the dubious bleakness of the 1930s and the publicity gloss of the 1980s, humour off-beam, deadly-dull side-tracking explanations, point of the film impossible to decipher. It's been worked at until there's nothing left, a psycho-sexual thriller which is so absolutely awful it might even have been interesting if it hadn't been so out of touch and pretentious. Mortal bore.'

l'effroi' (Malterre 2001).[13] Several reviewers, particularly web reviewers, supported the film strongly. Payen, for example, praised Beineix's close attention to the actors, pointing out that 'Beineix n'a jamais mieux filmé la fragilité d'Anglade, son inquiétude, le grain de sa peau transpirante, son regard aux aguets, la peur de sa propre mort' (Payen 2001),[14] and another web journal applauded the fact that the narrative proceeds like free association: 'La trame narrative prend des allures d'élaborations, d'associations libres, au gré des sursauts du psychanalyste paniqué ... ; un canevas burlesque et parfois surréaliste, comme une divagation de divan' (Pecnik 2001).[15] A professor of philosophy weighed in with a strongly supportive review in a national paper (Etchegoyen 2001), while American reviewers could not understand why Beineix had been yet again hounded by much of the French press:

> The reviews ranged from mediocre to merciless, accusing Beineix of making a confusing, self-indulgent, unfocused film about the arcane subject of psychoanalysis. Such reactions will probably seem baffling to moviegoers unencumbered by anti-Beineix baggage. In fact, *Mortel Transfert* is an extremely well-told and entertaining detective tale, full of suspense and burlesque humor and seen through the prism of an aesthetic sensibility that turns every frame into a rich tableau of light and shadow, color and composition. (Sancton 2001; see also Nesselson 2001)

Adaptation

As with his previous adaptations of novels, Beineix, who scripted this film himself, working through five versions (Beineix 2000a), stayed close to the original. There are only two major changes. In the novel, there are two secondary characters, Durand's psychoanalyst ex-wife and his son, dropped by Beineix for reasons of economic storytelling.

---

13 '*Mortel Transfert* exudes the mysterious and persistent charm of films which oscillate all the way through between irony and terror.'

14 'Beineix has never better filmed Anglade's fragility, his anxiety, the texture of his skin beaded with sweat, his hunted look, the fear of his death.'

15 'The narrative takes the form of elaborations, free associations, following the psychoanalyst's lurching panic; a burlesque and occasionally surreal tapestry, like the ramblings of the patient on the couch.'

Second, the inopportune visit by a dysfunctional family who claim that their daughter is anorexic is in the novel a visit by Durand's colleagues who expect to have their regular meeting to discuss psychoanalytic theory, a topic clearly too complex to convey without narrative dispersal in the film.

The other changes are minor, but some are revealing, nevertheless. Olga's Lancia becomes a yellow Porsche, while Durand's Volvo becomes a grey Cadillac, underlining Beineix's well-documented fascination for fetishistic cars. Durand has lunch with Hélène in a sushi bar, reminding us of the Japanese streak in Beineix's films.

Three further minor changes signal something more disquieting. In the novel, Durand becomes worried when one of his patients backs into his parked Volvo which has Olga's body in the boot, because this opens the boot. In the film, this event is transformed into a thief prising open the boot and running off when he discovers Olga's body. As he runs off, he runs into an advertisement for women's lingerie on bus-shelter. Second, when Durand visits Max Kubler's house, he hears voices which turn out to be politicians on the television, whereas in the film this becomes a sado-masochistic video. Finally, in the cemetery scene of the novel, where Durand goes to dump Olga's body, the man Durand meets is a Jim Morrison fan, not a necrophiliac making love to a rubber doll. As we shall see, the emphasis on fetishism and perversity is a key to the film.

Crossing boundaries

Mortel Transfert is not the only French film in recent years showing an interest in doctor–patient relationships. In Benoît Jacquot's *Le Septième Ciel* (1998), there is a similar three-way relationship between a kleptomaniac patient, Mathilde (Sandrine Kiberlain), an enigmatic hypnotist who remains unnamed (François Borléand), and who manages to fulfil his patient sexually without, apparently, touching her, and the patient's husband, Nico (Vincent Lindon), who consults the doctor in an attempt to understand his wife whom he cannot fulfil sexually. But whereas Jacquot's film is a drama, Beineix's is a comedy thriller, which ultimately provokes the spectator by its emphasis, as we shall see, on the primal scene and the pornographic, understood in its widest sense. This emphasis recalls the contention by several theorists that film is by its nature pornographic. Stanley Cavell, writing in the 1970s, pointed out how films are 'inherently pornographic' (Cavell 1971: 45), by which he meant that we are omnipotently invisible as we watch objects of desire tempting us with potentially erotic situations. More recently, Fredric Jameson opened an influential book with the same contention: 'the visual is *essentially* pornographic, which is to say that it has its end in rapt, mindless fascination', and that films 'ask us to stare at the world as though it were a naked body' (Jameson 1992: 1; his emphasis). The interest of Beineix's film, I shall be contending, is that it asks us to question our place as voyeurs of a naked body, and I shall further suggest that the body in question is our own. This might make the film sound rather indigestible, which is far from being the case. The film is primarily a comedy thriller.

The synopsis of *Mortel Transfert* above can only do partial justice to the comic elements of the film. Clearly, the narrative suggests farcical situations, such as the frustration felt by Durand in trying not simply to understand what has happened to him, but also to dispose of the unwanted corpse. Comedy is also evident in many details, such as Durand's strident red socks, his slowly deliberate 'oui, Madame' to encourage his patient's monologue, the bizarreness of the secondary characters, such as the frightened schoolteacher who suddenly becomes a determined kleptomaniac stealing from her pupils so as to gain revenge on their treatment of her, or the dysfunctional family with a daughter who is clearly not 'anorexic', played for laughs, or the deranged necrophiliac, who asks Durand if he can 'borrow' Olga, and who, zombie-like, repeats the same phrase, 'fais gaffe à tes couilles, mec'.[16] There are more obscure psychoanalytical in-jokes as well, such as Zlibovic's bow-tie, a reference to Jacques Lacan's favourite neck-tie, and frequently adopted by Lacanian psychoanalysts (Taubes 2001: 11). There is also the giraffe referred to by Durand in his conversation with Zlibovic, and which he retrieves at the end of the film; it lies beneath the couch as he and Hélène make love on his couch. It is a reference to a famous case of Freud's, Little Hans, and represents the penis, as it did for Freud's patient, and beyond that, the acquisition of an apparently unproblematic heterosexual masculinity (Taubes 2001: 12).

The film is typical of Beineix's earlier features in its visual richness. If *Diva* was a blue film, and *La Lune dans le caniveau* green,

16 'watch your balls, man.'

Mortel Transfert is a mixture of these two colours, cian, a glaucous blue-green, with splashes of vivid red in the paintings in Zlibovic's consulting room, echoed by Durand's trademark red socks, ridiculed by Olga, which represent Durand's 'touche de folie',[17] according to Jean-Hugues Anglade (from the film's website). Unlike Beineix's previous features, however, this film has many more close-up shots, particularly of Durand/Anglade, emphasising his face, his feet, his hands. There is also a recurring, haunting shot of Olga removing her shoes in slow-motion on Durand's couch, with a pink key-light on the wall behind. This visual detail is not the only one to suggest fetishism, as mentioned above in the section on adaptation. Indeed, the film's first shot is one of the most disquieting. We see a black splodge on a bright orange background, which, as the camera pulls back, turns out to be a painting (by Beineix himself) of a nude, and the black splodge is slowly recognizable as female pubic hairs. This, and the fascination for the sexually perverse, in Olga's accounts of her husband's beatings, the fetishistic shots of her removing her high-heeled shoes, and of her black stockings and garters, the SM video in their house, the lingerie of the bus-shelter advertisement, and, finally, the grotesque necrophiliac of the Père Lachaise cemetery, disturb, in the way that we might be disturbed when faced with a pornographic image.

They disturb the spectator as much as the vision of the wolves in his dream disturbs Durand. That vision is directly related, although he disavows it, to the primal scene, and it will be my contention that the vision/dream is a key to the film. The reason for this is that 'because films recreate the earliest primal scene experience or fantasy, they constitute a reposing of our most basic and implicit questions about origins' (Kline 1992: 1). The first shot of the vagina has as much to do with the question of origins as it does with the potentially pornographic. No wonder then that Durand hangs on, fascinated, to Olga's body, perverse embodiment of that aesthetic origin, always not quite managing to dispose of it. It is exactly analogous to what we do as spectators in this film, which (trans)fixes us in much the same way that 'the moviegoer will return again and again to the "scene of the crime" precisely because it constitutes *recreation*' (Kline 1992: 1; Kline's emphasis).

17 'touch of madness.'

The wolf dream forms the centre-piece of the film. It is a theatrical dream, which takes place in an excessively magnified version of Kubler's drawing room, with elaborate red draperies, and a large swing on which Max swings to and fro, taunting Durand. Durand subsequently talks to Zlibovic, his own psychoanalyst, about this dream. Zlibovic suggests that Durand has read Freud's case-history of the wolf man too often. Beineix in fact uses Freud's patient's drawing of the wolves sitting on a tree for the *mise en scène* of the dream (see figure in Freud 1955: 30), emphasising this link between the wolf man and Durand. Durand confesses to Zlibovic that he had for most of his life disagreed with Freud's interpretation of his patient's dream. For Durand, the wolves were relatively simple symbols of man's inhumanity to man. Some men, such as Kubler, he suggests, are 'wolves' who prey on weaker men. Freud's interpretation of the dream, however, is that it represents the repression of an early trauma, the child seeing his parents having intercourse, known as the *Urszene*, or 'primal scene'. During his session with Zlibovic, Durand realises that he has had the same dream throughout his life, and that it does indeed represent the repression of the primal scene. As a child, he felt contempt for his father, whom he considered weak, he says to Zlibovic, siding with his mother against his father. One afternoon, he sees them making love in their bedroom, his mother on top of his father, as if she is killing him, which is what he wants. He realises later, however, that far from getting rid of his father, his mother appears to behave even more tenderly towards him.

Durand associates this dream with his own problems as a psychoanalyst, suggesting to Zlibovic that he had fantasised crossing over from being the voyeur of the primal scene to being one of its principal actors, particularly in the case of Olga. The question we might ask, however, is whether he fantasises being the 'father' (so adopting Max Kubler's position, beating his wife, as Olga invites him to do), or the 'mother' (so adopting Olga's position, being beaten by Max, as happens in reality when Max roughs him up, injuring his arm). Neither the film's dialogue nor the original novel makes clear which position is his fantasy. A number of points suggest, however, a *feminine* (understood as passive) position. He realises that he is like his father, and therefore passive relative to his mother; he is beaten by Max at an earlier point of the film; he is fundamentally a voyeur listening passively to his patients, so passively indeed, that he has a tendency to fall asleep. Things happen to him during this film; only rarely does he seem to be in control. The film is therefore construct-ing a masochistic scenario, which, to the extent that we might identify ourselves with Durand, traps us too, until the resolution of the final scenes (not in the novel), where Durand makes up with Hélène on the Passage de Billy, a bridge over the Seine, followed by love-making on his couch.

This corresponds, but only partly, to the way Freud interpreted the facts of the wolf man's case. He explains how his patient had identi-fied with his father, longing masochistically for his father to beat him (a characteristic fantasy in young boys), and, by extension, longing for his father to make love to him. The primal scene, however, forces the young boy to see that intercourse with his father, that is, taking the place of his mother, involves castration, since he has seen that his mother does not have a penis. This leads him to repress his longing, which is transformed in the dream into fear of the wolf. Freud summarises the position reached by the boy in this way: '"If you want to be sexually satisfied by Father", we may perhaps represent him as saying to himself, "you must allow yourself to be castrated like Mother; but I won't have that." In short, a clear protest on the part of his masculinity!' (Freud 1955: 47).

There is a twist in the novel and the film, however: the wolf who is 'on top' is not the father, as in the wolf man case, but Durand's mother. It is the father who is in the more passive feminine position. The corollary of this is that Durand remains in the passive position, as we do with him. The construction of a feminised, masochistic prota-gonist is, as we have seen in earlier sections of this book, in keeping with Beineix's other main protagonists. Durand, like them, is relatively passive, and constantly threatened by stronger males, in this case Max, whom he fears, and Zlibovic, whom he respects, reminding us of a similar antagonism between Gorodish and Saporta in *Diva*. The interesting feature of this film, in contrast with *Diva*, is the direct appeal to a psychoanalytic structure integrated within the narrative, which forces us to confront more directly our own position. This is mainly because Durand is a psychoanalyst, a voyeur, like us, watching and listening to others, just as we do when watching the film. The emphasis on psychoanalysis also legitimises the film's fetishism and perversity; they are likely to be perceived by spectators as unsurprising in this context, even if the opening shot of 'rapt, mindless fascination'

(Jameson 1992: 1) with the vagina might be felt as shocking (but why? Because it is obscene? Or, simply because it is the 'scene of the crime'?).

Fetishism and perversity, however, are an integral part of the trap sprung by the film to implicate us more directly, since they force us to confront our status as voyeur-driven spectators, just as Durand is tempted by Olga to cross the line from being the psychoanalyst observer to the one who suffers, the patient in his turn, forced to confront and then question his voyeurism. As I explained in Chapter 4 of this book (devoted to *La Lune dans le caniveau*), Beineix's concern, once again, in this film, is to find a film language which approximates the unconscious. I am not claiming that this makes *Mortel Transfert* a great film, but it does give it the status of an experiment in film language, which disconcerts spectators and reviewers alike (as we saw above from the contradictory reactions to the film), just like dreams disconcert us by their incongruities, their shifts of tone, and their bizarre absurdities.

The film, then, encourages us to cross the boundary between voyeur and actor, between seeing and doing, between being distant and being there, between disembodied eye and the embodied I. It is, to recall Kline's term used above, a recreation (entertainment) wherein we recreate (originate) ourselves, 'moving in a kind of specular play of speculation between analyst and analysand' (Kline 1992: 7).

References

Anon. (2001a), 'Mortel Transfert', *Ça se passe comme ça*, January: 7.

Anon. (2001b), '*Mortel Transfert*', *Voici*, 8 January.

Anon. (2001c), '*Mortel Transfert*', *La Vie*, 11 January.

Anon. (2001d), '*Mortel Transfert*', *Le Nouvel Economiste*, 12 January.

Attali, Danielle (2001), '*Mortel Transfert*', *Le Journal du dimanche*, 14 January.

Beineix, Jean-Jacques (2000a), 'Jean-Jacques Beineix: "Adapter, c'est ce que fait tout lecteur quand il lit un livre"', *Synopsis*, November–December.

Beineix, Jean-Jacques (2000b), 'Jean-Jacques Beineix', France-Aéro 30: 22–26.

Beineix, Jean-Jacques (2001a), 'Beineix sur le divan', *Première* 286: 104–11.

Beineix, Jean-Jacques (2001b), 'Jean-Jacques Beineix: j'ai retrouvé le désir', *Le Journal du dimanche*, 7 January.

Cavell, Stanley (1971), *The World Viewed: Reflections on the Ontology of Film*. New York: The Viking Press.

Coppermann, Annie (2001), 'Le psy, le prolo et la grande Jeanne', *Les Echos*, 12 January.

Etchegoyen, Alain (2001), 'Beineix et la magie du septième art', Beineix et la magie du septième art, 24 January.

Freud, Sigmund (1955), *The Standard Edition of the Complete Psychological Works of Sigmund Freud, Vol. XVII (1917–1919): An Infantile Neurosis and Other Works*, London, The Hogarth Press.

Gaillac-Morgue (2001), 'Chaud divan!', *Paris-Match*, 11 January.

Guilloux, Michel (2001), 'Une beauté fatale sous le divan', *L'Humanité*, 10 January.

Heymann, Danièle (2001), 'Un cocktail trop secoué de macabre et de psychanalyse', *Marianne*, 15 January.

Jameson, Fredric (1992), *Signatures of the Visible*, New York and London, Routledge.

Kaganski, Serge (2001), '*Mortel Transfert*', *Les Inrockuptibles*, 9 January.

Katelan, Jean-Yves (2001), '*Mortel Transfert*', *Première* 287.

Kline, T. Jefferson (1992), *Screening the Text: Intertextuality in New Wave French Cinema*, Baltimore and London, The John Hopkins University Press.

Lalanne, Jean-Marc (2001), 'Beineix emberlificoté', *Libération*, 10 January.

Larcher, Jérôme (2001), '*Mortel Transfert*', *Cahiers du cinéma* 553: 90.

Loiseau, Jean-Claude (2001), '*Mortel Transfert*', *Télérama*, 10 January.

Malterre, Stéphanie (2001), 'Allez-y!: Diva SM sur un divan', *France-Soir*, 6 January.

Maupin, Françoise (2001), '*Mortel Transfert*: un cadavre sous le divan', *Figaroscope*, 10 January.

Menguy, Fabien (2001), 'Double Je', *A nous Paris*, 8 January.

Mérigeau, Pascal (2001), 'Fin de séance', *Le Nouvel Observateur*, 11 January.

Nesselson, Lisa (2001), '*Mortel Transfert*', *Variety*, 15 January.

Payen, Bernard (2001), '*Mortel Transfert*: Révélation', *Objectif Cinéma*, www.objectif-cinema.com/webmag/champ/travelling/pointdevue/j108.htm, accessed 22 February 2001.

Pecnik, Katia (2001), 'L'actualité passée à la loupe psy', *Psychonet*, www.psychonet.fr/index.phtml?id_rub=3&id_srub=45, accessed 22 February 2001.

Quéméré, Eric (2001), 'Décalages', *Zurban*, 8 January.

Royer, Philippe (2001), 'Beineix passe sur le divan', *La Croix*, 10 January.

Sancton, Thomas (2001), 'Prophet without honor', *Time Europe* 157/4, 24 January.

Sotinel, Thomas (2001), 'La dernière séance', *Le Monde*, 10 January.

Taubes, Isabelle (2001), 'Décryptage d'un polar psy', *Psychologies* 193: 10–12.

9

Conclusion

One of the disadvantages of presenting Beineix's films in their chronological order as I have done in this book is that a sense of coherence is more difficult to sustain. One purpose of this final chapter is to show, if only briefly, how Beineix's films form a coherent body of work. The notion of 'coherence' is, of course, problematic. It depends largely on the idea that a director's films, however heterogeneous in appearance, nevertheless have themes and styles in common which suggest the worldview of an auteur. It is a presumption which is peculiarly problematic in the case of Beineix.

The auteur and his signature

It is likely that for the youth audiences of the *cinéma du look*, the notion of the auteur played little part in their appreciation of Beineix's films, as the difference in audience figures between *Diva* and *La Lune dans le caniveau* suggests. And yet, Beineix, by his frequent and very personal public interventions against critics and producers, nourished the notion of the auteur, while at the same time frequently claiming that he was merely an illustrator of other people's ideas. Much of the critical establishment's work during the 1980s was directed at undermining any sense that he might be an auteur. For many critics he was no more than an ad-man pretending to make films, and arrogating to himself the status of 'auteur maudit', when in fact he was no more, for them, than a 'faiseur' (a practically untranslatable term used pejoratively in opposition to a real creator; it could be roughly translated by the word 'concoctor').

And yet Beineix's development of a personal style based on colour, artificial decor, emphatic music, and melodramatic romantic plots, as well as his obsessive return to fetish objects, fetish dialogue, and fetish structures, suggests the mark of an auteur, who, like Hitchcock, managed to combine the popular with the experimental, and familiar plots with an obsessive personal vision. Like Hitchcock, too, Beineix 'signed' his films with authorial signatures, and it is with these that I shall start.

A Beineix feature film does not only have as a signature the 'postcard' shot so criticised by the reviewers of the *Cahiers du cinéma*. It also typically has

- Ethnic actors: the diva; Gérard's stepmother; Frazier's wife; Jockey; Erostrate.
- Breakfast scenes: 'J'adore les scènes de petit déjeuner. Si Chabrol aime les déjeuners ou les dîners, moi c'est les petits déjeuners. Il y en a deux dans *Diva*. Trois autres dans *37°2 le matin*. Les tartines de beurre, les bols et le café avec deux jeunes filles en tenue légère c'est merveilleux' (Beineix 1992: 80).[1]
- Cars as fetish objects: the white Citroën of *Diva*; the red Ferrari of *La Lune dans le caniveau*; the yellow Mercedes of *37°2 le matin*; the black BMW of *IP5*; the yellow Porsche and grey Cadillac of *Mortel Transfert*. This, Beineix suggests, is a throwback to childhood: 'Il y a toujours (des voitures) dans mes films. C'est un reste d'enfance' (Beineix 1992: 196).[2]
- Churches: the magical cathedral of *La Lune dans le caniveau*; the church where Zorg catches Betty; the church where Roselyne has her inspiration; the 'cathedral' of the forest.
- The fetish 'zen' dialogue: Beineix calls his zen reference a fetish ('ma réplique fétiche sur le "zen"'; Beineix 1992: 170), and likens its use to Hitchcock's cameo appearances: 'Hitchcock s'amusait bien à apparaître dans ses films. Pourquoi ne m'amuserais-je pas moi aussi à ma façon?' (Beineix 1992: 170).[3] He is referring to

---

1 'I adore breakfast scenes. Chabrol may like lunches or dinners, me, it's breakfast. There are two in *Diva*. Three more in *37°2 le matin*. Buttered bread, bowls of coffee with two scantily dressed girls is wonderful.'

2 'There are always cars in my films. It's what's left of my childhood.'

3 'my fetish line on zen ... Hitchcock amused himself by appearing in his films. Why shouldn't I amuse myself as well in my own way?'

Gorodish's zen in the art of buttering bread, the neighbour's comment to Zorg when Betty has emptied his beach house that 'ça fait très zen chez toi';[4] Jockey's comment when experiencing difficulty in picking the lock of a Japanese car that 'faut être zen'.[5]

• Epiphanic moments, which are normally signalled by a combination of richly textured neo-romantic music and a very mobile camera, as for example in Gérard's first meeting with Loretta; Tony and Jockey's introduction to ecological mysticism as they and Léon Marcel embrace the trees in the forest.

These function much like Hitchcock's appearances in his films, as a 'signature' which marks the film as a 'Beineix film'.

More interestingly than Hitchcock's signature, however, most of the examples I have given suggest an ambivalence between the fetishised other (a woman, or a car, or both, as is the case with Betty and Loretta; an ethnic actor) and an empty space (the church, the house) which represents something spiritual in its broadest sense. As Beineix himself once said talking about the difference between Zorg and Betty, there is a tension in his work between baroque and zen: 'J'oscille entre le luxe, voire la luxure, et le jansénisme. Entre le baroque et le zen' (Beineix 1986: 23).[6] This tension between the fullness of the fetish and the emptiness that mirrors it can be mapped onto the other major paradox that informs his work, passion and derision, or, to put it another way, commitment and marginality.

Beineix's characters are obsessively passionate, single-mindedly committed to their vision of perfection, whether it be Jules and the perfect sound, Gérard and the perfect world where his sister's rapist will be punished, Betty and the perfect writer, Roselyne and the perfect act, Tony and the perfect love, Durand and the perfect analysis. They are so single-minded that their mode of operation is a heady mixture of tragedy and melodrama. In this respect, the frequent comic interludes in Beineix's films function as necessary releases of tension, which, since they are more often than not associated with secondary characters, serve only to isolate and emphasise the solitude of the hero. The hero himself is less of a hero than an anti-hero, weak, feminised, marginal, usually derisively self-deprecating, leading to a

4 'it's very zen in your place.'
5 'you have to be zen.'
6 'I swing between a taste for luxury, for the lustful even, and purity. Between baroque and zen.'

curious attitude of passionate detachment from his environment. Derision mocks the world because it does not come up to expectations, because it cannot deliver the ideal to which Beineix's characters aspire. His characters are not nihilists, however. They may deride, but they are implicated totally and obsessively in what they do, and the context in which they do it, while at the same time being distanced from it. This distance is analogous to allegory, a trope which says one thing while meaning another, so that one could say that these characters live their lives allegorically, as a pale shadow of the perfection they aspire to.

Beineix's films constantly gesture to a utopia formed from an amalgam of passion and emptiness, contradictory positions of total commitment and disgusted resignation and abnegation; as the advertising hoarding of *La Lune dans le caniveau* says, 'Try another world'. Beineix's emphatic and baroque use of colour, music and decor, his reliance on luxurious artifice, underlines the vacuity of the world and the desire for something better. As Lacan says of the baroque:

> Le retour baroque à tous les jeux de la forme, à tous ces procédés ... est un effort pour restaurer le sens véritable de la recherche artistique – les artistes se servent de la découverte des propriétés des lignes, pour faire resurgir quelque chose qui soit justement là où on ne sait plus donner de la tête – à proprement parler, nulle part'. (Lacan 1986: 162)[7]

The characters of Beineix's films have indeed lost their bearings, and find themselves 'nulle part', in a nowhere, a labyrinth from which there is apparently no escape, a structure whose interest is its 'constructed undecidability', 'the obvious pleasure of getting lost, of wandering, of renouncing that final principle of connection that is the key to the solution of the enigma' (Calabrese 1992: 139–40), as I explained in the introduction. The decorative in Beineix's films is, to recall Deleuze, a fabrication expressing the intensity of the spiritual. In other words, the baroque of Beineix's films is an attempt to approximate the world of purity which is just beyond reach, as *La Lune dans le caniveau* most perfectly in its necessary imperfections suggests. It is hardly surprising that Beineix's favourite geometrical trope

---

7 'The Baroque return to the play of forms, to all manner of devices (...) is an effort to restore the true meaning of artistic inquiry: artists use the discovery of the property of lines to make something emerge that is precisely there where one has lost one's bearings or, strictly speaking, nowhere' (Lacan 1992: 136).

should be the *asymptote*, 'quelque chose qui part tout doucement puis progresse très vite, en restant asymptotique, sans toucher son but' (Beineix 1989: 28).[8]

The auteur and his psychodrama

I suggested in the introduction that I would sketch out a psychodrama formed by Beineix's feature films. That psychodrama is no more peculiar to Beineix the film-maker than it is to his characters or to spectators viewing his films. It may be informed by what we might wish to call auteurist obsessions peculiar to Beineix, but what his films do, if we assume that as spectators we identify ourselves principally with his main protagonists, is to set up a structure of longing, of desire. This longing is constantly undermined by the real, represented most forcefully by figures of authority in Beineix's films. It is not just *IP5* which articulates an Œdipal trajectory, but all of the films. As I have explained elsewhere (Powrie, forthcoming), the feature films 'work through' the father, constructing his gradual fall from Gorodish the god, to Koenig the king, to Léon the fool, and, finally, Zlibovic, the frail psychoanalyst turned criminal, with only a brief respite as the son tries either to recreate a 'family' by an ethos of sibling collectivity (*37°2 le matin*) or to refuse it (*La Lune dans le caniveau*). Beineix's protagonists, who oscillate between anomie and revolt, and who are generally weaker than the father figures they struggle against, function as our perspective on the degradation of the father/establishment whom Beineix felt, and had reason to feel, as I hope this book will have made clear, was out to get him.

This degradation is enacted both through the narrative and individual images within the *mise en scène*. The 'sons' pull us into a narrative where they themselves constantly fade. They are replaced, one might argue, or at least accompanied, by what many reviewers of Beineix's films saw as an overemphasis on image at the expense of message or character. But these overemphatic images are distorted, consciously wrought images of what lurks as unrepresentable, the unconscious. It is no coincidence that Beineix has often said that he was trying to find

---

8 'something which starts off slowly then goes more quickly, while staying asymptotic, without ever reaching its goal.'

a language for the unconscious,[9] and still less of a coincidence that his return to feature film-making in 2001 was with a film about psycho-analytical transfer. The degradation of the 'fathers' and the wilting away of the 'sons' which occurs on one level, which we might call the macro-level of narrative, is thus paralleled at the micro-level of *mise en scène* and cinematography by moments in the films where excess breaks through, figuring the unconscious.[10]

Given the struggle against the father which the feature films represent, it is perhaps understandable that Beineix stopped making features in the early 1990s after *IP5*, which, as I explained in Chapter 7 of this volume, signals the ultimate fall and transfiguration of the patriarchal father into an Edenic feminised father. Curiously, the more personal Beineix's films became in the 1980s, the less they attracted audiences, in comparison with his more popular films, *Diva* and *37°2 le matin*. One reason for this, I would suggest, is that French cinema in the 1980s, as I have suggested elsewhere (Powrie 1997), shows a movement away from auteurist cinema. The need to pursue a personal vision, which we might consider the mark of an auteur, combined with a double bereavement (his mother and a close friend) forced Beineix into documentary film-making. As he put it in a 1997 interview, 'j'étais en crise. J'ai ressenti le besoin de voir la société' (Cornu 1997: 3).[11] If anything, the documentaries made by Beineix in the 1990s show even more clearly his obsession with loss and imprisonment in a cruel world.

Imprisonment and solitariness are the common themes of three of the four documentaries whether it be the Romanian orphans of *Les Enfants de Roumanie* (1992), the obsessive Japanese hobbyists of *Otaku* (1993), or the tragic story of the editor of *Elle* magazine, Jean-Dominique Bauby, who succumbed to locked-in syndrome, but fought to carry on communicating with eye movements so as to tell his story of gradual disintegration (*Assigné à résidence*, 1997). Obsession is common to the last two documentaries, and if we enlarge the idea of

9 'I wanted to make the subconscious materialize on the screen. I didn't want to be in the service of logic, of reality' (Beineix 1983: 17).

10 The position I am adopting here is broadly that adopted by Willemen in relation to Sirk during the 1970s, although I am not claiming the kind of leftist radicalism for Beineix that Willemen arrogated to Sirk. See Willemen 1971 and 1972/73.

11 'I was in crisis. I felt the need to see society.'

obsession from the subjects treated to the documentarist, it is also very evident in the documentary on the Romanian orphans as Beineix, who acts as interviewer, returns again and again to the same question: how could a mother abandon her child to an orphanage?

The other documentary, *Place Clichy ... sans complexe* (1994), tells the story of the Pathé-Wepler cinema, in Place Clichy, and its transformation from a single screen to multiplex. The documentary leans towards a nostalgia for the community that the old cinema used to support, and which appears to be dying, a community of which Beineix may well have felt part, since his production company offices were at the time just off Place Clichy in the Rue Biot (a road name to which the film frequently returns in autonomous inserts).

It is ironic that Beineix's films have been seen principally as part of the modernisation which the multiplex and a new type of audience might be considered to represent. What Beineix's documentaries highlight is the complexity of his work. His work, as Jameson and Greene have suggested, looks back as well as forward; it is as 'traditional' as it is 'postmodern'; it is dystopian as well as utopian. It celebrates marginality and obsession. In all of these respects, it is not, I would suggest, what critics during the 1980s claimed it was, style at the expense of message. Rather it is rooted in French film culture at the same time as it questions it, and the questions it asks have as much to do with social issues as they have to do with style.

References

Beineix, Jean-Jacques (1983), 'Man in the moon', *Film Comment* 19/4: 16–19.

Beineix, Jean-Jacques (1986), 'La Chasse aux papillons', *Télérama* 1891 (9 April), 22–23.

Beineix, Jean-Jacques (1989), 'Jean-Jacques Beineix: "Une réflexion sur l'artiste qui, comme un dresseur..."', *Le Quotidien de Paris* 2921, 10 April 1989: 27–28.

Beineix, Jean-Jacques (1992), '*IP5: L'Île aux pachydermes*, Paris, Dargaud.

Calabrese, Omar (1992), *The Neo-Baroque: A Sign of the Times*, Princeton, New Jersey, Princeton University Press. Originally published in Italy as *L'età neobarocca*, Rome, Laterza, 1987.

Cornu, Francis (1997), 'Jean-Jacques Beineix, de la fiction à la réalité', *Le Monde* 23 June, 3.

Lacan, Jacques (1986), *Le Séminaire. Livre 7: Ethique de la psychanalyse, 1959–60*, edited by Jacques-Alain Miller, Paris, Seuil.

Lacan, Jacques (1992), *The Ethics of Psychoanalysis 1959–60: The Seminar of Jacques Lacan. Book VII*, edited by Jacques-Alain Miller, translated by Dennis Porter, London, Tavistock/Routledge.

Powrie, Phil (1997), *French Cinema in the 1980s: Nostalgia and the Crisis of Masculinity*, Oxford, Clarendon Press.

Powrie, Phil (forthcoming), 'The God, the King, the Fool and ØØ: The Œdipal Trajectory in the Films of Beineix', *Gender in the French Cinema*, edited by A. Hughes and J. Williams, Oxford, Berg.

Willemen, Paul (1971), 'Distanciation and Douglas Sirk', *Screen* 12/2: 63–67.

Willemen, Paul (1972/73), 'Towards an analysis of the Sirkian system', *Screen* 13/4: 128–34.

Filmography

Statistical information for the feature films

	Release Date	Spectators in France	Spectators in Paris	Cost in French francs (millions)
Diva	11 March 1981	2,269,200	774,569	7
La Lune dans le caniveau	18 May 1983	616,940	186,347	24
37°2 le matin	9 April 1986	3,631,344	881,314	21
Roselyne et les lions	12 April 1989	412,543	123,568	40
IP5	12 June 1992	855,136	218,474	35
Mortel Transfert	10 January 2001			53

Director/Scriptwriter

Le Chien de Monsieur Michel (1977) 15 mins

First Prize at the Festival de Trouville 1978; nomination at the Césars for best short film

Production: Les Films 7
Script: J.-J.Beineix, based on a short story by André Rouyer
Main actors: Yves Afonso (Monsieur Michel), Denise Peron
Photo: Yves Lafaye
Editor: Monique Prim
Sound: Robert Connan
Music: Vladimir Cosma

Diva (1981) 117 mins

Best First Film, Best Décor, Best Lighting, Best Sound (Césars 1982)

Production: Films Galaxie, Greenwich Film Production, Antenne 2
Script: J.-J.Beineix and Jean van Hamme, based on a novel by Delacorta.
  Dialogues by J.-J. Beineix.
Producer: Irène Silberman
Main actors: Frédéric Andréi (Jules), Richard Bohringer (Gorodish),
  Gérard Darmon (Spic), Wilhelmenia Higgins Fernandez (Cynthia
  Hawkins), Thuy An Luu (Alba), Dominique Pinon (Le Curé)
Photography: Philippe Rousselot
Editing: Marie-Josèphe Yoyotte and Monique Prim
Sound: Jean-Pierre Ruh
Music: Vladimir Cosma

La Lune dans le caniveau (1983) 137 mins

Production: Gaumont, TFi Films Production, Société Française de
  Production de Cinéma, Opera Film Produzione
Script: J.-J.Beineix and Olivier Mergault, based on a novel by David
  Goodis
Producer: Lise Fayolle
Main actors: Gérard Depardieu (Gérard), Nastassia Kinski (Loretta),
  Victoria Abril (Bella), Vittorio Mezzogiorno (Newton), Dominique
  Pinon (Frank)
Photography: Philippe Rousselot
Art director: Hilton Mac Connico
Editing: Monique Prim and Yves Deschamps
Sound: Pierre Gamet and Bernard Chaumeil
Music: Gabriel Yared

37°2 le matin (1986) 121 mins

The director's cut was released in June 1991, lasting 183 min.

Best Film, Grand Prix des Amériques; Public Prize, Jury Prize at the
Festival des Films du Monde de Montréal 1986; Georges de Beauregard
Prize for the Best Producer 1986; Best Director and Best Actress at the
Golden Space Needle International Festival 1992; nominated Best
Foreign Picture at the Academy Awards; nine nominations at the Césars
(1986).

Production: Constellation Productions, Cargo Films, Centre National de
  la Cinématographie, Ministre de la Culture
Script: J.-J.Beineix, based on a novel by Philippe Djian
Producer: Claudie Ossard

Main actors: Béatrice Dalle (Betty), Jean-Hugues Anglade (Zorg),
    Consuelo de Haviland (Lisa), Gérard Darmon (Eddy), Jacques
    Mathou (Bob)
Photography: Jean-François Robin
Cameraman: Jean-Jacques Beineix
Art director: Carlos Conti
Editing: Monique Prim and Yves Deschamps
Sound: Pierre Befve and Dominique Hennequin
Music: Gabriel Yared

Roselyne et les lions (1989) 137 mins

Production: Cargo Films, Gaumont, Gaumont Production, ArtFinance
Script: J.-J.Beineix and Jacques Forgeas
Producer: J.-J.Beineix
Main actors: Isabelle Pasco (Roselyne), Gérard Sandoz (Thierry),
    Philippe Clévenot (Bracquard), Günter Meisner (Klint), Wolf
    Harnisch (Koenig)
Photography: Jean-François Robin
Cameraman: Jean-Jacques Beineix
Art director: Carlos Conti
Editing: Marie Castro-Bréchignac, Annick Baly, Danielle Fillios, Osvaldo
    Bargero
Sound: Pierre Befve and Dominique Hennequin
Music: Reinhardt Wagner

IP5 (1992) 119 mins

Production: Cargo Films, Société Nouvelle des Etablissements
    Gaumont, Gaumont
Script: J.-J.Beineix and Jacques Forgeas
Producer: J.-J.Beineix
Main actors: Yves Montand (Léon Marcel), Olivier Martinez (Tony),
    Sekkou Sall (Jockey), Géraldine Pailhas (Gloria)
Photography: Jean-François Robin
Cameraman: Jean-Jacques Beineix
Art director: Carlos Conti
Editing: Joëlle Hache
Sound: Pierre Befve and Dominique Hennequin
Music: Gabriel Yared

Les Enfants de Roumanie (1992) 26 mins

Documentary

Otaku (1993) 52 mins; video version 168 mins

Documentary. First Prize at the International Environment Festival 1995

Place Clichy ... sans complexe (1994) 26 mins

Documentary

Assigné à résidence (1997) 27 mins

Documentary. Certificate of Merit Award at the Chicago International Television Competition 1998; Emmy Award Nomination for the Best News Documentary 1998; Silver Spire Award at the San Francisco International Film Festival 1998

Mortel Transfert (2001) 122 mins

Production: Cargo Films
Co-producer: Odeon Pictures
Script: J.-J.Beineix, based on a novel by Jean-Pierre Gattégno
Producer: J.-J.Beineix Cargo Films
Main actors: Jean-Hugues Anglade (Michel Durand), Hélène de Fougerolles (Olga Kubler), Robert Hirsch (Zlibovic), Yves Rénier (Max Kubler)
Photography: Benoît Delhomme
Art director: Philippe Chiffre
Editing: Yves Deschamps
Sound: Pierre Befve and Patrice Grisolet
Music: Reinhardt Wagner

In development

Deal of the millennium

Feature film based on Marc Behm's novel *The Ice Maiden*
Author/director : J.-J. Beineix

Reproduction prohibited

Feature film based on a novel by Jean-Michel Truong
Author/director: J.-J. Beineix

Paris aux 2000 visages

Series of 52-minute documentaries by 20 directors; co-production with Pathé Television

The Demon

Feature film based on the novel by Hubert Selby Jr.
Author/director: J.-J. Beineix
Co-producer: Odeon Film.

As Producer

L'Accompagnement (1996) 26 & 52 mins

Documentary directed by Jackie Bastide; broadcast on France 2 ('Envoyé Spécial')

Le Courage des mères (1998) 52 mins

Documentary directed by Marie-Pierre Raimbault; broadcast on France 2

Les Gardiens de la cité (2000) 26 mins

Documentary directed by Marc Petitjean; co-producer Forum des Images; broadcast on Canal Plus July 2000

Bibliography

Books

Beineix, Jean-Jacques (1992), *IP5: L'Île aux pachydermes*, Paris, Dargaud. Storyboard: incomplete dialogue of the film with commentaries by Beineix, illustrated with drawings by Bruno de Dieuleveult.

Beineix, Jean-Jacques and Jacques Forgeas (1992), '*IP5, d'après L'Île aux pachydermes*, Arles, Actes Sud, coll. 'Scénario'. The novelisation of the film.

Leclère, François (1991), *Diva* (découpage), Paris, L'Avant-Scène Cinéma, 407. An essential tool which comprises a brief retrospective introduction, transcription of the dialogue, and a selection of extracts from reviews.

Parent, Denis (1989), *Jean-Jacques Beineix: Version originale*, Paris, Barrault Studio. The only full-length volume on Beineix. The first section is an account of the making of *Roselyne et les lions* (13–165); the second section is a brief history of Beineix (169–211); the final section is a compilation of comments by Beineix from interview, arranged alphabetically by theme (213–77). Some of these were published in *L'Evénement du jeudi* 231, 6–12 April 1989: 106–09.

Robin, Jean-François (1987), *La Fièvre d'un tournage: 37°2 le matin*, Paris, Séguier. An interesting account of the making of the film by the director of photography. There is a short introduction by Beineix.

Chapters of books or journal articles

Most of the following works have been summarised in the introduction and Chapter 3 on *Diva*

Bassan, Raphaël (1989), 'Trois néobaroques français', *Revue du cinéma* 449: 44–50.

Beugnet, Martine (2000), 'La folie-spectacle: *37°2 le matin* (Jean-Jaques Beineix, 1986)', in Martine Beugnet, *Marginalité, sexualité, contrôle: cinéma français contemporain*, Paris, L'Harmattan, 53–104. Argues that Betty, although presented as a rebel, is in fact a patriarchal stereotype of the hysterical and enigmatic muse who must be sacrificed for the hero to fulfil himself. Especially good discussion of the function of madness, the role of children, the way Betty is caught in multiple male gazes, and her role as mediator of images.

Dagle, Joan (1991), 'Effacing race: the discourse on gender in *Diva*', *Post Script* 10/2: 26–35.

Hagen, W.M. (1988), 'Performance space in *Diva*', *Film/Literature Quarterly* 16: 155–58.

Jameson, Fredric (1992), '*Diva* and French Socialism', in *Signatures of the Visible*, New York and London, Routledge, 55–62. Originally published in *Social Text* 6 (1982): 114–19.

Kelly, Ernece (1984), '*Diva*: high tech sexual politics', *Jump Cut* 29: 39–40.

Lang, Robert (1984), 'Carnal stereophony: a reading of *Diva*', *Screen* 25: 70–77.

Platten, David (1995), '*Betty Blue*', in *37°2 le matin*, Glasgow, University of Glasgow French and German Publications, 'Glasgow Introductory Guides to French Literature' no. 32. A sympathetic chapter on the film version in a book devoted to the novel.

Powrie, Phil (1997), '*Diva*'s deluxe disasters', in *French Cinema in the 1980s: Nostalgia and the Crisis of Masculinity*, Oxford, Clarendon Press, 109–20. Argues, against Jameson, that the films have very traditional concerns.

Revie, Ian (1994), 'Paris remythologised in *Diva* and *Subway*: *Nanas néopolarisées* and *Orphées aux enfers*', in *Mythologies of Paris*, Stirling, Stirling French Publications 2: 28–43.

Russell, David (1989–90), 'Two or three things we know about Beineix', *Sight and Sound* 59/1: 42–47.

White, Mimi (1988), 'They all sing ... voice, body and representation in *Diva*', *Literature and Psychology* 34/4: 33–43.

Yervasi, Carina L. (1993), 'Capturing the elusive representations in Beineix's *Diva*', *Literature/Film Quarterly* 21/1: 38–46.

Zavarzadeh, Mas'ud (1983), '*Diva*', *Film Quarterly* 36: 54–59. Reprinted with minor changes in Mas'ud Zavarzadeh, *Seeing Films Politically*, Albany, State University of New York Press, 1991, 216–27.

Sections of film histories

Austin, Guy (1996). *Contemporary French Cinema: An Introduction.* Manchester and New York, Manchester University Press, 119–25. Short but useful sections on each of the films in a chapter devoted to the *cinéma du look*; there is also a section on '*37°2 le matin* and the female spectator' (62–64).

Forbes, Jill (1992), *The Cinema in France: After the New Wave,* London, BFI/Macmillan, 62–66. Analyses *Diva* as a postmodern thriller.

Frodon, Jean-Michel (1995), *L'Age moderne du cinéma français: De la Nouvelle Vague à nos jours.* Paris, Flammarion. A first section (574–78) situates *Diva* and *La Lune dans le caniveau* negatively as examples of 'le Visuel'; a second brief section (700–01) dismisses the other three films.

Greene, Naomi (1999), *Landscapes of Loss: The National Past in Postwar French Cinema,* Princeton, New Jersey, Princeton University Press. Chapter 6 (159–89) shows how *Diva* and *La Lune dans le caniveau* construct a melancholy nostalgia for the cinema of the 1930s.

Hayward, Susan (1993), *French National Cinema,* London and New York, Routledge, 292–93. Very brief analysis of gender politics. *37°2 le matin* is memorably described as 'a high-tech designer clip-film about nymphomania'.

Prédal, René (1991), *Le Cinéma des français depuis 1945,* Paris, Nathan, 466–69. More balanced than Frodon (accepts Bassan's reappraisal), but finds the films more perverse than attractive.

Siclier, Jacques (1991), *Le Cinéma français, 2: de Baisers volés à Cyrano de Bergerac 1968–90,* Paris, Ramsay Cinéma, 256–59. The subtitle of this section, 'esthétisme et mégalomanie', says it all.

Wilson, Emma (1999), *French Cinema since 1950: Personal Histories,* London, Duckworth. A few pages on *37°2 le matin* (56–59), which focus on problems of female identification.

Dossiers of periodicals

The major film periodicals and dailies often carry large dossiers with articles, reviews and interviews when films are released.

La Lune dans le caniveau

Cinématographe 90, June 1983: 24–25. Two reviews.

Libération 13 May 1983. Three articles; review by Daney; interview with Beineix.

Le Matin 13 May 1983. Two articles; review by Perez; interview with Depardieu.

Revue du cinéma 385, July–August 1983: 22–25. Review; interview with Beineix.

37°2 le matin

L'Evénement du jeudi, 3–9 April 1983. Articles on Djian and Barrault; interview with Beineix.

Le Matin, 9 April 1986. Articles on Dalle, Djian, and Anglade; interview with Beineix.

Le Point 707, 7 April 1983: 109–11. Review by Frodon; article on Djian.

Première 109, April 1986: 13, 90–99. Review by Esposito; interviews with Beineix, Anglade, Dalle, Darmon, and de Haviland.

Le Quotidien de Paris 1985, 9 April 1986. Articles on Beineix, Djian, Anglade and Dalle; review.

Revue du cinéma 416, May 1986: 52–55. Review; interview with Anglade.

Monthly Film Bulletin 53/633, October 1986: 298–300. Review; interview with Beineix.

Télérama 1891, 9 April 1986: 20–25. Two reviews; interviews with Beineix and Anglade.

Roselyne et les lions

La Croix, 13 April 1989. Interview with Beineix, review.

L'Evénement du jeudi 231, 6–12 April 1989: 106–09. Extracts from Parent 1989, three short articles.

Le Monde, 13 April 1989. Interview with Beineix, review.

Le Quotidien de Paris 2921, 10 April 1989: 27–28. Interview with Beineix, article on the film, article on Pasco.

VSD, 6 April 1989: 80–83. Interview with Beineix, article on Le Portier.

IP5

Télérama 2213, 10 June 1992: 32–35. Two reviews by Murat and Trémois; interview with Beineix.

Première 184: 46–55. Interview with Beineix, articles on Yared, Martinez and Sall.

Studio 64: 17, 55–61. Review by Lavoignat, articles on Montand, Martinez and Sall, interview with Beineix.

Mortel Transfert

Psychologies 193: 8–13. Interview with Hélène de Fougerolles, article on film, interview with Beineix.

Interviews with Beineix

In common with many contemporary directors, Beineix has given a large number of interviews when his films were about to be or had been released, some of them in English (this has been indicated in the following list by an asterisk). The selection below represents very useful sources of information. There is a selective list of non-subscription terrestrial television interviews at the end of this section.

Diva

(1981), 'Réalisation', *Le Film Français* 1855: 26–27.
(1989), 'Jean-Jacques Beineix', in *L'Aventure du premier film*, edited by Samra Bonvoisin and Mary-Anne Brault-Wiart, Paris, Barrault, 148–59.

La Lune dans le caniveau

*(1983), 'Man in the moon', *Film Comment* 19/4: 16–19.
(1983), 'Au-delà du réel: une interview de Jean-Jacques Beineix', *Première* 74: 47–53, 165–66. On the making of *La Lune dans le caniveau*.
(1983), 'Les confessions d'un enfant du siècle et du cinéma', *Première* 75: 119–21, 130–35. A detailed account of Beineix's apprenticeship years.
(1983), 'Entretien avec Jean-Jacques Beineix', *Revue du cinéma* 385: 23–25.
*(1984), 'Jean-Jacques Beineix: An Interview with Michael Buckley', *Films In Review* 35/1: 29–33.

37°2 le matin

(1985), 'Jean-Jacques Beineix: le virage', *Starfix*, 30 November, 58–59.
(1986), 'Le choix de Beineix', *Première* 109: 90–99.
*(1986), 'Universal mariner', *Monthly Film Bulletin* 53/633: 300.
(1987), 'Interview', *Séquences*, 129: 40–47.
See also below, *version longue*

Roselyne et les lions

(1989), 'Beineix: tourner, ça fait mal', *L'Express*, 7 April, 128–29.
(1989), '"Quand l'homme asservit l'animal, il s'asservit lui-même"', *La Croix*, 13 April 1989.
(1989), 'Les cris et les rugissements de Beineix le révolté', *Le Journal du dimanche*, 9 April.
(1989), 'Beineix critique Beineix', *Le Monde*, 13 April 1989, IV.
(1989), 'Le dompteur d'images', *Le Nouvel Observateur*, 6 April, 106–07.
(1989), 'Jean-Jacques Beineix: "Une réflexion sur l'artiste qui, comme un dresseur..."', *Le Quotidien de Paris* 2921, 10 April 1989: 27–28.
(1989), 'Entretien', *Revue du cinéma* 448: 50–54.
(1989), 'Le dompteur est un artiste don't l'animal est la matière brute', *VSD*, 6 April 1989: 80–81.

37°2 le matin (version longue)

(1991), 'Beineix, intégralement', *Le Soir*, 31 July.

IP5

(1992), '*IP5*: Montand au pays des tagueurs', *Le Point* 1029, 6 June.
(1992), 'Le taggeur, le rappeur et le vieil aliéné', *Le Quotidien de Paris*, 10 June.
(1992), 'Le mal aimé', *Télérama* 2213, 10 June, 32–34.
(1992), 'Beineix: Je suis un asocial"...', *L'Evénement du jeudi* 11–17 June, 101.
(1992), '"Montand? Je ne l'ai pas trahi, je ne l'ai pas tué', *Le Nouvel observateur*, 11 June, 128–29.
(1992), 'Jean-Jacques Beineix: un cinéaste en quête de sagesse', *Le Figaro*, 12 June.
(1992), '*IP5* Le nouveau Beineix: Montand l'émotion', *Première* 184: 46–52.
(1992), 'Jean-Jacques Beineix: les racines du ciel', *Studio* 64: 59–61.

Mortel Transfert

(2000), 'Jean-Jacques Beineix: "Adapter, c'est ce que fait tout lecteur quand il lit un livre"', *Synopsis*, November–December.
(2000), 'Jean-Jacques Beineix: "L'inconscient n'a pas de réalité. Mais il faut bien le représenter"', *Art actuel*, December.
(2000), 'Jean-Jacques Beineix', *France Aéro* 30 December: 22–26.
(2000), 'Mortelle rencontre: Beineix et Ovidie font chacun leur cinéma', *Hot Vidéo* 126 December: 114–21.

(2001), 'Entretien: "La fin d'une analyse, c'est comme la fin d'un film ..."', *Ça m'intéresse*, January.

(2001), 'Autant en emporte le divan: Jean-Jacques Beineix et Jean-Hugues Anglade', *Ciné-Livre* 42 January: 54–59.

(2001), 'Le divan du monde', *Nova*, January.

(2001), 'Beineix sur le divan', *Première* 286, January: 104–10.

(2001), 'Entretien avec Jean-Jacques Beineix', *Psychologies* 193, January: 13.

(2001), 'Jean-Jacques Beineix: "Faisons d'abord respecter nos films"', *L'Express*, 4 January: 14–18.

(2001), 'Jean-Jacques Beineix: "J'ai retrouvé le désir"', *Le Journal du Dimanche*, 7 January.

(2001), 'Jean-Jacques Beineix: "Je suis un vieux Parisien"', *A nous Paris*, 8 January.

(2001), 'Beineix, le retour', *Figaroscope*, 10 January.

(2001), 'Mortel Beineix', *FranceSoir*, 10 January: 21–22.

(2001), 'Jean-Jacques Beineix: "Ni Freud ni Lacan', *Le Figaro*, 11 January.

(2001), 'Psychanalyse: l'inépuisable filon', *Panorama du médecin*, 11 January.

(2001), '"Le cinéma s'est donné à la télé"', *VSD*, 11 January.

(2001), 'Jean-Jacques Beineix sur le divan', *Impact Médecin*, 12 January.

(2001), 'De *Diva* au divan', *Elle*, 15 January: 46–49.

Television interviews

Date	Channel	Programme	Subject (where known)
27 October 1992	France 3	Faut pas rêver	
4 October 1993	France 2	Les 4 vérités	On GATT
12 October 1993	France 2	Journal de 13 heures	On GATT
8 December 1993	France 3	La marche du siècle	On GATT
19 May 1994	France 2	Envoyé spécial	Accompanies 'Otaku'
12 July 1995	France 2	Vélo Club	
14 December 1995	M6	Starnews	On TV screening of *37°2 le matin* (long version)
15 October 1995	France 3	Lignes de mire	On TV screening of *37°2 le matin* (long version)
10 May 1996	France 2	Les 4 vérités	On French cinema
12 May 1996	France 2	Polémiques no. 31	On French cinema
11 April 1999	France 2	Thé ou café	On Beineix's work
12 January 2001	France 3	On ne peut pas plaire à tout le monde	On *Mortel Transfert*
15–19 January 2001	TF1	Exclusif	Interviews with Beineix, Anglade and de Fougerolles
23 January 2001	France 3	Vie privée, vie publique	Beineix on Montand's death

Index